"As Schultz captures in his remarkable book, children with LD and ADHD often experience feelings of frustration, anger, helplessness, and low self-esteem—feelings that prompt them to avoid situations that they believe will lead to further humiliation. *Nowhere to Hide* describes how these disorders are manifested in the home and school setting, and, most importantly, offers a strength-based framework filled with many practical, realistic strategies that parents, teachers, and other professionals can use to help these youngsters become more competent, proactive, and resilient. Schultz's understanding and empathy for students with LD and ADHD as well as their parents and teachers are evident on every page of this easy-to-read book."

—**Robert Brooks,** Ph.D., clinical psychologist and faculty member, Harvard Medical School; coauthor, *Raising Resilient Children*

"It's been said that kids 'go to school for a living.' It is their job, their livelihood—their entire identity. When you meet a school-aged child in your community, your first question inevitably is, 'Hi, Jason. How's school?' For 10–15 percent of America's kids, the answer to that question is, 'Well, not too good.' These students fight the battle of learning disabilities and attention deficits every day. Through no fault or choice of their own, they become a daily source of puzzlement and frustration for the parents and teachers in their lives.

"Enter Jerry Schultz. In his new book, *Nowhere to Hide*, Dr. Schultz brings his unparalleled experience, knowledge, background, and wisdom to this issue. He provides the reader with comprehensible explanations of the latest neurobiological research and translates it into practical strategies that parents and professional can use to assist these students in reaching their fullest potential.

"By telling his story through the eyes of students he has evaluated, taught, and counseled, Jerry allows us a unique look at the day-to-day challenges faced by these kids and their families. His book will provide you with invaluable knowledge and insights that will assist you in delivering the quality services that these struggling students need—and deserve."

—**Richard D. Lavoie, M.A., M.Ed.,** educational consultant and author,
  The Motivation Breakthrough and *It's So Much Work to Be Your Friend*

NOWHERE TO HIDE

Why Kids with ADHD and LD Hate School and What We Can Do About It

Jerome J. Schultz, Ph.D.

Foreword by Edward M. Hallowell

JOSSEY-BASS
A Wiley Imprint
www.josseybass.com

Published by Jossey-Bass
A Wiley Imprint
989 Market Street, San Francisco, CA 94103-1741—www.josseybass.com

Jossey-Bass books and products are available through most bookstores. To contact Jossey-Bass directly call our Customer Care Department within the U.S. at 800-956-7739, outside the U.S. at 317-572-3986, or fax 317-572-4002.

Jossey-Bass also publishes its books in a variety of electronic formats. Some content that appears in print may not be available in electronic books.

Library of Congress Cataloging-in-Publication Data
Schultz, Jerome J.
    Nowhere to hide : why kids with ADHD and LD hate school and what we can do about it / Jerome J. Schultz.—1
        p. cm.
    Includes bibliographical references and index.
    ISBN 978-0-470-90298-1 (hardback); ISBN 978-1-118-09170-8 (ebk);
ISBN 978-1-118-09172-2 (ebk); ISBN 978-1-118-09173-9 (ebk)
    1. Attention-deficit-disordered children—Education—United States.   2. Hyperactive children—Education—United States.   3. Learning disabled children—Education—United States.   4. Classroom management—United States.   5. Education—Parent participation—United States.   6. Attention-deficit hyperactivity disorder—United States.   7. Learning disabilities—United States.   I. Title.
    LC4713.4.S44 2011
    371.94—dc23

                                                                                    2011017841

Printed in the United States of America
FIRST EDITION
HB Printing   V10008947_031919

I dedicate this book to my five wonderful grandchildren—David, Eli, Sophia, Ava, and Leah. These little miracles continue to enrich and expand my knowledge of child development, and the joy they give me is indescribable.

CONTENTS

FOREWORD

Think of this book as the friend you've been looking for for the longest while. Think of this book as a wise companion, a source of reassurance in the midst of uncertainty, clarity in the midst of confusion, and solutions where you've had only problems.

Jerry Schultz has got game! He knows the field of learning problems and ADHD inside and out. He has worked in the trenches for three decades. You have no idea how much that matters, but I do, because I have been working in those same trenches for those same years. It makes all the difference in the world. You cannot find a guide with more hard-won knowledge than Jerry Schultz.

That means you can trust what Jerry has to say as if he were your knowing pediatrician or savvy first-grade teacher. It means Jerry is not going to try to hustle you with pat answers or patented remedies. It means Jerry understands your pain, and the pain of your child or student. It means Jerry also knows a host of possible answers . . . not *the* answer but many answers.

One value of this book is that it distills much of what Jerry has learned into a single volume. Beyond providing knowledge, however, this book provides hope. It provides the kind of emotional uplift all of us so urgently need. And Jerry provides the best kind of hope: hope that grows out of the rich mine of real-life triumphs. Jerry has helped thousands of teachers, students, parents, and others triumph. He has helped them turn what seemed at first a shortcoming, even a disability, into an asset. He has mined the treasures embedded in what can seem like impenetrable rocks in the brain. But Jerry knows how to find the treasures. He is indeed a master of his trade.

Savor this book. Read each page slowly. Take in all that it has to offer. After you've digested it, keep it nearby, like a best friend. Like a best friend, it will always be there for you when you need it.

May 2011   Edward Hallowell, M.D.
                                              Sudbury, Massachusetts
                                              New York, New York

ACKNOWLEDGMENTS

Writing this book represents the fulfillment of a very important personal and professional goal. Included in the long list of people to whom I owe a deep debt of gratitude are the many gifted and talented teachers, colleagues, and mentors who have freely shared their knowledge and wisdom, helping me to shape my ideas and hone my clinical and teaching skills over the years. The list is much too long to include here. I'm a big believer in thanking people and telling them how much I love them before their funerals, so most of these people already know how I feel about them.

In a way, this book is my thank-you note to those who have given me the privilege of working with them over the years. While colleagues and friends have provided me with support and encouragement during my professional career, it is to the children and the families I have worked with over the past nearly forty years that I owe the greatest thanks. It is they who have taught me about living, struggling, coping, and succeeding with LD and ADHD and other special needs. It is these individuals who have invited me into the private space of their lives, who have helped me shape the thoughts and ideas that have informed my teaching, guided my clinical practice, and helped me fill the pages of this book.

In the year leading up to the publication of *Nowhere to Hide*, my first book, several people have taught me much about writing and publishing and helped to make this an interesting and enjoyable experience. My literary agent, Janice Pieroni of Story Arts Management, has shown enthusiastic support for the idea behind the book since its inception. Her personal interest in and understanding of the need for its publication have fueled many conversations that have helped me bring this work to fruition. Janice helped me build a bridge to the many people at Jossey-Bass and Wiley who have shepherded me along the road that took me from outline to oeuvre.

Acquisitions editor Marjorie McAneny initially sought me out to do this project because she felt that my interpretation of the challenges faced by kids with LD and ADHD would help parents and teachers appreciate the role that stress plays in their lives. It was Margie who graciously helped show me the ropes of the publishing business and became my home port and anchor as she ushered me through the stages of this project. My thanks go to Tracy Gallagher, her senior editorial assistant, who (among other important things) helped me track down the rights to the songs that I referenced in the book. Developmental editor Paula Stacey was both gentle and generous as she and Margie helped me get a better idea about how to turn my initial draft of the manuscript into something much more presentable. At that point, the manuscript and I were put in the capable hands of senior production editor Mary Garrett as she oversaw the copyediting process and the subsequent steps involved in getting this book produced.

Before writing this book, I had a pretty limited view about the role and value of a copyeditor. I want to extend a special thank-you to the incredibly talented Hilary Powers, who provided this final-stage review of my manuscript. I now see that this process is rather like submitting one's work for the literary equivalent of cosmetic surgery. Starting with a solid body of work, Hilary deftly wielded her semantic scalpel, making laserlike excisions of extraneous or confusing language, taking in a little here, suggesting a little filling in there—all of which helped me to create the finished product you now hold in your hands.

Although I know it will cause her to turn a little red, for although she deserves it, she never seeks public praise, I have to say here how grateful I am to my wonderful wife, Marlene. Her training and skills as a social worker have not only brought comfort and guidance to many clients and students over the years, they have enabled us to have hours and hours of great conversations about mental health, schools, kids, and families. In the early days of our marriage, she would scour my professional journals, looking for training opportunities for me that would lead us to new places and allow me to explore new horizons. She has always believed in me and always supports me when I set out for new adventures or take on new challenges. This book is the most recent excursion, and Marlene, who is my inspiration and my muse, was with me every step of the way. She helped me find the time to write and found articles and highlighted passages in all sorts of places that were relevant to the book. Most important, she served as first editor on everything I put into print. I could always count on her for an honest, intelligent, and sensitive appraisal of my work, and my readers will be thankful that she was there.

Introduction

In this book, I share what I have learned over the past thirty-five years about how kids with learning disabilities (LD) and attention-deficit/hyperactivity disorder (ADHD) cope with the stress and frustration caused by constantly being asked to do what they cannot do very well, or what they *think* they can't do well. I hope that you, like thousands of parents and teachers who have heard me talk about this in workshops or at conferences, will come to understand the neurobiological reason that many kids with LD, ADHD, or a combination of these disabilities do not improve fast enough or often enough, and why, despite all the interventions parents and teachers put in place, so many of these kids actually get *worse* over time.

My goal in writing this book is to help you understand the cause of the problem and to offer you a model for intervention that will give you and your children or students renewed hope.

Here's the crux of this book: When children or adolescents have unrecognized, undiagnosed, or misunderstood LD or ADHD, these students encounter an unending stream of academic and social challenges that other students don't seem to have. Because they don't know why they have these difficulties and because their efforts over the years have not made the problem better, they have no idea what to do and have little control over the challenges they encounter. As a result, thousands of intelligent, competent students face frustration and failure, which results in anxiety and leads to unrelenting stress that ultimately causes them to do what any organism does to protect itself—to fight, to run, or to try to find a place to hide.

This book is written to help you understand the neurological basis for this stress response, and why much of the negative behavior you see in children with LD and ADHD is actually the evidence of their desire to avoid failure. Most important, I wrote this book to share with you a method of intervention that can break this cycle and put kids on a path to competence and confidence.

WHY READ THIS BOOK

I assume that if you are reading this, you have, love, or teach a child with LD or ADHD. That is, you may be a parent of a child or adolescent who has significant difficulties with learning or attention. You may be a teacher of children with these challenges. The child you care about or care for has probably had at least one evaluation, if not multiple evaluations, including testing by a school psychologist, a comprehensive neuropsychological assessment, or a consultation with a pediatrician or a psychiatrist. Despite the efforts of many qualified and talented professionals, you do not seem to have found the answer to this child's problem. Your son or daughter or your student might have been given a formal diagnosis of specific learning disabilities or ADHD and be getting services under the provisions of an Individual Educational Plan—called an IEP, as specified in the Individuals with Disabilities Education Act (IDEA), a federal law first enacted in 1990—or a 504 Plan (Section 504 of the Rehabilitation Act of 1973).

Let me guess what you've done that hasn't worked:

Parents: you have attended countless meetings at your child's school, where well-meaning professionals have talked to you about your child's progress but have not told you how to fix the problem. You may have been called into the principal's office to discuss certain behaviors that are getting in the way of your child's learning, and your child's teacher's ability to teach. Perhaps you have taken your son or daughter to a psychologist for therapy. You may have hired specialized tutors to work with your child at school, or sent your son or daughter to a special summer camp offering interventions for children with disabilities or attention problems. You may be among the hundreds or even thousands of parents who have chosen to move to another town in order to get better special education services! You have done everything you know how to do, and although your child may be showing some progress, you know it's not enough, and you are worried.

Teachers: You and your colleagues have spent months or years trying to solve the mystery of why certain students resist your efforts to help them and spend much of their time trying to escape work that you believe they are capable of doing. Or you may be one of the growing number of teachers who have come to understand how extremely difficult it is to address the needs of severely learning disabled children or those with untreated ADHD in a regular classroom. In the days before "the inclusion movement," schools had many more resource rooms or self-contained classrooms for kids like those who are now in "full inclusion" programs nationwide. You may wonder how one special education teacher can address the needs of all the kids in a heavy caseload—when these students are located in classrooms all over the building. And while you may have become that special kind of hybrid teacher who has created a classroom that is inclusive both in spirit and in deed, and that adequately serves the needs of the kids this book is written about, you may have colleagues who are struggling to maintain sanity in a classroom filled with twenty-five to thirty-five challenging and diverse learners, let alone meet the intensive individual needs of children with significant LD or ADHD who have been placed there in the name of inclusion.

This all leaves us with a huge unanswered question: Why, despite the best efforts of so many professionals, is the current approach to education not having the intended effect on kids with LD and ADHD? The answer lies in the complex and miraculous workings of the human brain. While I'll offer a fuller explanation in subsequent chapters, the key point is that different events activate different regions of our brains. Because we're humans, stored information is always associated with some kind of emotion. Sometimes the associated feeling is positive, and sometimes it's relatively neutral (and therefore, more susceptible to forgetting). At other times, the memory is laced together with negative emotions, which as it turns out are very hard to get rid of. This is why (if you're old enough) you probably know exactly where you were when you heard the news about the explosion of the Space Shuttle *Challenger*. It's why you will probably never forget what you were doing on 9/11. Unfortunately, because of the terrors of war and large-scale tragedies that have befallen us as citizens of a complex world, most of us know what is meant by post-traumatic stress syndrome, or PTSD. It's easy to understand how horrific, traumatic events can stamp an indelible imprint on our brains. When this happens, the victim becomes hardwired to respond to any hint of the tragedy with a full-blown reaction, essentially reliving that event. This book addresses the chronic stress that is created by exposing a child to an unending flow of tasks that seem impossible to do, or do well. We know that stress, like bullying, changes the brain. Can't a book you find difficult to read, or a schedule you can't follow, harass you as unceasingly and as covertly as any bully? Like so many victims of peer abuse, kids with LD and ADHD can find no escape from this stressor: they have . . . *nowhere to hide*. Although the factors that cause chronic stress cannot be considered traumatic in the same way as the horrific events that lead to PTSD, research nonetheless shows that unabated stress can also be neurotoxic—harmful to the brain.

How You Know I Am Telling the Truth?

First of all, my mother always told me that lies always get you into trouble. I guess I was destined to be researcher when I was a kid, because I felt I had to test her hypothesis. The story about how I found out that she was right is too long to retell here (and dredges up many sad feelings from my limbic system). Let's just say that you and I might have different ideas about what "pain in the butt" means. (But that was long ago and far away.)

The other reason that you should (and will) believe me is that the ideas you read about in this book are absolutely supported by sound research carried out by some of the best minds in the country. Besides, they all have brain scanners and we don't, so how can we argue with them? An increasing number of highly regarded scientists have demonstrated that not only acute traumatic stress but also chronic unabated stress causes changes in the human brain that can rewire the way it deals with stress. That reorganization in the service of survival has a definite downside. It causes problems with learning and attention, and it impairs executive functions such as planning, memory, and organization.

Once I help you develop a basic understanding of the brain science that supports my thesis, I translate that scientific knowledge into practical, doable, and inexpensive strategies based on my many, many years of real-life experience with the kids you and I love and care about. I am certain that this will make a difference. My mother also told me to believe in myself, but she always added: "but you'd better be able to back it up." I guess she was a researcher too. I have four brothers and sisters. We were her lab mice, and we all lived, so I think she knew what she was talking about.

Have Hope!

Is your child's problem getting worse? Despite all the steps you have taken, and all the money and time you have spent trying to help your child, you may feel that the problem not only persists but may even be getting worse as your child grows older. Your son or daughter may not be as happy as in earlier years. The child who used to love school seems to be going into a tailspin of failure. Your daughter may say she hates school, or hates her teacher, or hates homework, or even that she hates *you!* Your ten-year-old son might be doing mean things to his little sister because she can read just about anything that she can put her hands on. A high school student may stop going to a particular class, or come to school and shut down for hours, or refuse to go to school altogether, retreating to an (all too often smoky) bedroom or basement lair. Your son may be spending more time slumped behind video games or computer screens, or texting incessantly, or doing just about anything he can to get out of doing schoolwork. Your little first-grader might have started to bite her nails or pull out her eyelashes, or your formerly sweet child may have started to get surly in the middle of fourth grade. Any of these sound familiar? To parody that famous Music Man . . .

> *Well, if so my friends, Ya got trouble . . .*
> *Right here in River city!*
> *With a capital "S"*
> *And that rhymes with "Mess"*
> *And that stands for STRESS.*

As a parent, you have met with your child's teachers year after year, and despite their high level of skill, their genuine concern, and their efforts to give your child a successful learning experience, they may seem as frustrated as you by your child's lack of progress. As a teacher, you too are concerned about students who, despite the best efforts of your school district, continue to have serious learning difficulties, and who are perhaps displaying an increase in challenging behaviors and fragile emotions. They may be talking back, refusing to do work, or acting surly. They may have been referred for a reevaluation to see if, in addition to LD or ADHD, they now meet the criteria for oppositional defiant disorder, or something more serious.

Why LD and ADHD Evaluations Are Not the Answer

LD and ADHD evaluations are necessary and helpful, but they don't help enough. Specialists in the field have developed many tools to help us diagnose and treat both conditions, and a lot of teachers, pediatricians, school psychologists, and neuropsychologists can do that very well. The real challenge lies in understanding and assessing the collateral damage to a child's sense of confidence and competence that can come from years of unabated stress created by these interrelated conditions. This book will help you reduce the impact of LD and ADHD by inoculating your children against stress by building a greater understanding of their particular kind of LD or ADHD. (Yes, there are different kinds.)

Some of the Practical Things in This Book

By teaching children how to more accurately appraise their products as well as the processes used to create those products, you will strengthen their will, their stamina, and, ultimately, their sense of control—the best anti-stress medicine there is. You'll learn how to help them make deposits into their own "self-concept account" (and how to get teachers and grandparents to make contributions to this fund too). You will help your children put their strengths and weaknesses in their proper perspective. You will learn how to help your children understand that they actually *are* able to make a difference in their own life and not be so dependent on others to define who they are and what they can or can't do. By doing the things that you'll learn about in the chapters that follow, you'll give each child a feeling of purpose, agency, and control that can transform stress from a large, frightening, and immobilizing fire-breathing dragon into a source of energy that can fuel achievement and build self-esteem from the inside out, for today and for a lifetime.

Why You'll Be Glad You Read This Book

If you are the parent of a child with LD, ADHD, or both, an adult who cares for or about a child with these conditions, or a professional who works with these kids, you are about to learn some things that can help you change a young person's life. A better understanding of the relationship between stress, learning, and attention can help a child who lives with fear, worry, anxiety, and frustration transform into a child who views life with a sense of hope and optimism that can lead to academic and social success. If you want to look back on someone's life in five, ten, or thirty years and say, "I really did something to make a difference for that child," keep reading. You'll be glad you did, and so will your child or your students.

A Brief Word About Music

During my teenage years, music was the backdrop for my life. In high school, music was my sport. I played saxophone in every instrumental group I could, including "pep" band, concert band, orchestra, dance band, and marching band. While I was tooting out the fight songs of famous football colleges with the band, the music of the sixties and seventies was playing on my car radio or a transistor radio (if that doesn't make sense—ask your parents!) and, almost incessantly, in my head. I learned a lot of things in high school, but the melodies and lyrics of those songs have stuck in my brain as if glued there. And the tunes and the lyrics of that period appear to be timeless. People of all ages seem to know the lyrics and the melodies even if they didn't grow up when the songs were originally sung.

I've woven references to that music into the chapters of this book for several reasons. If you know the lyrics or the tune of a song at all, your brain will start to sing or hum it as soon as you see the trigger of the lyrics—even if I've put in only a few words of it. This phenomenon makes a point that's relevant to this book: If you learn something when you (and your brain) are in a happy state (that is, relaxed, content, and not under stress), it's generally easier for you to remember it than something you learned while you were in a neutral or negative mood, or under a lot of stress. Who knows? Maybe the musical references peppered throughout this book will put you in a happy mood. If so, and if my hypothesis is right, the "Good Vibrations" (The Beach Boys, 1966) that you get may help you remember what you read.

It's not just because I love music—it's *all* about the brain.

Another reason I put the musical references in this book it that the lyrics help me tell my story about how brain function is affected by what happens to us. When your brain gets triggered by a printed word or phrase, or a song to hum or sing, it is using an intricate series of neural networks to cause the visual centers of your brain to communicate with the areas of the brain that have put these lovely little poems and their melodies away for safekeeping. On its way through this network, a flow of electrochemical energy passes through the areas of your brain that process your emotions. If the lyric is associated with a wonderful experience you had when you first heard the words and the music, that song becomes associated with positive emotions. You might resonate, for example, to the opening lyrics of a song made famous by Frankie Valli and the Four Seasons: "Oh, *what a night!*"

If, on the other hand, the lyrics or the melody of a song is firmly associated with an unhappy event, like the night you broke up with your first love, your brain registers and holds on to your negative emotional state at that time. Even after many years, you may tear up when you hear "Breaking Up Is Hard to Do," sung by Neil Sedaka (#1 on the Billboard Hot 100, August 11, 1962), which includes those incredibly emotional lyrics: "Come-a, come-a down dooby do, down, down." (Or, then again, you may want to fill in your own song here.) You might be interested to know that it was the hit recording "Nowhere to Run" sung by Martha and the Vandellas that found its way into my brain on a happy sunny summer afternoon in 1965 and remained there until it rose up from the depths of my memories to give me the inspiration for the title of this book, *Nowhere to Hide*.

Go ahead, sing it. Ya know ya wanna. Your brain can't help but respond to what your body sees, hears, touches, feels, smells, or otherwise senses. As you read this printed page, the occipital lobe of your brain is picking up the visual images that your eyes are sending its way. These images are little more than meaningless combinations of curved and straight lines and angles. To make sense of these little symbols called letters, and the way they are organized into groups called words and then into sentences and so on, your brain needs to activate an incredibly complex network of neurons to find the centers of the brain (the auditory cortex, among others) that have stored the sounds and words that help the visual symbol make sense. People who live in remote villages with no access to print materials have the potential to learn this sound-symbol association, but unless it is taught to them, they do not become literate. In efficient well-trained readers (and those without learning disabilities), this process is almost instantaneous. Rather amazing, don't you agree?

A ROAD MAP FOR READING THIS BOOK

Allow me to tell you a bit about the terrain into which you are about to venture. *Nowhere to Hide* is divided into five parts. Part One is called "The Neurobiology of Stress." Chapter One, "Stayin' Alive: Understanding the Human Brain and How It Responds to Stress," is where I provide you with a quick, introductory tour of brain anatomy. A book on the impact of stress has to include at least an introduction to how the brain is built and how it does some of the things it can do. It also has to explain how this miraculous little organ holds up (or breaks down) under pressure. In Chapter Two, "Stress Goes to School," you'll see what happens to the brains of kids with LD and ADHD when they are confronted with tasks they can't handle, and you'll begin to understand why I'm so concerned about the harm that can come to the brain when the child has an inadequate understanding of LD, ADHD, and the stress connection.

Part Two of the book is called "Making Sense of LD and ADHD." In Chapter Three, "What's in a Name? Clearing Up Misperceptions About Learning Disabilities," I take you on a historical journey, tracing the genesis of the term *learning disability* and the evolution of this condition over time. I also tell you a bit about the development of laws that govern the education of students with this condition.

In Chapter Four, "Demystifying ADHD," you'll take a parallel tour of the history and development of the condition that today is known as attention-deficit/hyperactivity disorder, or ADHD. I try to clear up some of the common misconceptions about both of these conditions, and you'll learn how they may overlap. I also invite you to look ahead, to get a glimpse of what the future holds for these conditions, as definitions and classification schemes undergo anticipated modification with the publication of a new version of a diagnostic handbook widely used by psychiatrists and other mental health specialists.

Chapter Five, "Decoding Stress with Neuropsychological Evaluations," focuses on breaking the stress cycle in students with LD and ADHD. In it I draw upon my thirty-plus years of experience to explain the role that neuropsychological assessment plays in understanding the specific nature of the learning and attentional skills of individual children and adolescents, and how that knowledge helps teachers and other professionals create educational environments in which students can reduce stress by gaining increased mastery over their learning and social environments.

Part Three is called "How Kids 'Save FASE' and DE-STRESS." Accordingly, Chapter Six shows you how the negative behaviors often exhibited by students with LD and ADHD are apt to be symptoms of underlying stress that's created by chronic exposure to tasks these kids can't master. This chapter is called "Nowhere to Hide: How Negative Behaviors Help Kids 'Save FASE.'" In it, I explain the cycle of Fear, Avoidance, Stress, and Escape (FASE) that's exhibited by many kids who question their own competence, and why I refer to these behaviors as Saving FASE. Chapter Seven, "From Distress to DE-STRESS: Breaking the FASE Cycle and Putting Kids on the Path to Competence," is the keystone chapter, the one that holds all this information together and offers much hope for change. In presenting the DE-STRESS model of intervention, I share a set of principles and many practical, research-based strategies designed to help parents and teachers break the stress-learning logjam and help students move to a position of confidence that comes from competence.

In Part Four, "Special Messages for Teachers and Parents," you'll find Chapter Eight, "Making Schools Stress-Less and Success-Full for Students with LD and ADHD," and Chapter Nine, "Parents and Families: Home Is Where the Heart (and the Heartache) Is," which respectively offer teachers and parents deeper interpretations of the DE-STRESS model and describe even more practical strategies that they can implement to increase self-awareness, build competence, instill a sense of confidence, and reduce the toxic stress that impedes the success of far too many students with LD and ADHD. The book's Conclusion, "All's Well That Ends . . . *Well* . . . ," offers some parting words of advice and hope.

In this book you'll learn about the negative impact that chronic stress has on learning, happiness, and actual brain function, particularly in the brain of a child or adolescent with under-recognized or untreated learning, attention, or social problems—and what to do about it. If you are a parent, you'll find suggestions that are based on best practices in special education and psychology that will help you create learning environments at home, in the community, and in the school that will take your son or daughter down a path that leads away from or around stress, and winds its way toward greater confidence and competence. If you are a teacher, you'll find out just how important success and a sense of mastery are to brain health, and how what you do, what you say, and how you say it may make all the difference in the world to the future of a student with LD, ADHD, or other special need. In the chapters that follow, you'll learn how to help children stop their brains from doing what they're built to do under stress, and start doing more of what they do when . . . well . . . when they're happy. Let's begin by taking a look at the brain and how it handles stress.

Author's Note: The cases I present in this book are based on fictional characters. While students I've worked with over the years have displayed all of the characteristics or behaviors I discuss in this book, any similarities to any persons (children, parents, teachers, or other professionals) living or dead are clearly coincidental. If you think you are reading about yourself or your child here, that just means the message is hitting home.

PART ONE

The Neurobiology of Stress

1

Stayin' Alive

Understanding the Human Brain and How It Responds to Stress

> Worry is like a rocking chair. It gives you
> something to do, but it gets you nowhere.
> —Erma Bombeck

The brain is the control center for all of our thoughts, actions, attitudes, and emotions. It's the pilothouse on the riverboat of our lives. It's Mission Control for all of our flights into space or time. It's the air traffic controller that helps us navigate and reroute our paths based on incoming and outgoing information and how we're feeling about it at the time. It's the John Williams of our personal symphony. It's the Mother Ship to our Starfleet; it's . . . (Uh, sorry, I got carried away there, but I think you get my point!)

As I was working on the drafts of this chapter, my own brain was very active, to say the least. I kept hearing in my head the words of the old Jack Scott favorite (#5 on the charts in 1960), asking me that musical question: *"What in the world's come over you?"* The song also wondered if I could ever change my mind. At first I took this message from the deep memory stores of my brain to be a protective warning about the writing task upon which I had embarked. But alas, this melodious warning was, as they say, too little and too late. Madly typing away, I banished the tune from my head. I had an unquenchable desire to tell the story of the impact of stress in the lives of kids with LD and ADHD, not to mention the fact that I had a signed book contract sitting in a folder on my desk.

The cognitive and emotional centers of my brain collaborated nicely to keep my fingers moving on the keyboard, but I understood why that song kept popping up. I was not without my own stress about writing this chapter. To say "I wrote the book on stress" is not the same as saying I had conquered it. (In fact, it's a double-entendre. Get it? . . . I wrote the book *while* stressed . . . never mind.)

Seriously! How was I ever going to write an introduction to the brain, the most complex organ in the human body, that you, my reader, would *want* to read, and that you would *understand?* Hundreds of thousands of textbooks and scholarly articles contained deep and dense discussions by brilliant scientists all over the globe who were trying to explain the mysteries of this incredible organ, and I had to do it in 70,000 words!

You'll learn in this book that the best way to combat stress is to gain some control over whatever it is that threatens you. My own stress level began to go down dramatically as I realized I didn't have to tell the entire story. I just needed to focus on the parts and systems of the brain that are most involved in the perception and processing of stress. As a neuropsychologist, I find this part of the story incredibly interesting, and hope you will as well. Trying to tell the story of stress without putting it in the context of the brain is like writing a novel without giving the characters a setting in which to act out their dramas. Without context, the reader can't see where the action is taking place.

This helps explain the perception of the many parents, kids, and even teachers who tend to view the behaviors that result from stress not as brain-based, brain-generated reactions but as premeditated oppositional or even defiant *mis*behaviors. Putting the characters of this story—the symptoms of stress—in the context of the brain and central nervous system makes it possible to understand their nature and their purpose in a way that makes scientific sense. So . . . stay with me as I set the stage for an amazing tale about how the brain deals with stress, and how the presence of neurologically based ADHD and LD put a special spin on the story.

THE HUMAN BRAIN: A BRIEF TOUR

To most people, the brain is terra incognita, a priceless piece of neurological real estate that we're glad we own but tend to take for granted unless or until something bad happens to it. So let's take a brief tour, just so you can appreciate the inestimable value of this miraculous organ called the brain. (If you're very familiar with brain anatomy and function, you might want to skip this overview and move on to "The Stress Response Explained," later in this chapter. You can always return to this section if subsequent reading reveals that you need a refresher.)

The average adult human brain weighs about three pounds (a kilogram and a half), which is a little bigger than a small cantaloupe or a large grapefruit, depending on the growing season. It starts out substantially smaller, of course, but as certain kinds of cells develop and change as a child moves into adulthood, the brain grows in size. As a result of *myelination* (the development of the outer coating of the long stem of brain cells, or neurons), and the proliferation of glial cells (the term *glial* comes from the Greek word for glue), which hold the brain together and feed it, an adult brain is about three times heavier than it was at birth. This is why you occasionally have to buy new hats.

The largest and most recognizable part of the brain is the large dome-shaped cerebrum, which is the outermost layer of brain tissue. If you lift off the skull and look down on the brain from above, it looks rather like what you see when you lift half the shell off a walnut. However, the cerebrum is not stiff like a nut; it has a thick, jelly-like consistency that allows it to literally bounce around inside the skull, which is why it's so important to protect the head from encounters with immovable objects.

A sheet of neural tissue called the *cerebral cortex* forms the outermost surface of the cerebrum. It includes up to six layers, each one different in terms of the arrangement of neurons and how well they connect and communicate with other parts of the brain. The cortex is distinguishable by its many little ridges (called *gyri*) and valleys (*sulci*). In terms of space, the cortex is an economically arranged region that folds in on itself many times. This results in a very large but mainly hidden surface area that contains more neurons than any other part of the brain.

Gray Matters

The term *gray matter* usually evokes an image of the cortex, because that's the part most visible in pictures of the brain. In fact, gray matter makes up not only the cerebral cortex but also the central portion of the spinal cord and areas called the *cerebellar cortex* and the *hippocampal cortex*. This dense tissue is packed full of neuronal cells, their *dendrites* (branching, root-like endings), *axon terminals* (the other end), and those sticky glial cells I mentioned earlier. The cortex is the area of the brain where the actual processing of information takes place. Because of its relative size and complexity, it's easy to understand why it plays a key role in memory, attention, perceptual awareness, thought, language, and consciousness.

A Division of Labor

A central groove, or fissure, runs from the front to back of the cortex, dividing it into right and left hemispheres. In general, the left hemisphere controls functions on the right side of the human body and the right hemisphere controls the left side, but there are significant exceptions and much sophisticated interaction *between* the two hemispheres. This communication between the left and right hemispheres is facilitated by the *corpus callosum,* a wide, flat bundle of axons located in the center of the brain, beneath the cortex. Think of it as the Lincoln Tunnel, connecting Manhattan and Jersey City. (I'll leave it to you to decide which one represents which hemisphere.)

The corpus callosum makes up the largest area of so-called white matter in the brain. White matter is made of bundles of axons each encased in a sheath of myelin. These nerve bundles lead into and out of the cortex and the cerebellum, and branch to the "old brain," the hippocampus. About 40 percent of the human brain is made up of gray matter, and the other 60 percent is white matter. It's the white matter that facilitates communication between different gray matter areas and between the gray matter and the rest of the body. White matter is the Internet of our brains. (Al Gore did not invent it.)

Evolution, tempered by experience, has employed gray matter to build what might be considered very well-developed "cognitive condos" that sit above the hippocampus. This arrangement is very important to a discussion of stress. Our old or primitive brain was primed for survival in our ancestors' environment. It's interesting to note that the brains of lower vertebrates like fish and amphibians have their white matter on the *outside* of their brain. We are blessed (and cursed) with lots of gray matter that gives us the ability to think things through (especially if we are anxious). Frogs and salamanders and their pond-side friends don't *think* about danger so much—they just get out of its way! (And while I can't be sure, I don't think that they have nightmares about giant human children armed with nets.)

How do you feel about that? In case you ever get this question on *Jeopardy* or in a game of Trivial Pursuit, the limbic system is made up of the amygdala, the hippocampus, the cingulate gyrus, fornicate gyrus, hypothalamus, mammillary body, epithalamus, nucleus accumbens, orbitofrontal cortex, parahippocampal gyrus, and thalamus. These structures work together to process emotions, motivation, the regulation of memories, the interface between emotional states and memory of events, the regulation of breathing and heart rate, the production of hormones, the "fight or flight" response, sexual arousal, circadian rhythms, and some decision-making systems. Pretty impressive job description, eh? The word *limbic* comes from the Latin word *limbus*, which translates to "belt" or "border," because this system forms the inner border of the cortex. The limbic system is part of the old brain and developed first, followed by the new brain: the cortex, which is sometimes referred to as the *neocortex*. Put *very* simply, the limbic system feels and remembers; the cortex acts and reacts. And they communicate with each other. Why is this important? The limbic system figures prominently in what's called the stress response, which is a central player in this book.

These days, both our old and new brains are activated when we're under stress. The primitive part, the limbic system (notably the hippocampus), sniffs out danger well before the new brain (the neocortex) actually processes it. The old brain responds first, acting as a sort of fire alarm system. It is the neocortex, and in particular, the frontal lobe (the prefrontal cortex), that helps us make sense of the alarms.

The cortex is made up of four major sections, arranged from the front to the back. These are called the *frontal, parietal, occipital,* and *temporal* lobes. Each of the four lobes is found in both hemispheres, and each is responsible for different, specialized cognitive functions. For example, the occipital lobe contains the primary *visual* cortex, and the temporal lobe (located by the temples, and close to the ears) contains the primary *auditory* cortex.

The frontal lobes are positioned at the frontmost region of the cerebral cortex and are involved in movement, decision making, problem solving, and planning. There are three main divisions of the frontal lobes. They are the *prefrontal cortex*, the *premotor area*, and the *motor area*. The frontal lobe of the human brain contains areas devoted to abilities that are enhanced in or unique to humans. The prefrontal cortex is responsible for planning complex cognitive behaviors, the expression of personality, decision making, and social behavior, as well as the orchestration of thoughts and actions necessary for a person to carry out goals. A specialized area known as the *ventrolateral* prefrontal cortex has primary responsibility for the processing of complex language. It is more commonly called *Broca's area*, named for a nineteenth-century French physician who determined its role.

In humans and other primates, an area located at the forward part of the prefrontal cortex is called the *orbitofrontal cortex*. It gets its name from its position immediately above the *orbits*, the sockets in which the eyes are located. The orbitofrontal cortex is very involved in interpreting rewards, decision making, and processing social and emotional information. For this reason, some consider it to be a part of the limbic system.

The *amygdala*, a part of the limbic system, is a brain structure that is responsible for decoding emotions, especially those the brain perceives as threats. As we evolved as a species, many of our alarm circuits have been grouped together in the amygdala. Not surprisingly, many regions of the brain send neurons into the amygdala. As a result, lots of sensory messages travel instantaneously to the amygdala to inform it of potential dangers lurking in our neighborhood. The amygdala is our guard dog.

The amygdala is directly wired to the hippocampus, also a part of the limbic system. Since the hippocampus is involved in storing and retrieving explicit memories, it feeds the amygdala with strong emotions triggered by these recollections. Why is this important? If a child has a negative experience in school, like being terribly embarrassed when asked to read in front of the class, the hippocampus just won't let go of this memory, and it shouts it out to the amygdala. Since the amygdala has signed a no confidentiality agreement, it sends a warning to the rest of the brain to go into protection mode. A rather amazing arrangement, don't you think?

What's really interesting about this is that the hippocampus specializes in processing the context of a situation. As a result, the child under stress generalizes the entire situation and uses it as justification for anxiety or stress: "Hey, they're telling me to go to social studies class." Even though not everything about social studies may be a threat—perhaps just the fact that they read out loud in there—the hippocampus sends out a general alert. So the student responds by protesting the whole enchilada: "No way I'm going there."

The amygdala is also wired to the *medial prefrontal cortex*. Want to know why this is important? This is the area of the brain that seems to be involved in planning a specific response to a threat to safety. Here's how it works: the child is hit with the gigantic *Titanic* news (which may be just "social studies coming up next" to the rest of the group, but it's "Submerged iceberg ahead!" to the kid worried about perceived horrors there). This two-way communication between the prefrontal cortex and the limbic system (particularly the amygdala) enables us to exercise conscious control over our anxiety. The emotion-cognition connection allows us to feel that we can do something about the danger that lies ahead. The child is then faced with the necessity of choosing a course of action that looks best for getting out of danger. This seems very protective but tends to be counterproductive, because the very mechanism that allows us to create an escape plan can actually create anxiety. "Oh crud—now we have to *do* something!" The brain not only allows us to imagine a negative outcome, which can help us avoid danger, it makes it possible for us to imagine dangers that do not actually exist. This is a problem for children who have ADHD, and a huge problem for students who have both anxiety disorders and ADHD. If you do a brain scan of a person with ADHD while putting on pressure to perform in a certain way, you see that this "to do" order results in a *decrease* in activity in the prefrontal cortex (instead of increasing it, as it does in most people). This helps explain why kids with ADHD don't respond well to lists. These are read as "thou shalt" messages. What helps some of us stay organized sends some kids with ADHD up the wall.

The Thalamus Bone's Connected to the . . .

Of course, it's not really a bone; it's a plum-shaped mass of gray matter that's multilayered and multifaceted. The thalamus, another part of the limbic system, sits on top of the hypothalamus which, in turn, sits on top of the *brain stem*, which is in the center of the base of the brain. This is a great location for the thalamus because it acts as a relay system that sends nerve fibers upstairs to all parts of the cerebral cortex as well as many *subcortical* (underneath the cortex) parts of the brain. The thalamus receives information from every sensory organ and its associated neurons except the *olfactory* (smell) system. The hypothalamus gets information from the eyes, the ears, the skin, and the tongue, and it forwards these messages to the corresponding areas of the cortex where they are processed. In terms of stress, this relay system is how the brain knows that it's in a dangerous environment.

That Stinks!

There's a bulb-shaped brain structure (called, as you might guess, the *olfactory bulb*) that has the specialized task of making sense of scents. Think about this: you can't see when you are sleeping, but you can *smell*. This is awfully helpful at night, especially when there's a fire. And when you get hold of a bad piece of fish. That's probably why the nose gets its own special receptor. It's another example of how sensitive the brain is to changes in the environment, and how it's always on alert!

Amazing Related Fact: Because a dog has about 200 million smell cells in its nose (versus 5 million in the human nose), it can pick up much fainter scents. Scientists tell us that salmon, too, have remarkable noses. By smelling the ocean, they can swim their way back to the exact stream in which they were born years before.

The Little Brain Down Under

The tour continues . . . Sitting under the occipital and temporal lobes of the brain is the *cerebellum*. It's about the size of a child's fist. Because it looks like a separate brainlike structure attached to the underside of the cortex, the cerebellum is sometimes referred to as the "little brain." It's connected to the brain stem, which in turn connects the brain to the spinal cord. The cerebellum used to be relegated to the very simple role of helping us maintain balance when we walk or run, but modern neuroscience has found that the cerebellum plays a much larger and more important role than that. Like the hypothalamus, it is involved in cognitive functions, including attention and language, as well as the ability to hold mental images in the "mind's eye." This part of the brain is important to the discussion of stress, since recent research has shown that the cerebellum also plays a key role in regulating responses to pleasure and to fear—strong forces when it comes to loving school or hating it.

The BeeGees song "Stayin' Alive" reached #1 on the pop charts in 1977. Maybe it was the beat, maybe it was John Travolta's dancing. Or maybe it's that the Gibb brothers' central lyric is quite literally always playing in our head. Keeping us safe—that is, "stayin' alive"—is the primary mission of the brain. The brain works very fast and very hard—mostly in the background—to do just that. It's exquisitely positioned close to ears, eyes, nose, and mouth so the signals from those sensory organs get into it without delay. Everything we encounter in our daily lives gets sent, incredibly fast, from our ears, nose, mouth, skin, and eyes to our brain for processing. The brain controls the other organ systems of the body, either by activating muscles or by causing secretion of chemicals such as hormones. That three-pound mass of gray and white matter somewhat miraculously uses this unending and potentially overwhelming stream of information to change our physical position, our pattern of thought, and our feelings or emotions—all in the service of keeping us alive. After all, a brain without a body is, if you will forgive me, nobody at all.

Now that you have had a brief introduction to this marvelous and complex organ called the brain, it will be easier to understand what happens to the brain under stress.

THE STRESS RESPONSE EXPLAINED

Stress was put on the map, so to speak, by a Hungarian-born Canadian endocrinologist named Hans Hugo Bruno Selye (ZEL-yeh) in 1950, when he presented his research on rats at the annual convention of the American Psychological Association. To explain the impact of stress, Selye proposed something he called the General Adaptation Syndrome (GAS), which he said had three components. According to Selye, when an organism experiences some novel or threatening stimulus it responds with an alarm reaction. This is followed by what Selye referred to as the recovery or resistance stage, a period of time during which the brain repairs itself and stores the energy it will need to deal with the next stressful event.

What is critical to the impact of stress on kids with LD or ADHD is the third stage of the GAS proposed by Selye. He said that if the stress-causing events continue, neurological exhaustion sets in. This phenomenon came to be referred to popularly as *burnout*. It's a state of mind characterized by a loss of motivation or drive and a feeling that you are no longer effective in your work. When this mental exhaustion sets in, a person feels emotionally flat, becomes cynical, and may display a lack of responsiveness to the needs of others. Does this sound like any kids with LD or ADHD that you know?

What's going on behind the scenes to cause this exhaustion? When humans are confronted by physical or mental stress or injury, an incredibly complex and critically important phenomenon rapidly takes place. First to be put on alert is the *hypothalamus*, which is situated deep inside the brain, under the thalamus and just above the brain stem. It's only about the size of an almond, but plays a crucial role in linking the nervous system to the endocrine system. The hypothalamus is particularly interesting because it controls the production of hormones that affect how the body deals with stress. When danger looms, the hypothalamus sends a nearly instantaneous chemical message down the spinal cord to the adrenal glands, which are located just above the kidneys. This first message signals the production of a stress hormone called *adrenaline*, also called *epinephrine*, which is released into the blood stream. *Norepinephrine* also plays a role here. The interaction of these two hormones controls the amount of glucose (sugar) in the blood, speeds up the heart rate, and increases metabolism and blood pressure, all of which get the body ready to respond to the stressor.

Meanwhile, the hypothalamus has been closely monitoring these changes, as well as the source of the stress, and now releases something called a *corticotrophin-releasing hormone* (CRH). CRH travels along the neurons that go from the hypothalamus into the *pituitary gland*. This important gland, which is located at the base of the brain just above the roof of the mouth, releases something called *adrenocorticotropic hormone* (ACTH) into the bloodstream. ACTH travels down to the adrenal glands. This triggers the adrenal glands to release another hormone called *cortisol*. (Seriously, folks, isn't this just *amazing*?)

Some cortisol (it's a steroid, by the way—you've probably used cortis*one* cream to quell some itch) is present in the bloodstream all the time. Normally, it's present at higher levels in the morning and much lower at night. Incidentally, recent research has found that the opposite is true in some children with autism, a finding that might shed light on this condition. A little cortisol is a good thing. It can give you that quick burst of energy that comes in handy for survival purposes. For a brief period, it can enhance your memory and help boost your immune system. The right amount of cortisol helps keep your body systems in a healthy balance, and it can fight against inflammation and even lower your sensitivity to pain—all good things when you've been injured or if you're going into battle against a single stressful opponent. But as often happens, too much of a good thing is, well . . . you know.

The stress response described here temporarily turns down or modifies nonessential bodily functions and activates the ones we need to keep us safe and healthy. It's a wonderfully efficient system, and it's fine-tuned to do its job well. Our brains and bodies are exquisitely designed to handle occasional acute stresses or injuries. However, they're not well-equipped to handle ongoing or chronic stress.

Hans Selye's research on the impact of stress in rats formed the foundation on which most subsequent studies about stress were built. Over time, and with the aid of sophisticated brain imagining technology, Selye's hypothesis has been scrutinized and expanded. He believed that all types of stress resulted in the same reaction in the brain, but we now know that this process is much more complex. For example, contemporary research shows that the brain responds in different ways based on its perceptions of the degree of control that a person has over a stressful event. Here's how this plays out in the brain.

The more stress people are under, or *think* they are under, the greater the amount of cortisol that's pumped into the blood by the adrenal glands. If too much cortisol is produced (as in acute stress) or is maintained at high levels in the bloodstream for too long (as in chronic stress), it can be very harmful. This hormone can cause a variety of physical problems, including blood sugar imbalances like *hypoglycemia* (a disturbance in the functioning of the thyroid), a decrease in muscle tissue and bone density, and high blood pressure: It can also make the body susceptible to disease by lowering immunity and inflammatory responses in the body and making it harder for wounds to heal. Prolonged exposure to excessive amounts of cortisol has been implicated in the rise of obesity because too much cortisol has been shown to be related to an increase in the amount of abdominal fat. Being overweight can lead to a host of other problems, including a decrease in "good" cholesterol (HDL) and an elevation of "bad" cholesterol (LDL) as well as metabolic disorders, heart attacks, and strokes. Most important to our discussion of stress in the lives of students with LD and ADHD is that too much cortisol can cause brain changes that result in impaired cognitive performance.

The Human Brain Likes to Be in Balance

Fortunately, the brain has some built-in safety systems. Too much cortisol in the blood signals the brain and adrenal glands to decrease cortisol production. And under normal conditions, when the stress is overcome or brought under control (by fighting, fleeing, or turning into an immobile statue, *or by mastering the threat*), the hypothalamus starts sending out the orders to stand down. Stop producing cortisol! Event over! Under *continuous* stress, however, this feedback system breaks down. The hypothalamus keeps reading the stress as a threat, furtively sending messages to the pituitary gland, which screams out to the adrenal glands to keep pumping out cortisol, which at this point begins to be neurotoxic—poison to the brain.

Bruce Perry and Ronnie Pollard, a well-respected psychiatrist-neurologist team, have contributed much to our understanding of the impact of stress and how it affects this sense of balance, or *homeostasis*, in the brain. Sometimes when stress is so intense, the delicate interaction among the brain systems designed to handle it are thrown off balance. Other researchers have also shown that intense, acute, or traumatic stress presents such a shock to the brain and the stress response system that it actually reorganizes the way the brain responds to stress. For example, neuroendocrinologist Bruce McEwen and neuroscientist Frances Champagne have shown that repeated activation of the stress response can result in physical changes, caused by too many inflammatory proteins being pumped into the bloodstream. The research of Michael Meany, a neurobiologist at McGill University, shows that adverse early childhood events (traumas) can actually change the chemistry of DNA in the brain. By a process known as methylation, little chemical markers attach themselves to the genes that control the stress hormone receptors. This makes it hard for the brain to regulate its response to stress.

Let me explain it this way: It's rather like the keys of a piano being hit so hard that the impact puts the strings out of tune. The piano still plays, but it plays differently. While another hard hit on the keys might have broken a tuned piano wire, the now-slack wire can withstand another hit . . . and another. If the hits are even harder, the wire stretches more. You can almost hear the piano (and the brain under acute stress) saying, "Go on, hit me again! I can take it." But the cost is that both are out of tune and the melody is never quite the same. In the human nervous system, this kind of adjustment or *adaptation* protects the brain from harm by changing the way it responds to stress. Perry and Pollard point out that repeated exposure to stress—chronic stress—results in a new way of coping with a continuous stressor, but it is *less effective*. Not a good thing.

Both repeated traumas and chronic stress can result in a number of biological reactions. Neurochemical systems are affected that can cause a cascade of changes in attention, impulse control, sleep, and fine motor control. Other researchers have zeroed in on specific parts of the brain that are affected by stress, and their work shows us just how refined and complex this process is. For example, Walker, Toufexis, and Davis suggest that an area of the brain called the *bed nucleus of the stria terminalis* plays a role in certain types of anxiety and stress responses. Although this area is not thought to be involved in *acute* traumatic events, these authors have shown that it is responsible for processing the slower-onset, longer-lasting responses that frequently accompany *sustained* threats. (Aha!) These authors further posit that the physiological reactions in this area may persist *even after* the threat goes away. (Ah-HA!!) Why is this relevant? Even when teachers and other professionals try to get these kids to move forward, the memory of past traumatic events lingers on—and impedes efforts to lead students to a higher level of competence.

All of this research has incredible significance in the discussion of kids who are under stress as a consequence of their LD and ADHD. It also has implications for students with other disorders, such as Asperger syndrome and autism. Pollard and Perry tell us that chronic activation of certain parts of the brain involved in the fear response, such as the hypothalamic-pituitary-adrenal (HPA) axis, can wear out other parts of the brain such as the hippocampus, which is involved in cognition and memory. Again, *cognition and memory:* two of the most important building blocks for successful learning, attention, and social communication.

What's Bullying Got to Do with It?

The underlying thesis of this book is that chronic stress changes brain chemistry and therefore brain function. This connection is made even stronger by a burgeoning amount of provocative new research that sheds light on the adverse impact of bullying on the brains of victims. Dr. Martin Teicher, a neuroscientist at McLean Hospital, a Harvard teaching hospital, scanned the brains of young adults who reported that they had been bullied by peers when they were younger. The brain cells in their corpus callosum, that fibrous bundle of tissue that connects the two hemispheres of the brain, showed evidence of cellular changes that were not seen in a comparable group of students who had not been bullied. The neurons in this part of the brains of victims had less myelin, that is, less of the protective coating that covers the nerves. Since myelin facilitates communication between cells, reduced myelin results in a slowdown in the transmission of brain signals. Rapid and efficient transmittal of neurological impulses in the brain is a prerequisite for effective learning and memory.

Here's the reason this is so important to the discussion of stress: because of the differences that many children with LD and ADHD exhibit (impulsive behavior, poor receptive and expressive language, poor social perception, and so on), they are more likely than other children to be victims of bullying. This is borne out both by research and by clinical observation.

What *is* clear is that a slowdown in neural transmission in the still-developing brains of young people affects learning, memory, and emotional reactivity. Dr. Tracy Vaillancourt, a psychologist at the University of Ottawa, and her colleagues found that both occasional and frequent bullying can recalibrate the amount of the stress hormone cortisol produced by a group of twelve-year-old victims. Interestingly, she also found that boys who had been bullied had very high levels of cortisol, while corresponding levels were abnormally *low* in girls who had been harassed. The exact reasons are yet unclear, but we do know that the amount of cortisol is reset or recalibrated in people and animals that are in a state of chronic stress. If girls are neurobiologically more vulnerable to stress, this might account for the difference. Dr. Vaillancourt points out that high levels of cortisol can damage and even kill neurons in the hippocampus. The impact of stress damage can be seen in the results of formal testing. Dr. Vaillancourt found that bullied teens performed more poorly than their peers on tests of verbal memory. She concludes, "Bullying likely diminishes a person's ability to cope with stress, possibly placing them at risk for psychopathology and ill health."

And here's another interesting piece of information generated by Martin Teicher's work that relates to Dr. Vaillancourt's. While Teicher did not determine a cause-and-effect relationship, he found that students who had been verbally or physically harassed reported more psychiatric symptoms, including depression and anxiety, than their bully-free classmates.

While additional research is necessary, it is impossible to avoid wondering whether the disability-bullying-stress connection is a significant factor in the lives of many of the children you and I care for and care about.

TO FIGHT, FLEE, OR FREEZE—THAT IS THE QUESTION

With a better understanding of the neurobiology of stress, the LD-ADHD-stress connection becomes clear. Students with learning disabilities or ADHD, confronted with the stress created by exposure to tasks that are *in reality or in their perception* too difficult (and thus threatening), exhibit the protective behavior of any organism under extreme stress: *They fight, they flee, or they freeze.* When these kids don't understand why they can't do what other kids can do (master the stressor), and they can't see any way to get out of a situation that won't go away, they begin to shut down. Trapped in this situation, from which there is no apparent exit, they may lash out with words or fists. They may tear up papers, throw books, or overturn desks. As much as they love their teacher, they may bite the hand that feeds them. If they override their impulse to act up or act out to escape the stress caused by a feeling of cognitive incompetence, these kids may freeze like the proverbial deer in the headlights.

Now that I've redefined No-Brainer as Know-Brainer . . . let's move on to Chapter Two, where I introduce a few kids who will help illustrate how this plays out in the classroom. Let's see what happens when stress goes to school.

2

Stress Goes to School

If your eyes see a tiger cut out of paper or a tiger ready to pounce, it's your brain that gives that information meaning and tells you which you need to fear. When what you encounter is read by your brain as good, pleasurable, satisfying, or soothing, you get the *go* signal to approach. If it's a new or different experience—something you haven't encountered before—your brain is able to access a vast network of neurons to help you decide whether you should enter this new territory. By allowing you to compare the new experience with the memories of previous encounters, this mechanism makes it possible for you to decide if it's safe to approach or engage. And you can make other choices; whether to dip a toe in the water or jump in the deep end of the pool. Let's see how this plays out in the classroom.

ALL THE CLASSROOM'S A STAGE

Eli, who has had prior success solving quadratic equations, looks at a page filled with problems and says to himself: "This is a piece of cake!" or "These are like solving mysteries" and eagerly puts pencil to paper. Stimulated by the task, Eli's limbic system is calling up many positive memories. Eli gets excited, not stressed,

---

by the idea of doing math. Not only does he believe he will be successful at most of what he'll be expected to do, he knows that he'll be able to find out how to do the rest by asking his teacher for help, or by analyzing his errors to see where he went wrong. He also knows that even if he gets one or two of the problems wrong, it's not the end of the world. He always gets more right than he gets wrong, and what's more, he can usually fix all of his mistakes. For Eli, errors, while mildly irritating, are not a reason to crumble in defeat. Errors are challenges to be confronted and overcome. He is most often the master of this domain; *he is in control.*

And then there's Julie, a student who has mastered the six-times tables, who approaches a page filled with 6's and 7's with a cautious optimism, thinking to herself: "I can do the *sixes* . . . so I *probably* can figure out the sevens." She is invoking the power of past successes to help her face this new challenge. She is also doing what other confident students do—building a bridge between the known and the new, and stepping out, albeit cautiously, onto that bridge with the feeling that she'll get safely to the other side. It has always been this way for her. Success leads to success. Bridges keep getting built. And if they start to crumble, she does not fall into the abyss below. She hops gingerly back to the edge, surveys the scene, restocks her supplies, and looks for another way across. Oh, if we could only package what these kids have and give it to kids who don't! (By the end of this book, you'll have more ideas about how to do just that.)

Incoming!

In the same way that your brain helps you approach those tasks or experiences that have the look, feel, or smell of success, it also lets you know when a threat has broken through your protective perimeter fence. Informed by one or more of your sense organs, the brain serves as your radar or distant early warning system, continuously scanning the physical and emotional horizon for incoming experiences that might be harmful to your survival. All mammals share this capacity to process information and instantaneously categorize it as good or bad, safe or harmful, helpful or hurtful—and steer the body that contains the brain to do what it must to protect itself.

More Brain Biology

Recall that the amygdala is the brain structure responsible for decoding emotions, especially those the brain perceives as threats. It's a message center; signals travel almost instantaneously from many parts of the brain to the amygdala to inform it of potential dangers lurking in the neighborhood. Just like a guard dog.

The amygdala is directly wired to the hippocampus, which specializes in processing the context of a situation. Even if you tell a student specifically why success is likely ("You did this homework with me—you know this information cold!") or try to minimize the fear ("just try to relax . . ."), a child under stress regards the entire situation—the idea of going to class—as justification for anxiety. Since the hippocampus is involved in storing and retrieving explicit memories, its connections to the amygdala may be the origin of strong emotions triggered by particular memories. So if a child has had a negative experience in school, like being terribly embarrassed when asked to read in front of the class, it's the hippocampus that just won't let go of this memory.

Bye, Bye Birdie

Sometimes there are system overrides that allow the brain to bypass its warning message and to act in some way that will not necessarily keep the harm at bay. For example, a nesting blue jay is biologically programmed to fly away from her nest if a potential predator comes close—and not to engage the enemy, because to do so would defeat her goal of leading it away from the nest and her chicks. To attack the intruder might also place the safety of Mrs. Jay in jeopardy. She could die in this encounter, leaving her babies unprotected in the short term and unfed in the long term. The consequence? The end of this branch of the Jay family! So if momma Jay sees a human approach the nest, or a toothy jaw, hooked beak, or taloned foot comes dangerously close to those beautiful little eggs or recently hatched chicks, she'll fly away, noisily drawing the villain away from her downy little darlings. At that moment, the intruder looks in her direction, attention turned from the nest to her raucous departure. If this evasive strategy doesn't work, Mrs. Jay is likely to take a more aggressive approach by swooping down on the head of the trespasser.

The blue jay's instinctive behavior sheds some light on the intensity with which students can react to threatening situations in the classroom. Kids under academic stress do the same thing. When avoidance or diversion ("I have to go to the bathroom") doesn't work, when the demands to perform persist despite the student's attempt to escape (the threat continues), things can get intense pretty quickly. Protective diversion turns to defensive attack.

Threats That Lurk and Loom

Consider Cesar, a fifth grader with ADHD and LD who will tell you he "hates everything about school." On a daily basis, he can be observed joking around in the classroom, going on frequent trips to the nurse's office, drawing on his desk, or throwing paper wads when he thinks the teacher isn't watching. Viewed from the perspective of threat avoidance, this is to be expected. He's being defensive and self-protective. Cesar does these things just to get out of doing work that he thinks will make him look or feel incompetent. Wouldn't you? Have you ever called in sick when you were unprepared for class or work?

However, in Cesar's school the date for state-required standardized tests is fast approaching, and Cesar has been told that he has to pass them in order to move on to the next grade. As the infamous day approaches, preceded by much discussion about the importance of the exams and the many hours of in-class preparation, Cesar feels increasingly trapped. Backed into a corner, he does what any threatened animal does when it has no place to escape when faced with a predator—he lashes out. Trapped by the demands of a situation he cannot control, this otherwise very nice and appealing little boy becomes rude and uses language not often heard in the classroom. He may even get physically aggressive with those in power—those who have the ability to put him in harm's way; those who are forcing him to move toward danger. His behavior isn't the willful negativity that in some circumstances might earn the label of oppositional defiant disorder. It's neurologically based survival behavior switching on during a time of acute stress. This is the main point of this book: kids who are threatened by the demands of their environments try to escape. If they can't, they fight! If we understand how the human brain works, this reaction is predictable, and more important, it is *preventable*.

WHAT'S GOING ON IN CESAR'S BRAIN?

Step into the Wayback Machine . . .

Some years ago, Bell Labs created a Prestige Science Film Series for kids. One film that I showed often when I taught middle school science was called *Hemo the Magnificent*, which was written and directed by Frank Capra and starred Dr. Frank Baxter and Richard Carlson. A delightful and captivating interaction between live humans and animated characters, it was created to explain the human circulatory system. While this film is dated a bit (the TV producer character smokes cigarettes throughout the show!), and the religious overtones about how this all came to be are obvious, it's now a classic that still entertains and educates (at least as far as 1957 science allows) on YouTube.

Ladies and Gentlemen . . . Neuro the Magnificent!

I wish there were a similar film that would describe the relationship between stress and learning the way "Hemo" explained how blood sustains life by tracing its flow through the human circulatory system. Since there's not, I'll invoke the spirit of Hemo, and have *Neuro the Magnificent*'s resonant voiceovers explain what happens when Cesar is confronted by a stress-inducing activity.

Lights . . . Camera . . . Action!

Cesar's teacher asks the class to take out the homework they did last night. Cesar tried to do the homework, but since he found it difficult and upsetting, the only thing he has in his backpack is a crumpled piece of paper. Let's take a look into Cesar's brain:

The frontal lobe of the left cerebral hemisphere is responsible for understanding or giving meaning to Cesar's experiences. It allows him to categorize, analyze, and problem-solve. The left hemisphere can organize information and also remember sequences of events, so it plays a major role in connecting current experiences to past learning. Cesar's LD and ADHD have made learning excruciatingly difficult, and his left hemisphere knows that because it's been communicating with the other side of his brain. The role of Cesar's right hemisphere is to recognize and process nonverbal information and handle emotional memory. As soon as the teacher mentioned homework, Cesar's right hemisphere went into high gear, initiating a rapid but very complex process. Not only is the right hemisphere layering emotions that the limbic system just sent up onto the current task ("take out your homework"), the left hemisphere is now conjuring up an image of the events of last night, which involved a frustrated, teary interaction with Cesar's mom, who was trying to get him to do work he believed was too difficult. So now his brain is awash in a biochemical bath of negative emotions.

In a rather miraculous way, the left hemisphere plays a role in inhibiting some of these emotional responses. In kids with *successful* learning histories, it tells the right hemisphere, "Calm down, don't worry so much. You've done this before." However, in Cesar's case, he has faced this moment many times before, and it usually hasn't turned out well. So right hemisphere says to left hemisphere: "Calm *down?* That's easy for *you* to say. Our boy's gonna freak out about this."

So what do you think Cesar's doing right now? *"Mr. Producer, can we get a look into that classroom again?"*

Cesar is slumped down in his chair, wishing he could slip quietly under his desk. He is not reaching for his homework. He is not hearing the words of his teacher; he is having a "Charlie Brown moment"— hearing only a muted series of noises coming from her head. "Wak-wak-wa-wah-wah . . ."

Back to Cesar's Brain

Focus on the very front of the brain, on that area called the prefrontal cortex. You might remember that this part is involved in processing information, maintaining attention, and monitoring the hormonal responses generated by input from the senses. It's divided into three distinct zones. The lateral prefrontal cortex helps assess various alternatives to a problem or a dilemma and choose the strategy to use to get out of a situation. The orbito-frontal cortex is the part that makes it feasible to defer immediate gratification and dampen emotions in the short term so as to be able to think and plan for the longer term. If it activates, it allows kids like Cesar to think: "If I wait and don't respond to this right now and think about my options, things might turn out better." Still another section of the prefrontal cortex, the ventromedial cortex, is thought to be one of the sites in the brain that process risk and fear as they figure in decision making.

In Cesar's brain, these areas are working at warp speed. His ears are listening to the teacher's droning and to the sound of classmates as they begin to go into learning mode; his eyes are scanning the room, noting that a majority of the kids are reaching, seemingly unafraid, for their homework. His hypothalamus goes on high alert and begins sending a rapid stream of messages down the spinal cord to the adrenal glands, telling them to pump out some adrenaline, since Cesar may have to take some evasive action. His eyes are looking for the door to the classroom. His limbic system is getting bombarded with emotion-laden messages. When this happens, his brain gets stuck; he can't think flexibly about different ways to solve his dilemma. Not being able to figure things out means not being in control. Not being in control and having no way out *defines* stress.

Cesar feels a compelling need to tell someone how he feels, but he can't find the words to do it. Even if he could, he'd be too frightened of the consequences. He might incur the anger or frustration of his teacher, and he's likely to be on the receiving end of the whispers, snickering, or outright laughter of his classmates. He has been down this road before. So he sits quietly, but his body is on alert. His nervous system is under siege, but you have to know what to look for to see that. If we zoom the camera and microphone in on Cesar, we notice his increased heart rate, tense muscles, sweaty palms, and shallow breathing. We might notice his eyes darting back and forth, scanning the landscape for danger, or looking down at the desktop to avoid a face-to-face confrontation.

The Language-Stress Connection

Among all the other things it does, the left prefrontal cortex is the part of Cesar's brain where language is received, interpreted, and generated. After about the age of four in children whose language develops well, the left prefrontal cortex, with its decision-making and interpretive functions, takes a front seat to the emotion-generating right prefrontal cortex. This development allows language (both internal self-talk or outwardly expressed communication) to be used to process and modulate the emotion-laden messages coming from the right hemisphere. The left prefrontal cortex plays a role in toning down the activity of the limbic system and throwing cold water on negative responses such as "There's no way I can do this!" Under ordinary circumstances, the prefrontal cortex neutralizes negative messages rather quickly, notably by sending out signals to adjust the production of cortisol, and of dopamine, norepinephrine, and serotonin, three neurotransmitters that are important in mood regulation. This intricate chemical process helps cope with negative events or thoughts. But in the brains of kids who are under chronic stress, making that adjustment is sometimes difficult.

It turns out that old negative memories have a long shelf-life, and Cesar's got plenty of them. He's a fourth grader (though he's nearly eleven; he has repeated a grade) who has a language-based learning disability. He also comes from a bilingual family where English is not the first language used in the home. He has difficulty with syntax and grammar in both English and Spanish, and his expressive language is disorganized and inefficient. As a result, he has learned to keep quiet to avoid being misunderstood and perhaps ridiculed. His perceptual-motor skills are well developed, and he has become very good with his hands. This is seen in his artwork, which is very expressive, and also in the boxing ring at the local boys' club. Since he cannot use language as easily as other kids to override his emotional impulses, he's more likely to respond physically, *inside the ring and out.*

In Cesar's brain, his hypothalamus is monitoring this homework scenario as it unfolds. It doesn't sense a good outcome here, so it sends out more messages, this time to the pituitary gland, urging it to prod the adrenals to create more cortisol. The adrenal glands are now on autopilot, churning out some very potent corticosteroid. *Heart rate and blood pressure up, breathing shallow, blood to legs, no blood to stomach (no need to waste time digesting food now), pupils widen (to see the danger more clearly), muscles tense, ready to sprint.*

Cut!

I hope this little foray into cinema-land gives you a better appreciation of what happens to a boy's brain when confronted with stress. But note that this scenario describes but a single episode in Cesar's day. It's a clip from the full-length feature of his life. The actual film goes on and on and on. The scene described here is followed by others like it, in a relentless flow of episodes that bear witness to the fact that this is a *chronic* problem.

ACUTE STRESS VERSUS ENDLESS STRESS

Brief periods of mild or predictable stress are a part of everyone's experience. These encounters help get ready to cope with the demands of day-to-day life. Stress, and the body's reaction to it, is an adaptive mechanism. The body's survival actually depends upon the ability to mount a response to stress. But prolonged, severe, or unpredictable stress is problematic. As you learned earlier, brain development can literally be altered by these experiences, resulting in negative impacts on the child's physical, cognitive, emotional, and social growth.

Why Transitions Are So Difficult

When kids like Cesar walk into school, they may be on high alert. Because they have been burned so many times, they may be thinking about what's coming next, even during activities that are designed to be fun. This helps explain why kids with LD and

ADHD have such major problems with transition. Getting ready for the next class or activity often means moving from a zone of comfort and control over some activity (and the pleasure that brings) into a zone of incompetence and worry. As Shore tells us, "Chronic stimulation of the brain's fear response means that the regions of the brain involved in this response are frequently activated. When they are, other regions of the brain, such as those involved in complex thought, cannot also be activated and are therefore not 'available' to the child for learning."

Shore's research focuses on children who have been exposed to traumatic stress. Clearly, the worse the event, the more serious the risk to body and brain. Shore and other researchers differenti-ate single or multiple exposures to stress from stress that goes on unabated. The longer the event goes on, the more likely the child is to endure brain changes that, while destructive to memory and cognition, make it easier to deal with the unending onslaught of stressful stimuli. I'm not making the case here that not being able to read or to gain control over the executive functions that allow for an organized, satisfying experience in school con-stitutes traumatic stress. However, my clinical experience has shown me that the inability to develop a feeling of mastery over one's learning environment or bring order into a life that is frag-mented and chaotic at its neurological core does constitute chronic stress.

It's clear that chronic stress activates neural pathways and overdevelops the regions of the brain involved in anxiety and fear responses. What is most chilling about this fact is that this overactivation of fear *often results in the underdevelopment of other neural pathways and other regions of the brain.* This means that the brain is so busy protecting itself that the way it works actu-ally changes. As a result, it can't do what it needs to do in school.

It's indisputable that children who have experienced trau-matic stress, such as sexual or physical abuse, focus their brain's energies on staying alive and finding help. I contend that the brains of children who experience chronic exposure to stress are also engaged in the business of survival. I believe this explains what's happening in the brains of students who spend every day in school feeling stupid, ashamed, embarrassed, and harassed—by the demands of teachers, of books, of homework. They also experience as chronic stressors their own comparison to the omnipresent classmates who seem to fly through the school day and its challenges, and even seem to have fun doing it.

Family: Gotta Love 'Em, But . . .

Transitions from school to home can also add to the chronic stress felt by some children with LD and ADHD. Some kids arrive home every day only to be taunted by a younger sister or brother whose organization skills or learning abilities have outshone theirs for years! In a child who has been trained by experience to be on the lookout for trouble, even the sympathy of a capable sibling can be perceived as a veiled insult to self-esteem. On the weekends, a child may spend time with Grammy and Grandpa, whose loving but worried and sad glances at each other do not escape the gaze of a child who looks up from struggling to read a book to them. These kids dread back-to-school nights because they do not want their parents to see their messy cubby or their disorganized drawing or poorly spelled essay hanging on the classroom wall next to the work of some budding Rembrandt or Hemingway.

Assaults to a child's self-concept and self-confidence range from subtle and passive to overt and active—but they are ubiquitous; they are always there, or always lurking around the corner. For many children with LD, ADHD, or both who are not in environments that grasp this problem and know how to deal with it, there is no relief from these insidious forces. There is, indeed, *nowhere to hide*.

Stress Can Lead to Anxiety and Depression

Research has shown that early traumatic experiences can interfere with the development of the subcortical and limbic systems. Trauma can give rise to extreme anxiety and eventually depression. In its most severe form, early trauma can even cause difficulty forming attachments to other people. Chronic activation of the neural pathways involved in the fear response can create permanent memories that shape a child's perception of and response to the whole environment. This may help to explain why children with learning disabilities and attention deficits have such a difficult time letting go of the memories of earlier encounters with people or materials that challenged their competence. Without appropriate intervention, these negative interchanges and the emotions that accompany them stack up, backing the child further and further into a corner.

WHY SPECIAL EDUCATION MAY NOT BE THE SOLUTION

This next comment may be taken as unkind, but it's based on many years doing observations in hundreds of classrooms, and is relevant to the discussion of stress at school. Some children with ADHD and LD have been put into self-contained special education classrooms in which the major modification made to their programs was *to make them easier*. Sometimes this is done in the name of making the environment less stressful. Theoretically, this approach does reduce the stress, but it creates another problem. If children are allowed or encouraged to work at a level that is consistently below their ability, this may certainly shut off the fear response. However, it also confirms the students' belief that they are less capable than other kids—and this class is the living proof of that. *Dumbing down shall not raise thee up.* Unless what's special about the education of these kids is that it teaches them how to face ever-increasing challenges with a sense of confidence that's fueled by competence, it just isn't the right kind of special. In Chapter Eight (primarily for teachers) you'll find out whether your classroom or program is one of the many that challenges kids to do their personal best. In that chapter, I share techniques that can promote this kind of special education in every class, every day.

A CHALLENGE

Let me end this chapter with a call to action. Knowing what we know about the brain and how it responds to stress, and how that stress changes a brain in ways that make learning and attention even harder for kids with LD and ADHD, we must do the following:

1. Make sure that parents, teachers, and the kids themselves understand the connection between stress, LD, and ADHD.
2. Make sure that we equip students with the skills they need to recognize the negative impact of stress on performance.
3. Teach children in a manner that leads to mastery.
4. Teach students how to advocate for themselves, by helping them understand how they learn, what gets in the way, and what they can do about it.

The first two chapters of this explore the neurobiological basis of stress and how it looks in school. The next three are designed to help you reach goal #1. You'll learn what's really meant by LD and ADHD, and you'll develop a better understanding of the relationship between these two conditions. You'll see why knowing how to explain LD and ADHD in a way that kids can understand is a prerequisite for teaching them how to deal with stress. Read and learn . . . and change lives.

Making Sense of LD and ADHD

PART TWO

Making Sense of LD
and ADHD

3

What's in a Name?

Clearing Up Misperceptions About
Learning Disabilities

This chapter and the next answer questions about LD and ADHD and their relationship to each other. Despite the massive amount of information that has found its way into print, electronic media, and videos, or perhaps because of it, there continues to be a lot of confusion about these conditions. In my interactions with students, teachers, and parents, I continue to hear questions like these: *Is ADHD a learning disability? What is dyslexia, anyway? Isn't that when you reverse letters and numbers? Are all learning disabilities alike? What's "executive functioning" and what does it have to do with ADHD and LD?*

The list of important questions goes on and on. Both the definitions and the group of people who need to be educated about these conditions are constantly changing. Only with a clear understanding of these conditions can parents, teachers, and other professionals confidently create an effective plan to help children overcome their challenges. While definitions of LD and ADHD are moving targets—concepts that change as a result of new research, the publication of new diagnostic tools and guidelines, or the political climate—I can try to give you a better understanding of how things stand today and how they got that way.

I focus on learning disabilities in this chapter and then move on to an exploration of ADHD in Chapter Four. While there is significant overlap between the two, separating the discussions underscores the fact that these are unique conditions, each with its own history, definitions, and representative organizations.

EXPLORING THE CONNECTION

Before going down these separate but related paths, let me first say just a little about the relationship between LD and ADHD, so as to help weave these two chapters together.

ADHD and LD are distinctly different conditions. ADHD is one of the most common chronic conditions of childhood. It affects from 4 percent to 12 percent of school-aged children, a total that includes about three times as many boys as girls. It is a brain-based disability characterized by some combination of inattention, impulsivity, and distractibility. Despite the "H" in the name, it is only *sometimes* accompanied—and generally made more severe—by hyperactivity.

It's generally acknowledged among teachers and clinicians that there is no such thing as pure ADHD (or pure LD, for that matter). It's a much more complex issue. We know that many children with ADHD also have learning disabilities. Depending on the source of the information, there is a 30–50 percent overlap in these two conditions. According to a recent study by K. Yoshimasu in the journal *Pediatrics*, which controls for many of the variables that have made previous studies suspect, fully half of children with ADHD may experience problems with reading. This new research underscores the need to consider the presence of LD when ADHD is suspected and vice versa. If one condition is addressed and the other ignored, the problem will not be dealt with adequately.

We say that ADHD and LD often coexist, and (while I think the use of the term is a bit too macabre) we sometimes refer to them as *comorbid conditions*. It's important to point out that while these two conditions do often occur together, that does not mean that one *causes* the other. Rather, the LD and ADHD *interact* with one another in different ways in different people. This unfortunately adds to the confusion about the nature of both conditions, making the separate discussion in this part of the book especially useful.

HOW MANY CHILDREN HAVE LEARNING DISABILITIES?

The U.S. Department of Education reports that of the six million children in special education, half are identified as having a specific learning disability (SLD). This is about 4 percent of all school-aged children. Up to 90 percent of children identified as SLD have reading as their primary area of difficulty. Estimates of the actual number of students vary from source to source, reflecting variations in the definition or the methods used to collect the data, or both.

All Learning Disabilities Are Not Alike

Doing a headcount of students with LD is further confounded by the fact that there are several different kinds of learning disabilities. According to the International Dyslexia Association, dyslexia is a specific type of learning disability, and is by far the most common. These difficulties are typically the result of a deficit in the *phonological* (relating to sound) component of language—primarily a reading problem that has its roots not in the ears nor in the eyes but, you guessed it—in the brain. Because the hallmark problem in dyslexia is difficulty making sense of the sounds of letters in isolation or in combination, or understanding or using the written or spoken word, it is generally regarded as a language-based learning disability. Dyslexia is said to exist if problems in reading and spelling persist despite the presence of at least average intelligence and exposure to effective teaching. In other words, it's not attributed to a cognitive delay or to poor or interrupted teaching. The underlying difficulty with phonemic analysis can understandably lead to problems with reading comprehension; it's hard to understand what you read in a halting, inefficient manner. As a result of this difficulty with comprehension, children and adults with dyslexia may have a limited vocabulary and may not have acquired information that comes from reading books.

The core characteristics of dyslexia are common to all individuals who have been diagnosed with this condition, but the problems it causes can range from mild to severe, or may emerge or worsen with exposure to increasingly more difficult language. This is why young adults who have a history of previously compensated LD may run into difficulty when they move into the higher grades. When they were younger, the reading and spelling abilities of these kids may have been impaired but functional— perhaps because of practice or specialized educational intervention. They may also have relied on their ability to use visual cues (how words look), rather than auditory cues (how they sound), to read and spell. Some students are taught a core group of short, common words that provide clues to other longer words that may include these smaller "sight words."

Kids with dyslexia typically don't like reading, writing, or spelling very much, but they may excel in the nonreading components of math, the arts, or lab sciences. As they advance through high school, college, or graduate school, however, they may eventually reach a point where they are overwhelmed by the complexity of the vocabulary they encounter, or by the volume of reading they have to do. Spell-check features on a word processor may simply not be enough to handle the sophisticated language of law school or medical school. It is at this time that some of these students, not understanding the problem they have, drop out of advanced degree programs, despite their intellect and aptitude. A fortunate few are referred by enlightened advisors for a comprehensive assessment of their neurocognitive profile, in order to learn strategies that will help them manage the demands of a challenging, complex curriculum. Which, incidentally, many are able to do.

Other Kinds of Learning Disabilities

There is also a very specific type of LD that is characterized by impairments in functions carried out mainly in the right cerebral hemisphere. Because the left hemisphere (which is involved in language processing) is not primarily involved, this condition has been given the sometimes confusing name of Nonverbal Learning Disability (NVLD or simply NLD). This means that it is not a verbal learning disability but another kind. It's the kind of LD that can impair performance on visual-spatial tasks like form-copying or create difficulty with organization and planning. In essence, students with NVLD can't see how things are sequenced or how they go together. They tend to have very well-developed verbal skills, and many can write or talk, although often in a rambling or disjointed manner, about a topic of their choice. When they are asked to write an organized essay about something the teacher assigns, however, these students often freeze up because they can't envision a way to put their abundant ideas into an organized, cohesive story. Clinicians generally agree that a brain difference causes this difficulty. I believe that anxiety or stress, caused by the pressure of having to do something that is incredibly challenging, exacerbates this problem.

Students with NVLD have a difficult time making sense of social situations, and they may behave in a quirky, awkward manner when pressed to navigate the difficult terrain of social interactions. Some professionals believe that NVLD falls at the mild end of the autism spectrum, because of the rigid cognitive style and social challenges seen in students with Asperger syn-drome, which is generally regarded as "high-functioning" autism. These students find it very difficult to get with the flow of a conversation or to read the social cues of fellow classmates. In many students, finding themselves at this intersection triggers the stress response described in Chapter Two.

There Are More?

Several other types of learning disabilities besides dyslexia and NVLD have been identified, and their names convey some hints regarding the skills or abilities involved. For example, *dyscalculia* (dis-kal-*kyool*-ya) is a specific learning disability that impacts performance in the nonreading components of math.

Dysgraphia is another type of LD, characterized by difficulty with fine motor skills such as motor memory, muscle control, and coordinated movement. This results in difficulty in recognizing and forming letters, numbers, and words on paper, and in copying or drawing designs.

A related condition is called *dyspraxia*. This is a motor coor-dination problem that can affect the planning of movements and coordination because brain messages are not being accu-rately transmitted to the body. The diagnosis and treatment of both dyspraxia and dysgraphia generally fall into the domain of an occupational therapist. In the *Diagnostic and Statistical Manual of Mental Disorders* (DSM-IV), dysgraphia is regarded as a "Disorder of Written Expression" defined by "writing skills [that] . . . are substantially below those expected given the per-son's . . . age, measured intelligence, and age-appropriate educa-tion." Be aware that the term is often used, as in the preceding example, to include all disorders of written expression. Other groups, such as the International Dyslexia Association, use the term *dysgraphia* exclusively to refer to difficulties with *handwrit-ing*. While dysgraphia is always considered a type of learning disability, dyspraxia *may* be referred to as a learning disability because it does not affect overall intelligence or ability, but has an impact on certain specific skills. Officially, dyspraxia falls under the category of "Developmental Coordination Disorder" in the DSM-IV.

Is it dysgraphia or something else? While a student who has dysgraphia can have difficulty putting thoughts on paper, it's very important to determine whether that difficulty has its roots in the relatively pure perceptual-motor-integration weakness that is at the core of dysgraphia, or from other factors. For example, poor executive functioning (the organizational aspects of planning and executing written work) or a language-processing deficit (for example, the inability to hold a sequence in memory long enough to get it down on paper) can both create difficulties in writing. We know that individuals with cerebral palsy, a condition that presumes injury or damage to the motor area of the brain, may be unable to carry out the mechanical aspects of drawing or printing effectively. This does not mean, however, that their ability to *process* language is impaired.

The same kind of analysis can be applied to spelling. Words can be spelled incorrectly because the writer does not know the sequence of the sounds that make up the word, or how to line up the symbols for those sounds in proper order. Spelling problems might also be due to poor motor sequencing (knowing and remembering which letter goes first) or coordination (how to construct the letter). It is easy to see the confusion that exists around the use of the term *dysgraphia*, which underscores the importance of good clinical judgment in making this diagnosis. This clarification is critical, since interventions have to be matched to the problem—not to the label.

With the exception of the conditions just discussed, and the use of the term *language-based LD* as an alternative to dyslexia, no other specific learning disabilities are uniquely named. For example, there is no *science LD* or *history LD*; rather, the learning disability is described by its characteristics and the impact it has on the person's functioning. If a learning disability has not been defined as dyslexia or NVLD, dysgraphia or dyscalculia, you should expect it to be described in this way: "Sam has a learning disability that is characterized by a weakness in visual-perceptual-motor integration and ability to organize complex visual symbols. This constellation of deficits has a significant impact upon his ability to . . ." The nature of the LD as well as its functional impact must be spelled out.

LET ME BE SPECIFIC

Although the federal government's definition of LD refers to a "specific" learning disability (sometimes written as SLD), it's only *specific* if a qualified diagnostician defines and describes its specificity. Also, if the dyslexia or dyscalculia or NVLD label is used, that is *not* a sufficient descriptor. An evaluator or diagnostician should be expected to describe the extent and nature of the impact of that specific learning disability on day-to-day performance *at that time in the child's development* and *in different environments*, including school, home, and social interactions. Anything less than that is what I would consider to be a partial or incomplete diagnosis.

Ralph Waldo Emerson said, "Fear always springs from ignorance." In the context of this book, that translates to *what we don't know about LD, ADHD, and stress can make us worry.* My purpose in writing Chapters Three and Four is to reduce your worry and anxiety by providing you with the latest, most accurate, and most understandable explanation of the conditions that are discussed throughout this book. This also establishes a common understanding of the historical, conceptual, theoretical, and semantic roots of these terms, as well as a common language to use to talk about these conditions.

Emerson's insight about lack of knowledge (ignorance) fomenting fear can also be directly applied to students with learning disabilities. When kids understand that they have a learning disability and what they can do about it, they don't experience as much stress when they encounter difficult or frustrating tasks. So, as someone who may be responsible for explaining a learning disability to a child, it will be helpful for you to have an appreciation of the history and evolution of these conditions. That's what you'll find in the pages that follow.

LD: A BRIEF HISTORY

In 1998, Kenneth Kavale and Steven Forness, two well-respected researchers in the field of LD, published an article on LDOnline .org titled "The Politics of Learning Disabilities." In this well-researched, thorough, and justifiably edgy paper, the authors provide a concise historical tour of the evolution of both the name and concept of *learning disability*. They offer their interpretation of the various controversies that have surrounded the legitimacy of the LD diagnosis, and make recommendations to the scientific, medical, and educational community.

Their historical analysis of the LD literature points out that unlike intellectual disability (once known as mental retardation), which was regarded as a generalized learning failure, LD has historically been thought of as a constellation of identifiable factors not related to intelligence that impeded learning in very specific ways. Kavale and Forness also report that the study of learning disabilities (although without that name, which came much later) was originally the domain of medicine (notably neurologists), and not schools (nor, as increasingly became the case, politics).

There is general agreement in the professional community that the term *learning disability* was first introduced by Dr. Samuel

Kirk, professor of special education at the University of Illinois, in either 1962 or 1963 (the date is subject to some debate) at the first meeting of what shortly thereafter became the Association for Children with Learning Disabilities (ACLD). This event marks the founding of the largest national organization devoted to the study and treatment of LD, now known as the Learning Disabilities Association of America (www.ldaamerica.org), commonly referred to as "LDA."

With early roots firmly planted in a biological (that is, neurological) explanation of these *specific* learning difficulties, the study of learning difficulties started off on a firm (that is to say, science-based) footing. Early neurologists observed that if a brain is damaged, say in an accident or a war, or by disease, the behavior exhibited by the person who owns that brain changes. If a person whose brain is injured is fortunate enough not to die, the consequences of the injury are varied and range in severity. In other words, if it doesn't kill you, a spear through the brain on the battlefield, depending on where it enters and exits your head, might result in difficulties walking or talking, or it might lead to dramatic mood changes.

This phenomenon was clearly illustrated in the classic case of Phineas Gage, a railroad foreman who had a steel tamping rod blown completely through his skull in an explosion on September 13, 1848. Incredibly, Gage lived, but his abilities and personality were permanently impaired by the very traumatic injury to his brain. Over the years, as technology has advanced, scientists have been able to examine Gage's skull (which is on display at a museum at Harvard) and retroactively study the behavioral and emotional effects of having the emotional (limbic) system of Gage's brain disconnected from the thinking and decision-making part (the frontal lobes).

This case and others like it revealed that damage (real or presumed) in certain areas or the brain can affect the emotions of a person or impair or wipe out mathematical, writing, spelling, or reading abilities. In 1896, in the *British Medical Journal* article "Congenital Word Blindness," W. Pringle Morgan published the first recorded description of a brain-based impairment in reading:

> Percy F . . . aged 14 . . . has always been a bright
> and intelligent boy, quick at games, and in no
> way inferior to others of his age. His great
> difficulty has been—and is now—his inability to
> learn to read.

FAST FORWARD TO THE PRESENT

The work of Dr. Albert Galaburda (chief of Behavioral Neurology at Beth Israel Deaconess Medical Center and Emily Fisher Landau Professor of Neurology and Neuroscience at Harvard Medical School), has contributed much to the neurobiological understanding of learning disabilities. In the 1980s, Dr. Galaburda was studying preserved brains that had been willed to his lab by dyslexic individuals. While the left hemisphere (specifically, the temporal planum) is larger than the right in most people's brains, Dr. Galaburda found that the two parts were just about equal in the brains of four adults with dyslexia. Dr. Galaburda and his colleagues pointed out that considering that only 20 percent of normal brains are symmetric, the chances of finding four consecutive symmetric brains are less than one in five hundred. This finding confirmed the presence of something unique about the brains of adults who have a history of dyslexia. Upon further visual examination of density patterns, Dr. Galaburda saw that the neurons in this part of the brain are more tightly woven together, resulting in the smaller size of the brain tissue. This happened because the neurons had grown, or migrated, in a way that was different from the elegant and organized path taken by those in the brains of nondyslexic patients. Dr. Galaburda's research did not say that the symmetry he found *caused* the LD, but only that there was a verifiable relationship. It may be that the LD (caused by something else) actually *created* this type of brain.

In 2005, Dr. Galaburda gave an interview for the website of the Nancy Lurie Marks Family Foundation, which funds much important brain research. In this interview, He spoke of his work on the genetic basis of LD:

> [At this time] there have been 4 dyslexia susceptibility genes discovered . . . all of which are involved in brain development. Three are involved in neuronal migration, which my lab showed to be abnormal in dyslexia. . . . The future of dyslexia research, therefore, seems bright to me. We are in a position to clear up a lot of details in the pathway (or set of pathways) by which a gene mutation changes brain development in specific ways that can explain difficulties in phonological processing.

Dr. Galaburda's work establishes a genetic basis for dyslexia. It is conjecture on my part, but this research makes it plausible to think that the other types of LD discussed earlier in this chapter are *variants* of dyslexia, and that they manifest themselves differently based on the particular genetic signature of each condition. Perhaps future studies will validate this hypothesis. At any rate, there appears to be no doubt about the genetic and biological basis of learning disabilities.

Kavale and Forness traced the evolution of the term *learning disabilities* as it moved from the science laboratory into the classroom, and eventually into the realm of politics. Because of Galaburda's groundbreaking work and the research of others, the presumption of brain damage (at least brain difference) had gained a foothold as LD established a strong presence in schools, its arrival accelerated by federal legislation. Because brain-imaging techniques were not typically available outside the research laboratory, school-based interpretations of LD were based on a *presumption* of what was called "mild brain injury." The attempted diagnosis of LD via paper-and-pencil tests left the field open to criticism, based on the fallibility of the assessment tools and those who administered them. Kavale and Forness highlighted this degradation of the LD diagnosis:

> As foundation concepts of LD were ignored, classification increasingly became predicated on poor academic performance alone, and other factors (e.g., neurological dysfunction, process deficits, underachievement) were assumed rather than explicitly validated. Under such circumstances, it is easy to see how the LD concept lost its integrity, and an increasing number of students became eligible under these limited and less-than-rigorous criteria.

The absence of clear criteria, coupled with a mandate (initially backed by federal and state funds) to identify and serve more students with special needs, led to a massive increase in the numbers of students identified as having LD. In 2010, the U.S. Department of Education informed Congress that since the passage of Public Law 94–142 in 1975 (now the Individuals with Disabilities Education Act), the population of students identified as having a learning disability has increased by 200 percent. This means that almost one million children (ages six through twenty-one) have some form of a learning disability and receive special education in school. In fact, one-third of all children who receive special education have a learning disability.

This situation created fertile ground for critics of the relatively newly identified condition of LD. In 1987, Gerald Coles, an educational psychologist, wrote a widely read and controversial book called *The Learning Mystique: A Critical Look at "Learning Disabilities."* Coles challenged the core assumption that a learning disability is a neurologically based condition, arguing that the logic underlying the presumption of neurological damage was flawed. The fact that brain damage causes functional deficits like reading problems, he said, does not prove that a reading disability (that is, dyslexia) was *caused* by brain damage. One very positive consequence of the doubt cast on the validity of LD as a brain-based disorder has been the promotion of research about the neurological underpinnings of this disorder. The results of this scientific inquiry continue to be fruitful.

Subsequent research has been supported by the increased availability of sophisticated brain-imaging techniques. These include functional magnetic resonance imaging (fMRI), which measures changes in blood flow to different parts of the brain in response to carrying out different tasks. Positron emission tomography (PET scanning) measures the uptake of radioactive glucose molecules when certain areas of the brain are activated. In addition, enhanced versions of traditional electroencephalographs (EEGs), known as quantitative electroencephalographs, or qEEGs, have been used with increasing frequency in recent years.

Numerous studies using these advanced technologies have shown that the learning problems of some children (and adults) are clearly related to (that is, at least associated with, if not caused by) differences in brain structure and function. Brain-imaging techniques showing a pattern of activation in the brains of students with dyslexia different from that seen in their non-dyslexic peers have allowed researchers to identify those at risk for dyslexia at a very early age with a high degree of accuracy.

Many researchers have contributed to this discussion of the neurological underpinnings of LD, but a groundbreaking book by Sally Shaywitz, M.D., *Overcoming Dyslexia: A New and Complete*

Science-Based Program for Reading Problems at Any Level, has helped keep the topic on the front burner. Her decisive and incisive exploration of the neurological basis for dyslexia has resulted in a better understanding of who has dyslexia, and who (even though unable to read well) does not. I put this book in the category of "required reading" for anyone—whether a teacher, a parent, or someone with dyslexia (using the CD version, perhaps)—who wants to understand (in very readable language) the way the brain of a dyslexic person functions—and the research that allows us to know this. The book includes many valuable recommendations about strategies and materials that have been shown to improve reading and spelling in individuals with this condition. In an article titled "Dyslexia and the Brain: What Does Current Research Tell Us?" Roxanne F. Hudson, Leslie High, and Stephanie Al Otaiba review and distill Dr. Shaywitz's work. These authors summarize the brain-imaging work of Shaywitz and others in this way:

> Imaging research has demonstrated that the brains of people with dyslexia show different, less efficient, patterns of processing (including under and over activation) during tasks involving sounds in speech and letter sounds in words. In summary, the brain of a person with dyslexia has a different distribution of metabolic activation than the brain of a person without reading problems when accomplishing the same language task. There is a failure of the left hemisphere rear brain systems to function properly during reading. Furthermore, many people with dyslexia often show greater activation in the lower frontal areas of the brain. This leads to the conclusion that neural systems in frontal regions may compensate for the disruption in the posterior area.

The future use of brain-imaging technology holds much promise for a better understanding of LD and related disorders. The problem is that the equipment and techniques now available in some labs are too expensive, or require too much advanced training, to be employed on a large-scale basis by schools or even in pediatricians' offices.

The burgeoning numbers of students identified as LD and the consequent impact on federal and local budgets have generated much debate. In their article, Kavale and Forness show how the apparent overidentification of students with LD has led to a "politicalization" of the diagnosis and has generated dialogues that ranged from civil rights on one hand to Marxist philosophy on the other. "The Politics of Learning Disabilities" makes for fabulous reading. Teachers and other LD specialists who are not aware of this history are missing the context for the work they are doing today with kids with this condition. It's a "must read" for them.

Currently, the diagnosis of a learning disability is typically carried out by trained and experienced school psychologists, educational psychologists, or a rapidly growing cadre of clinical neuropsychologists who have specialized training in the assessment of pediatric learning disabilities. However, while they employ some common practices, these professionals have failed to come up with a way to consistently and *definitively* diagnose learning disabilities. While IQ test results tend to be consistent over time, their utility in diagnosing LD has come into question. IQ tests are used to evaluate a variety of neurocognitive processes that are known to be important for efficient learning. The scores from a bunch of little tests (subtests) are translated into an IQ score. If one or more of the processes tapped by these subtests is deficient, as a consequence of differences in the brain of a person with learning disabilities, then guess what? The IQ score is affected. The very deficits that characterize the LD can pull down the overall IQ score. That's why you see in so many psychological

WHAT'S IN A NAME?

and neuropsychological test reports phrases like *"because of the variability in test scores on the Wechsler Intelligence Scale for Children, Version IV, the Full Scale or overall IQ may be an underestimate of this student's actual intellectual capabilities."* We should ask: Well, is it or isn't it?

The variability of other test scores over time has eroded confidence in both the diagnostic batteries that are used and the clinicians who administer them. A team assessment of LD, a common practice in schools and clinics, helps establish a multi- or trans-disciplinary (across professional borders) view of a child. This collaborative approach, in which many clinicians provide input from their various clinical perspectives, provides a system of checks and balances that increases the validity of the findings, and can lead to more effective programming for students with LD.

CONFLICTING DEFINITIONS

The residual ambiguity about a definitive diagnosis has led to much confusion in schools. Parents may question the validity of the LD diagnosis, or conversely, may encounter schools that do not agree with the findings of an outside evaluator who has made this diagnosis. Untold amounts of money and time have been spent in courtrooms and clinics trying to resolve differences of opinion between schools and parents. This situation has led to the development of a cottage industry that has created lucrative careers for attorneys, advocates, psychologists, and other professionals who are hired to help resolve such differences. In my view, this is very unfortunate. If the money that has been spent on litigation and redundant, inconclusive testing had been used to support better education for children or better training for teachers, I believe that the quality of U.S. education for all children would have improved substantially. A pithy and provocative discussion of the history and misinterpretations of special education law, and the evolution of special education from a civil liberties argument to an era of litigation and entitlement, can be found in a concise little book by special education attorney Miriam Kurtzig Freedman, M.A., J.D., called *Fixing Special Education: The 12 Steps to Transform Our Broken System*. This book is available at www.schoollawpro.com.

It's the Law, Sir

While I understand and respect the reasons behind the anti-labeling movement, a diagnostic label is required and must be specified on the IEP order for a child to access special education services. The labels of LD and ADHD are as much a part of the legal landscape as mountains and canyons are features of the earth's surface. While we might refer to such landforms as "high and low places on the earth," naming specific high and low points helps us find them on maps. The same thing is true about naming the condition of LD. In this vein, it's important to understand how various organizations define learning disabilities, since for better or worse, we have to do it, too. It's the law.

How the Feds Define an SLD

The Department of Education (DOE) is the U.S. government agency that funds public education programs for students with learning disabilities, sometimes in coordinated efforts with the Department of Health and Human Services. The law governing special education, called the Individuals with Disabilities Education Act (IDEA 2004, implemented in 2005) uses the same definition of SLD as a previous special education law, the original Education for All Handicapped Children Act of 1975:

> The term "specific learning disability" means a
> disorder in one or more of the basic psychological

processes involved in understanding or in using
language, spoken or written, which disorder may
manifest itself in the imperfect ability to listen,
think, speak, read, write, spell, or do
mathematical calculations. Such term **includes**
such conditions as perceptual disabilities, brain
injury, minimal brain dysfunction, dyslexia, and
developmental aphasia.

Most definitions of LD have what's referred to as an exclusionary clause, telling us what LD is *not*. In the federal definition, this reads as follows:

Such term **does not include** a learning problem
that is primarily the result of visual, hearing, or
motor disabilities, of mental retardation, of
emotional disturbance, or of environmental,
cultural, or economic disadvantage.

When Congress reauthorized IDEA in 2004, the representatives made an effort to align it with each state's definition of "adequate yearly progress" under the No Child Left Behind Act of 2001 (NCLB). Together, NCLB and IDEA are supposed to hold schools accountable for making sure students with disabilities achieve high standards. We'll see.

The Discrepancy Model Morphs in IDEA 2004

While there were no changes in the definition of SLD in IDEA 2004, there were changes to the ways that schools can determine that the student's SLD is severe enough to have a significant impact on performance in school. This is a key difference. In older versions of IDEA, a diagnosis of learning disability required that a student display a "severe discrepancy" between different areas of performance or between intellectual ability (generally interpreted to mean IQ) and achievement (how well a student was doing in certain skills related to school success). Prior to 2004, for students to be considered learning disabled (and for their school to receive federal and state funds to support their education), deficits (performance that was below expectation when compared to IQ) had to exist in one or more of the following areas: oral expression, listening comprehension, written expression, basic reading skill, reading comprehension, and mathematical calculation or mathematical reasoning.

However, this discrepancy requirement, which had been on the books since 1977, has been seriously questioned by many groups. Consider, for example the plea made to a commission studying special education policy by Wade Horn, the former assistant secretary for the Administration for Children and Families (ACF) at the U.S. Department of Health and Human Services (DHHS):

> I would like to encourage this Commission to
> drive a stake through the heart of this
> overreliance on the discrepancy model for
> determining the kinds of children that need
> services. It doesn't make any sense to me. I've
> wondered for 25 years why it is that we continue
> to use it and overrely on it as a way of
> determining what children are eligible for
> services in special education.

The discrepancy requirement was deemed to be especially unfair to students whose first language was not English or those who come from different cultural backgrounds. It was also thought that it could take a very long time for these discrepancies to evolve, and as a result, appropriate interventions would be delayed. The current law now *allows* schools to identify a discrepancy, but it no longer requires that they do so. If there is a discrepancy, the school's job is to explain it by using a variety of strategies, including the judicious use of tests. Most important, schools not only have to explain the discrepancy, but must come up with a way to narrow this gap between achievement and potential.

All Learning Disabilities Are Not Created Equal

Whose definition of LD is the right one?

When it comes to defining a learning disability, many groups have offered an interpretation that reflects a particular point of view or value system. This has added to the confusion about what really constitutes a learning disability. As noted earlier, although science has not yet proven that brain differences *cause* dyslexia, the brains of people who are reading disabled are different from those of others who are not.

Another factor that makes the diagnosis (and the understanding) of learning disabilities so difficult is that there are different types of learning disabilities. They are alike in that they are all presumed to have their origin in the way the brain processes information coming in through the senses. They are different in the way that they affect the person who has the condition. Let's look at the organizations that carry the most weight in the field of LD, and see how each of them approaches the issue of definition.

The Learning Disability Association of America (www.ldaamerica.org), the largest and oldest organization dedicated to improving the lives of individuals with LD, defines LD in this way:

> A learning disability is a neurological disorder
> that affects one or more of the basic
> psychological processes involved in

understanding or in using spoken or written language. The disability may manifest itself in an imperfect ability to listen, think, speak, read, write, spell, or to do mathematical calculations.

Every individual with a learning disability is unique and shows a different combination and degree of difficulties. A common characteristic among people with learning disabilities is uneven areas of ability, "a weakness within a sea of strengths." For instance, a child with dyslexia who struggles with reading, writing and spelling may be very capable in math and science.

Learning disabilities should not be confused with learning problems which are primarily the result of visual, hearing, or motor handicaps; of mental retardation; of emotional disturbance; or of environmental, cultural or economic disadvantages.

Generally speaking, people with learning disabilities are of average or above average intelligence. There often appears to be a gap between the individual's potential and actual achievement. This is why learning disabilities are referred to as "hidden disabilities": the person looks perfectly "normal" and seems to be a very bright and intelligent person, yet may be unable to demonstrate the skill level expected from someone of a similar age.

A learning disability cannot be cured or fixed; it is a lifelong challenge. However, with appropriate support and intervention, people with learning disabilities can achieve success in school, at work, in relationships, and in the community.

In 1999, The National Joint Committee on Learning Disabilities defined learning disabilities in this way:

> Learning disabilities is a general term that refers
> to a heterogeneous group of disorders manifested
> by significant difficulties in the acquisition and
> use of listening, speaking, reading, writing,
> reasoning, or mathematical abilities. These
> disorders are intrinsic to the individual, presumed
> to be due to central nervous system dysfunction,
> and may occur across the life span. Problems in
> self-regulatory behaviors, social perception, and
> social interaction may exist with learning
> disabilities but do not by themselves constitute a
> learning disability. Although learning disabilities
> may occur concomitantly with other
> handicapping conditions (for example, sensory
> impairment, mental retardation, serious
> emotional disturbance), or with extrinsic
> influences (such as cultural differences,
> insufficient or inappropriate instruction),
> they are not the result of those conditions or
> influences.

Under the federal IDEA act, the term used to describe LD is "specific learning disability," one of thirteen categories of disability recognized under that law. This term was defined earlier in the chapter.

The American Psychiatric Association offers another way to define LD. This organization publishes a guide to diagnosis and treatment called *The Diagnostic and Statistical Manual of Mental Disorders: DSM-IV*, which was published in 1994 and is due to be updated as DSM-V in May 2013. This manual is used not only by psychiatrists but also by clinical psychologists,

neuropsychologists, and other professionals responsible for diagnosing various mental and emotional disorders. It is very important that these clinicians understand the nature and characteristics
of learning disabilities, since it is estimated that 35 percent to
50 percent of students seen in mental health clinics have learning disorders. It is interesting to note that the term *learning disability* does not actually appear in DSM-IV. There is a section
called "Learning Disorders" that includes general guidelines for
the diagnosis of "Reading Disorder," "Mathematics Disorder,"
"Disorder of Written Expression," and "Learning Disorder Not
Otherwise Specified." That will probably change in DSM-V.

As of early 2011, the proposed criteria for the diagnosis of
learning disabilities in DSM-V were as follows:

> A. A group of disorders characterized by
> difficulties in learning basic academic skills
> (currently or by history), that are not consistent
> with the person's chronological age, educational
> opportunities, or intellectual abilities. Basic
> academic skills refer to accurate and fluent
> reading, writing, and arithmetic.
>
> Multiple sources of information are to be
> used to assess learning, one of which must be
> an individually administered, culturally
> appropriate, and psychometrically sound
> standardized measure of academic
> achievement.
>
> B. The disturbance in criterion A, without
> accommodations, significantly interferes with
> academic achievement or activities of daily living
> that require these academic skills.

The APA website cites the rationale for the proposed changes
in DSM-V:

Learning disabilities interfere with the acquisition
and use of one or more of the following academic
skills: oral language, reading, written language,
mathematics. These disorders affect individuals
who otherwise demonstrate at least average
abilities essential for thinking or reasoning. As
such, learning disabilities are distinct from
intellectual disability.

Also, the categories of "Learning Disorder Not Otherwise Specified" and "Disorder of Written Expression" are recommended for removal from DSM-V due to "lack of evidence that they are discrete learning disabilities."

A Story to Make a Point

Nate had received a diagnosis of ADHD from his pediatrician and for the past year had been taking a small dose of Ritalin, which helped him focus and be more attentive in school. He was referred for a neuropsychological evaluation because his scores on standardized reading achievement tests were very low—much lower than this bright ten-year-old's performance in math and verbal abilities would suggest. He very much wanted to attend the private school where his older brother had gone, but his scores on these tests raised a flag of concern for the admissions office.

Nate's word reading (decoding) skills were great. He could read real and nonsense words like a pro, showing that his phonemic analytical skills were well-developed. As I customarily do when I begin the quest for answers to this kind of mystery, I administered the Wechsler Intelligence Scale for Children, version four (the WISC-IV, commonly referred to as the "WISK"). In addition to the Full Scale Intelligence Quotient (FSIQ), the WISC-IV allows the user to generate four Composite/Index scores. These are: Verbal Comprehension, Perceptual Reasoning, Working Memory, and Processing Speed. Each of the Index

(continued)

Scores is computed from scores on several subtests in each of these "domains."

"AHA!" A Discrepancy! Case Closed

Not surprisingly, given his history, Nate earned a Verbal Comprehension Index score in the superior range. His knowledge of word meanings and his ability to converse fluently with me about some very interesting topics was outstanding. In contrast, his Perceptual Reasoning and his Working Memory Index scores were just in the average range. Curiously, his Processing Speed Score was also in the Superior Range. The difference between his index scores was "statistically significant," meaning that a difference of this size only occurs once in a great while. If I had been using a discrepancy analysis as the basis for a diagnosis of LD, I could have stopped there and made the call. I could have explained Nate's reading difficulty as a sort of "cognitive friction" reflected in these intertest differences or discrepancies, and assigned the LD label. But my gut (filled with thirty-five years of experience) told me that just didn't seem right.

So we took a little break and I silently reflected while sipping my half-caf, no-fat sugar-free vanilla latte (definitely *not* the drink for those with expressive language problems to order) at the Starbucks next door: *"Hmmm. He's got a high processing speed score on two tests that measure how well he does 'under the clock.' His decoding skills are great. His ADHD is well-controlled. He's motivated. You'd think he'd read quickly. Well, he doesn't. He tells me he seldom finishes these reading tests, which present him with progressively more difficult passages. Why?"*

Back at the testing table, I'm thinking this boy doesn't have a learning disability, but I'm still puzzled by his slow pace of reading. So turning toward him, I consult the resource I always consult in such difficult cases—the student! "Nate," I ask, "do you have any idea why you read so slowly?" He replied: "I don't read slowly, really. I want to do really well, so I sometimes reread a sentence twice, sometimes three times, because I know that I miss stuff a lot. It just takes me a lot of time to do that."

Aha! Now it all makes absolute sense. Here's a verbally advanced little boy. He's learned from the past that his pre-Ritalin inattention caused him to read but not process words or phrases or whole sentences. Because he's smart and motivated, he had learned to reread as a way to compensate for, dare I say overcome, the negative impact of attention on a reading task. Do you see how the discrepancy, if we had just stopped there, might have defined this boy as a kid with a learning disability? A thoughtful analysis, aided in great part by this boy's accurate self-appraisal (and not the tests!) makes it clear that he doesn't have LD. He's a bright boy with effectively controlled ADHD who has learned from experience that if he slows down and rereads, he'll be able to focus better and comprehend more. He's a highly motivated lad. He's hanging on to old habits that continue to slow him down but help him comprehend better. Intervention designed to speed up his reading might work very well, and that's one of the things I recommended.

You can see how challenging it sometimes is make the call. If the test scores are given too much credence, they can tempt a clinician to confirm an erroneous diagnosis. Had I stopped the evaluation process before my latte, I might have missed the diagnostic boat.

> The real tragedy is that conceptualizations of LD have not changed over 30 years despite the completion of significant research in the past 15 years. What we know from research now needs to be implemented.
> —G. Reid Lyon, Jack M. Fletcher, and colleagues, from "Learning Disabilities: An Evidence Based Conceptualization"

THE GENESIS OF THE RTI

In 2004, in response to the criticisms lodged against IQ testing and the discrepancy formula, Congress announced that the criterion of a gap between intelligence and achievement *could still be used*, but that it was not *required* for a diagnosis of learning disability. The updated IDEA encouraged schools to use identification techniques that were related to classroom instruction. This correspondence between assessment and how the student was doing "on the ground" made a lot of sense. It was in this spirit that the federal government promoted the concept of "Responsiveness to Intervention" (also known as "Response to Intervention," or "RTI"). The RTI program is designed and delivered by general education staff in collaboration with special educators and other specialists such as school psychologists, and is based on what is considered to be reliable research.

In this model, teachers informally assess children's need for specialized services by carefully observing their individual responses to specialized interventions. Students who do not respond to well-planned and well-implemented interventions thereby provide what is regarded as evidence that they are "at risk" for learning disabilities. As a result, they receive a series of increasingly intensive, individualized instructional or behavioral interventions that meet the criteria of being "best practices" in education. The RTI is not designed to be diagnostic, but aims to reduce formal diagnostic assessments that many see as unwarranted, unhelpful, expensive, and unnecessary.

The problem is that the interventions are supposed to be *scientific, research-based interventions*, and it's not clear about how those methods are supposed to be created or disseminated to schools across the country. In my view, this is like telling surgeons that a certain problem could be fixed by a specialized form of surgery that has been used successfully at a few hospitals around the country. How are doctors to be trained in the use of this new, proven technique? And how many times must they perform the surgery to be really good at it? In the field of education, it's hard to identify models of instruction that have consistently proven to be effective. Even when we do, how long does it take a "best practice" in education to trickle down to the classroom? Who pays for the new materials? How is the approach taught? Who supervises its implementation and how is its continuing effectiveness monitored?

Because the implementation and monitoring of RTI are so challenging, we see pockets of competence in schools across the country—but nothing like a uniform system of instruction being consistently and appropriately implemented in different cities and towns. We are headed in a good direction, but are far from having a scientific approach to education that results in the eradication of severe learning disabilities, a tacit goal of the architects of the RTI approach. The discussion about this issue will continue. If you are interested in tracking the issues, you might want to check out the white paper on RTI that is available on the LDA website (www.ldanational.com).

Now that I've explored the LD landscape, let's move on to a brief tour of the world of ADHD. Oh, if only there were a blood test for all this!

4

Demystifying ADHD

After reading Chapter Three, I hope you have a better understanding of learning disabilities. In this chapter, my goal is to help clear up some misconceptions about ADHD and replace them with the knowledge you need to understand this condition well enough to help kids who have it.

PEOPLE ALREADY KNOW ABOUT ADHD (OR DO THEY?)

It's fairly common to hear someone proclaim, "I have ADHD!" The condition is often invoked as an explanation—or increasingly, in movies and stand-up comedy, as an *excuse*—for behaviors that have gotten someone in trouble. It's a very well-recognized condition. If you asked twenty friends, adults *or* kids, most of them could tell you the hallmark characteristics of the condition: inattention, hyperactivity, and impulsivity. Why is this so widespread?

We're constantly being bombarded by messages about this condition in the newspaper, on TV talk shows, in movies, and in the electronic media. Feed "ADHD" to Google and you can read what pops up for months and not make a dent. Check out the titles of any of several popular magazines that beg you to buy them (who *does* buy these, anyway?) as you move down the check-out line at the supermarket. It almost seems like you could zip through any one of these publications with their screaming fonts and hyperbolic titles and diagnose yourself, your partner, or your kids between loading your stuff onto the conveyor belt and handing your fistful of coupons to the cashier.

Because the terminology has been so popularized, and because so many people have the condition, in some ways it's easier to understand ADHD than it is to understand LD.

SO WHAT *IS* ADHD?

ADHD is a neurobiological condition that usually begins in childhood and may continue into adulthood, even though the way it presents itself may change. *Neurobiological* simply means having its roots in the central nervous system (brain and nerves). The term *neurobehavioral* is often used to describe ADHD, and this means that it's a brain-based condition, the effects of which are seen in human behavior.

Children and adults who have ADHD exhibit some combination of these symptoms: difficulty focusing, sustaining, or shifting attention; distractibility; and impulsivity. As I mentioned in Chapter Three, hyperactivity, although the most visible component of this mix of symptoms, is not always present. The condition ranges in severity from mild to severe; it may vary from situation to situation, and it generally changes its nature as a child matures.

Viewed through a positive lens, this condition can result in energy-fueled explorations of a person's environment that sometimes lead to the generation of new ideas, products, or thoughts. Many children with ADHD are creative, upbeat, funny, and fun to be around, even if they are hard to keep up with! More often, though, these traits—especially in the extreme—place the child at the mercy of uncontrolled impulses. The absence of brain brakes or filters can lead to difficulties in academic performance, family interactions, and social relationships.

Picture a little boy staring out the window of a classroom watching the leaves fall in unique spirals to the ground—*during a math lesson*. Or think about a girl hitting the field hockey ball toward the wrong goal—*in a championship game*. Imagine a child so engrossed in a book that the teacher's request to get into line for lunch just doesn't register. How about the child who is so captivated by a video game that it can't be put down? What about the intelligent high school student who can't stay focused on a history assignment, and who is chronically distracted by (or attracted to, depending on your point of view) the incessant flow of Facebook alerts on a cell phone that causes significant separation anxiety if not in reach 24/7. What about the child who has FFS or "Flat Forehead Syndrome"? (This is what you get when you hit your forehead repeatedly with the heel of your hand, usually while saying something like "Not again! How could I be so *stupid?*")

"FFS" is of course fictitious. But the image of this gesture is the metaphor for the kids I worry most about—intellectually capable students with ADHD who are chronically making mistakes about things that other kids routinely get. Kids who act first and think later. Unaddressed or unchanneled, ADHD can turn a life into a chaotic storm of regrettable impulsive acts and errors of judgment that have a very long shelf-life.

How Many Kids Have ADHD?

ADHD is the most commonly diagnosed neurobehavioral disorder of childhood. The National Institute of Mental Health estimates that 3 percent to 5 percent of children have ADHD. A report by the Centers for Disease Control and Prevention (CDC) presented the results of the National Survey of Children's

Health, which indicated that the national estimate of children aged 4–17 years with parent-reported ADHD had increased from 4.4 million in 2003 to 5.4 million in 2007. This represents an increase of approximately a million children, and translates roughly to one in every ten children in the United States having parents who have reported that their child has had this diagnosis at some point. When we look at increases like this, we have to consider the possibility of variations in the diagnostic criteria, the availability of professionals with the experience and training to make the diagnosis, the age at which the label is assigned, and the environment in which the behaviors are observed. While it's clear that more students are identified with this condition than ever before in history, it's difficult to say that more of these kids are being born. Perhaps it is only that more are being counted, because more people have been trained to observe the characteristics of the condition and make the diagnosis.

The publication of *Driven to Distraction* (1994) and its sequels, *Answers to Distraction* (1996) and *Delivered from Distraction* (2005), by Edward "Ned" Hallowell, M.D., and John Ratey, M.D. catapulted ADHD into the public awareness and offered guidance and direction for millions of readers with ADHD and those who care for and about them. Dr. Ratey's subsequent research on the effects of exercise in the lives of individuals with ADHD has underscored the importance of regular physical activity on brain development and function, and on increasing positive emotions and optimistic outlooks. Dr. Hallowell's many works have emphasized the importance of focusing on ADHD not as a disability but rather as a condition characterized by traits such as high energy, intuitiveness, creativity, and enthusiasm that has enabled many children and adults (including himself) to make significant contributions in their schools, their neighborhoods, their places of work, and their relationships.

Is ADHD a New Condition?

As a matter of fact, this condition, or rather the behaviors that are commonly associated with it, were recognized over a century ago. In *Driven to Distraction*, Hallowell and Ratey did a great job describing the evolution of this disorder. They cite the early work of George Frederic Still, M.D., who in 1902 described a group of children who displayed many of the characteristics that we associate with ADHD today. In this same section, they reproduce the poem "Fidgety Phillip," which appeared in 1904 in the prestigious British medical journal *Lancet*. Hallowell and Ratey describe this rhyming tale of a very active boy as "what might be the first published account of ADHD in the medical literature." While the name may be new (and I'll trace a bit of the evolution of that later on), the condition has been recognized for quite some time.

Who Are the Role Models for ADHD?

Cartoonist Hank Ketchum (1920–2001) portrayed Dennis ("the Menace") seated in the corner, voicing the lament of many kids with ADHD, as he says: *"By the time I think about what I'm gonna do, I already did it."* Calvin, of Calvin and Hobbes, has been regarded by many as the "poster child" for ADHD. Even poor Winnie the Pooh has been diagnosed with this condition. In a clever tongue-in-cheek feature in the December 2000 issue of the *Canadian Medical Association Journal (CMAJ)* titled "Research of the Holiday Kind," authors who named themselves Sarah-the-Shea, Ann-the-Hawkins, Janet-the-Kawchuk, Donna-the-Smith, and Kevin-the-Gordon presented a spoof-disguised-as-article called "Pathology in the Hundred Acre Wood: A Neurodevelopmental Perspective on A. A. Milne." In this pseudo article, a holiday gift for the journal's readers, the authors offered a tentative diagnosis of this famous and well-beloved bear:

> We begin with Pooh. This unfortunate bear
> embodies the concept of comorbidity. Most
> striking is his Attention Deficit Hyperactivity
> Disorder (ADHD), inattentive subtype. As
> clinicians, we had some debate about whether
> Pooh might also demonstrate significant
> impulsivity, as witnessed, for example, by his
> poorly thought out attempt to get honey by
> disguising himself as a rain cloud. We concluded,
> however, that this reflected more on his
> comorbid cognitive impairment, further
> aggravated by an obsessive fixation on honey.

And then, of course, there's the wildly (emphasis on *wild*) successful actor Jim Carrey, who regards his apparent ADHD as both an asset and a liability. On his website, he recalls: "There was a time when people said, 'Jim, if you keep on making faces, your face will freeze like that.' Now they just say, 'Pay him!'" He also poignantly explains the costs of being the frenetic funny man: "I tend to stay up late, not because I'm partying but because it's the only time of the day when I'm alone and don't have to be performing." And on his interpersonal relationships: "I'm a hard guy to live with. I'm like a caged animal. I'm up all night walking around the living room. It's hard for me to come down from what I do."

Many of the popular figures mentioned on page 277 had a combination of ADHD and LD. I think it's the *overlap* of these two conditions that has shaped the character of many of the people who are held up as models of success. The LD can create a history of academic difficulty that encourages children to move toward alternative ways to meet their need for recognition and feelings of competence. The ADHD can pull away the curtain of self-censure, and make the resulting comedy more spontaneous and often much funnier.

WHAT'S IN A NAME? IS IT *ADD* OR *AD/HD* OR *ADHD?*

This next section walks you through the evolution of the name of this condition. It's important to clear this up, since there continues to be confusion about what to call it. As you'll see, this confusion is caused in great part by the morphing of the terminology over time. In the 1994 version of the *Diagnostic and Statistical Manual of Mental Disorders* (DSM-IV), ADHD is described a "Disruptive Behavior Disorder" characterized by the presence of a set of chronic and impairing behavior patterns that are characterized by abnormal levels of inattention or hyperactivity, or a combination of both. This is the definition that was current as of the time of the publication of this book.

Looking Backward

The original 1968 version of the DSM made no mention of ADHD, but it described a "hyperkinetic reaction of childhood," which was a precursor of the current definition. In 1980, the manual was revised and published as DSM-II. "Hyperkinetic Reaction of Childhood" was changed to "Attention Deficit Disorder" (ADD), and the term that is used colloquially today was born. The most notable change in DSM-II was that the condition was now viewed *primarily* as a problem of attention, and hyperactivity took a back seat. Accordingly, in this version, two subtypes of ADD were now described; one referred to as ADD/H, (or ADD with hyperactivity), and the other designated as ADD/WO (ADD without hyperactivity). There was much debate in the professional community around this classification, especially regarding the deemphasis on hyperactivity. For the next seven years, the diagnosis went back and forth like a Ping-Pong ball.

Time Marches On

In the next revision of the manual in 1987 (DSM-IIIR), there was another name change, and hyperactivity attained more prominence. In this version, the disorder was called "Attention Deficit Hyperactivity Disorder" (ADHD), a title that consolidated all of the symptoms into a single disorder. In DSM-IIIR, there were no subtypes of ADHD. This version pretty much said that a child (or adult) who did not exhibit hyperactivity simply could not have the disorder. During this period of my career, I advised a lot of inattentive kids to start jumping up and down in class so they would get diagnosed. (Just kidding!)

Research Prevails!

After the publication of the DSM-IIIR, a variety of studies were published supporting the existence of ADD without hyperactivity (surprise!). One very beneficial outcome of this public acknowledgment was that increased attention began to be paid to girls who had this type of inattentive ADHD, many of whom had previously flown cluelessly under the radar of classroom teachers. The definition was modified *again* in the fourth, most recent edition of the manual (DSM-IV), which was published in 1994. In this version, the name was mercifully *not* changed from ADHD, but the symptoms were once again divided into two categories—inattentive and hyperactive/impulsive. Three subtypes of the disorder were now identified as: "AD/HD, Primarily Inattentive"; "AD/HD, Primarily Hyperactive/Impulsive"; and "ADHD, Combined Type." Notice that the full "name" of the condition was "Attention-Deficit/Hyperactivity Disorder," abbreviated as AD/HD. (Note the introduction of the slash mark, a reminder perhaps that it may be an either-or condition—or both.)

The revised DSM-IV definition was an attempt to describe the way ADHD really showed up in students. The American Academy of Pediatrics and the American Academy of Child and

Adolescent Psychiatry both use the DSM-IV criteria as a guide to the diagnosis of ADHD. This is important to know, since in most cases (unlike LD, which can be diagnosed by schools), ADHD is considered to be a medical condition (in fact, a psychiatric disorder) and has to be diagnosed by a medical professional. The main reason for this is that LD is not treated with medication but by educational intervention, and ADHD is very often treated with medication. The manual urges clinicians to use caution when considering an ADHD diagnosis, pointing out the challenge of accurately diagnosing this condition in children who are younger than four or five years of age because of the wide range of behaviors exhibited by children at that developmental level. In the next box are the diagnostic criteria for AD/HD, as they appeared in DSM-IV.

Diagnostic Criteria for Attention-Deficit/Hyperactivity Disorder

(A) Either (1) or (2):

    (1) six (or more) of the following symptoms of inattention have persisted for at least 6 months to a degree that is maladaptive and inconsistent with developmental level

Inattention

    often fails to give close attention to details or makes careless mistakes in schoolwork, work, or other activities

    often has difficulty sustaining attention in tasks or play activities

    often does not seem to listen when spoken to directly

    often does not follow through on instructions and fails to finish schoolwork, chores, or duties in the workplace (not due to oppositional behavior or failure to understand instructions)

    often has difficulty organizing tasks and activities

(continued)

---

often avoids, dislikes, or is reluctant to engage in tasks that require sustained mental effort (such as schoolwork or homework)

often loses things necessary for tasks or activities (e.g., toys, school assignments, pencils, books, or tools)

is often easily distracted by extraneous stimuli

is often forgetful in daily activities

(2) six (or more) of the following symptoms of hyperactivity-impulsivity have persisted for at least 6 months to a degree that is maladaptive and inconsistent with developmental level:

Hyperactivity

often fidgets with hands or feet or squirms in seat

often leaves seat in classroom or in other situations in which remaining seated is expected

often runs about or climbs excessively in situations in which it is inappropriate (in adolescents or adults, may be limited to subjective feelings of restlessness)

often has difficulty playing or engaging in leisure activities quietly

is often "on the go" or often acts as if "driven by a motor"

often talks excessively

Impulsivity

often blurts out answers before questions have been completed

often has difficulty awaiting turn

often interrupts or intrudes on others (e.g., butts into conversations or games)

(B) Some hyperactive-impulsive or inattentive symptoms that caused impairment were present before age 7 years.

(C) Some impairment from the symptoms is present in two or more settings (e.g., at school [or work] and at home).

(D) There must be clear evidence of clinically significant impairment in social, academic, or occupational functioning.

> (E) The symptoms do not occur exclusively during the course of a Pervasive Developmental Disorder, Schizophrenia, or other Psychotic Disorder and are not better accounted for by another mental disorder (e.g., Mood Disorder, Anxiety Disorder, Dissociative Disorder, or Personality Disorder).

Change Is in the Wind, Again

The next revision of the DSM will have its debut at the APA's annual meeting in San Francisco in May 2013. Some changes in the definition of AD/HD are anticipated in the new version, which will be known as DSM-V. The most significant change that is being proposed is that ADHD will be regarded as two separate disorders, ADD and ADHD, rather than as subtypes of the same condition. One argument in favor of this change was the fact that DSM-IV's diagnostic guidelines list more criteria for inattention than hyperactivity, rather than treating each with equal weight. The fact that a child could be considered hyperactive at one time and not at the next evaluation also raised questions about the validity of the criteria. Concerns were expressed about the age of onset (seven years or older) in DSM-IV, which was viewed by critics as arbitrary. Reviewers cited research that showed that the condition is usually first noticed or recalled (by a parent thinking back to when the symptoms were prominent) between the ages of seven and twelve, and that the complexity of this condition makes it difficult to differentiate it from other conditions that occur at earlier ages.

A LITTLE BIT OF THIS, AND A LITTLE BIT OF THAT: MORE ABOUT COMORBIDITY IN ADHD

Research as well as observation in clinics and schools reveals a high degree of comorbidity (the presence of coexisting conditions) among children and adolescents with ADHD. Frequent comorbid conditions include oppositional defiant disorder, conduct disorder, depression, anxiety, developmental disorders, and, as was discussed in Chapter Three, learning disabilities. This underscores the importance of looking carefully for other conditions in addition to or besides ADHD that can explain the symptoms. Clinicians have to consider whether the attention-related symptoms are primarily caused by ADHD, or if they are secondary to (or caused by) another condition. For example, children with bipolar disorder have clear difficulties with attention, especially when they are in the manic state associated with this serious mood disorder. In fact, a history of attention difficulties and a diagnosis of ADHD are often precursors of the bipolar diagnosis. ADHD diagnosed in children of adults with bipolar disorder might mean that these children are at high risk for the development of that condition. In some cases, ADHD may mask bipolar disorder, so that the more serious emotional disorder is misdiagnosed, or the ADHD may be incorrectly diagnosed and treated as bipolar disorder. This points to the importance of a differential diagnosis by a skilled clinician, or better yet, a team of experienced professionals.

BACK TO THE FUTURE

The proposed description of ADHD, as found on the website of the American Psychiatric Association and slated to appear in the new DSM-V is presented verbatim here. There may be some differences in the final version, but you will note that this definition retains the inattention/hyperactivity differential, but offers much more specific diagnostic criteria than previous versions.

Proposed Discussion of the Disorder

The disorder consists of a characteristic pattern of behavior and cognitive functioning that is present in different settings where it gives rise to social and educational or work performance difficulties. The manifestations of the disorder and the difficulties that they cause are subject to gradual change being typically more marked during times when the person is studying or working and lessening during vacation.

Superimposed on these short-term changes are trends that may signal some deterioration or improvement with many symptoms becoming less common in adolescence. Although irritable outbursts are common, abrupt changes in mood lasting for days or longer are not characteristic of ADHD and will usually be a manifestation of some other distinct disorder.

In children and young adolescents, the diagnosis should be based on information obtained from parents and teachers. When direct teacher reports cannot be obtained, weight should be given to information provided to parents by teachers that describe the child's behavior and performance at school. Examination of the patient in the clinician's office may or may not be informative. For older adolescents and adults, confirmatory observations by third parties should be obtained whenever possible.

A. Either (1) and/or (2).

1. **Inattention**: Six (or more) of the following symptoms have persisted for at least 6 months to a degree that is inconsistent with developmental level and that impact directly on social and academic/occupational activities. **Note:** for older adolescents and adults (ages 17 and older), only 4 symptoms are required. The symptoms are not due to oppositional behavior, defiance, hostility, or a failure to understand tasks or instructions.

   (a) Often **fails to give close attention to details** or makes careless mistakes in schoolwork, at work, or during other activities (for example, overlooks or misses details, work is inaccurate).

   (b) Often has **difficulty sustaining attention** in tasks or play activities (for example, has difficulty remaining focused during lectures, conversations, or reading lengthy writings).

   (continued)

(c) Often **does not seem to listen** when spoken to directly (mind seems elsewhere, even in the absence of any obvious distraction).

(d) Frequently **does not follow through** on instructions (starts tasks but quickly loses focus and is easily sidetracked, fails to finish schoolwork, household chores, or tasks in the workplace).

(e) Often has **difficulty organizing tasks** and activities. (Has difficulty managing sequential tasks and keeping materials and belongings in order. Work is messy and disorganized. Has poor time management and tends to fail to meet deadlines.)

(f) Characteristically avoids, seems to dislike, and is **reluctant to engage in tasks that require sustained mental effort** (such as schoolwork or homework or, for older adolescents and adults, preparing reports, completing forms, or reviewing lengthy papers).

(g) Frequently **loses objects** necessary for tasks or activities (e.g., school assignments, pencils, books, tools, wallets, keys, paperwork, eyeglasses, or mobile telephones).

(h) Is often **easily distracted** by extraneous stimuli (for older adolescents and adults may include unrelated thoughts).

(i) Is often **forgetful** in daily activities, chores, and running errands (for older adolescents and adults, returning calls, paying bills, and keeping appointments).

2. **Hyperactivity and Impulsivity:** Six (or more) of the following symptoms have persisted for at least 6 months to a degree that is inconsistent with developmental level and that impact directly on social and academic/occupational activities. **Note:** for older adolescents and adults (ages 17 and older), only 4 symptoms are required. The symptoms are not due to oppositional behavior, defiance, hostility, or a failure to understand tasks or instructions.

(a) Often **fidgets** or taps hands or feet or squirms in seat.

(b) Is often **restless** during activities when others are seated (may leave his or her place in the classroom, office or other workplace, or in other situations that require remaining seated).

(c) Often **runs about** or climbs on furniture and moves excessively in inappropriate situations. In adolescents or adults, may be limited to feeling restless or confined.

(d) Is often **excessively loud** or noisy during play, leisure, or social activities.

(e) Is often **"on the go,"** acting as if "driven by a motor." Is uncomfortable being still for an extended time, as in restaurants, meetings, etc. Seen by others as being restless and difficult to keep up with.

(f) Often **talks excessively**.

(g) Often **blurts out an answer** before a question has been completed. Older adolescents or adults may complete people's sentences and "jump the gun" in conversations.

(h) Has **difficulty waiting his or her turn** or waiting in line.

(i) Often **interrupts or intrudes** on others (frequently butts into conversations, games, or activities; may start using other people's things without asking or receiving permission, adolescents or adults may intrude into or take over what others are doing).

(j) Tends to **act without thinking**, such as starting tasks without adequate preparation or avoiding reading or listening to instructions. May speak out without considering consequences or make important decisions on the spur of the moment, such as impulsively buying items, suddenly quitting a job, or breaking up with a friend.

(k) Is often **impatient**, as shown by feeling restless when waiting for others and wanting to move faster than others, wanting people to get to the point, speeding while driving, and cutting into traffic to go faster than others.

(l) Is **uncomfortable doing things slowly and systematically** and often rushes through activities or tasks.

(m) Finds it **difficult to resist temptations or opportunities**, even if it means taking risks (a child may grab toys off a store shelf or play with dangerous objects; adults may commit to

(continued)

a relationship after only a brief acquaintance or take a job or enter into a business arrangement without doing due diligence).

B. Several noticeable inattentive or hyperactive-impulsive symptoms were present by age 12.

C. The symptoms are apparent in two or more settings (e.g., at home, school or work, with friends or relatives, or in other activities).

D. There must be clear evidence that the symptoms interfere with or reduce the quality of social, academic, or occupational functioning.

E. The symptoms do not occur exclusively during the course of schizophrenia or another psychotic disorder and are not better accounted for by another mental disorder (e.g., mood disorder, anxiety disorder, dissociative disorder, or a personality disorder).

Specify Based on Current Presentation

Combined Presentation: If both Criterion A1 (Inattention) and Criterion A2 (Hyperactivity-Impulsivity) are met for the past 6 months.

Predominately Inattentive Presentation: If Criterion A1 (Inattention) is met but Criterion A2 (Hyperactivity-Impulsivity) is not met *and* 3 or more symptoms from Criterion A2 have been present for the past 6 months.

Predominately Hyperactive/Impulsive Presentation: If Criterion A2 (Hyperactivity-Impulsivity) is met and Criterion A1 (Inattention) is not met for the past 6 months.

Inattentive Presentation (Restrictive): If Criterion A1 (Inattention) is met but no more than 2 symptoms from Criterion A2 (Hyperactivity-Impulsivity) have been present for the past 6 months.

Tracing the evolution of ADHD as a diagnosis makes it clear that the behaviors associated with this condition have remained fairly consistent over decades, even centuries, even as the name has changed. It is important to point out that many of the symptoms of ADHD are seen in the typical behavior of children and adolescents. For a child to be given the ADHD diagnosis, the core symptoms of inattention, hyperactivity, and impulsivity must be severe enough to impair functioning in school, at home, and in social situations. Symptoms of ADHD usually show up in childhood and often continue, usually with a decrease in hyperactivity, through adolescence and adulthood. Unless a person has an accident or injury that affects brain function, ADHD does not spontaneously appear in adolescence or adulthood. However, the symptoms associated with ADHD may be the *consequence* of disease or injury to the brain.

CHADD: INFORMATION, SUPPORT, AND ADVOCACY

According to its website, CHADD (Children and Adults with Attention-Deficit/Hyperactivity Disorder) is "the nation's leading non-profit organization serving individuals with AD/HD and their families." The organization has more than sixteen thousand members in two hundred local chapters throughout the United States. These chapters offer support for people affected by the condition either directly or by the need to care for affected individuals. CHADD produces the bimonthly *Attention!* magazine (for members) and sponsors an annual conference. The site mentions the National Resource Center on AD/HD (NRC) as the CDC-funded national clearinghouse for evidence-based information about the condition, and it explains that CHADD was founded in 1987 "in response to the frustration and sense of isolation experienced by parents and their children with AD/HD."

The CHADD website describes the condition as "a neurobiological disorder that is characterized by developmentally inappropriate impulsivity, inattention, and in some cases, hyperactivity." It goes on to explain:

> Although individuals with AD/HD can be very
> successful in life, without appropriate

identification and treatment, AD/HD can have
serious consequences. These consequences may
include school failure, depression, conduct
disorder, failed relationships, and substance abuse.
Early identification and treatment are extremely
important. Until recent years, it was believed
that children outgrew AD/HD in adolescence.
This is because hyperactivity often diminishes
during the teen years. However, it is now known
that many symptoms continue into adulthood. If
the disorder goes undiagnosed or untreated
during adulthood, individuals may have
trouble at work and in relationships, as well as
emotional difficulties such as anxiety and
depression.

SETTING THE RECORD STRAIGHT ABOUT EXECUTIVE FUNCTIONS

Current research indicates that the frontal lobe, basal ganglia, caudate nucleus, and cerebellum, as well as other areas of the brain, play a significant role in ADHD because they are involved in complex processes that regulate behavior. These higher-order processes are sometimes referred to as *executive functions*. Executive functions include such processes as inhibition, working memory, planning, self-monitoring, verbal regulation, motor control, maintaining and changing mental set, and emotional regulation. An Internet search quickly reveals that there is considerable confusion about the use of the term. Some people speak of an executive function *deficit*, almost as if this were a separate, specific condition. This term is sometimes erroneously viewed as a type of learning disability. I regard weak executive functions as a manifestation of learning disabilities, which vary from individual to individual. Some individuals consider executive function deficits (sometimes referred to as an executive dysfunction disorder) as synonymous with ADHD. All people have executive functions. Depending on the individual, these range from relative weaknesses to relative strengths. In my view, which I believe is supported by prevailing professional use, executive functions that are so poor as to impair day-to-day performance at school and at home are often associated with or characterize both learning disabilities and ADHD. They are symptoms—not a separate disorder.

ADHD as an Inhibition Deficit

Dr. Russell Barkley is a respected international expert in the field of ADHD whose continuing research and voluminous writings help us understand the true nature of this condition. According to his model, the core deficit in ADHD is a difficulty *inhibiting* responses, or the brain's ability to put the brakes on impulses. What might be considered an inhibition deficit has a cascading impact on the other executive functions. In other words, how can the brain remember, plan, monitor the environment, control muscles, maintain or change its mind-set, or regulate emotions if the impulse to act, to do, or to react or respond is always active, working in the foreground of thought and action? It's like trying to read a book in a waterfall—difficult and not very satisfying. The key to success, according to Barkley's model, is to teach the person the skills needed to override impulses. Behavior therapy and often medication can help in this regard.

The Genetic Basis of ADHD

ADHD tends to run in families. Dr. Joseph Biederman and his colleagues at the Massachusetts General Hospital studied families of children with ADHD and found that more than 25 percent of first-degree relatives (parents, siblings, uncles, and aunts) in the families of children who had ADHD *also* had ADHD. In families in which children do not have ADHD, only about 5 percent of other family members had this condition. Studies conducted by psychiatrist Dr. Dennis Cantwell compared adoptive children with hyperactivity to their adoptive and biological parents. Hyperactive children resembled their biological parents more than they did their adoptive parents with respect to hyperactivity.

Since identical twins have the same genetic make-up, if one twin has ADHD, there is a very strong likelihood that the other sibling also has it. This has been demonstrated in several studies. For example, Dr. Florence Levy studied almost two thousand families with twins in Australia and found that 82 percent of the identical twins had ADHD. It showed up in only 38 percent of the fraternal (non-identical) twins.

Twin studies have confirmed the important role that genes play in causing ADHD, but these studies haven't yet identified the specific genes linked to the disorder.

Spotlight on Environmental Toxins

Because ADHD is a brain-based problem, its symptoms can be caused or exacerbated or triggered by exposure to toxic substances in the developing fetus and by acquired brain injury due to trauma or disease. For example, research shows that children with higher than normal levels of pesticides in their urine were more likely to meet the diagnostic criteria for ADHD. We can only wonder about the neurological impact of the approximately eighty thousand chemicals that are poorly regulated or not regulated at all by government agencies in the United States. Fortunately, organizations dedicated to the study of factors related to LD and ADHD, such as the Research Committee of LDA, are monitoring the impact of pesticides and other chemicals including lead and other heavy metals on brain development. CHADD also monitors research and government actions regarding the connection between exposure to environmental toxins such as lead and cadmium. More information about these important efforts can be found at the websites of CHADD and LDA.

The Dopamine Connection

An increasing number of studies carried out in recent years have focused on the brain chemical dopamine, which has been found at lower than normal levels in those with ADHD. Some specific genes have been identified, including the dopamine genes DAT1 and DAT4. (DAT stands for Dopamine Active Transporter.) The gene that encodes or programs the DAT proteins is located on human chromosome 5. The DAT1 and DAT4 transporters are responsible, respectively, for excitatory and inhibitory neuro-transmission. This means they control the flow of dopamine molecules into and out of the synapse, or the space between neurons. If this process is disturbed by genetic impairment, then not enough dopamine is found in the synapse, and the nerve impulses that are related to (among other things) attention and activity are impaired. This process happens in all attention-related areas of the brain except for the prefrontal cortex, where a similar agent, the norepinephrine active transporter (NAT) takes on that function.

Nora Volkow, M.D., of the National Institute on Drug Abuse in Bethesda, Maryland, has carried out research on adults with ADHD which she believes has applicability to children and adolescents. Her research shows that individuals with ADHD who carry a specific type of dopamine receptor gene respond better to the drug methylphenidate (Ritalin) than those without the genotype. This research has shed new light on the effectiveness of stimulant drugs, which increase levels of dopamine in the brain. Dr. Volkow's research also found evidence of low levels of dopamine in the hippocampus and amygdala in individuals with ADHD. As you may recall from Chapter One, these areas of the brain are part of the limbic system, which are involved in emotional responses as well as consolidating and retrieving memories. Aha!

WRAP-UP

I hope that tracing the evolution of ADHD and the way it has been described over time has helped to clear up some of the confusion that surrounds this condition, the most common neurobehavioral disorder of childhood. A review of the research about ADHD makes it fairly clear that scientists believe that there is no single cause for ADHD. Most professionals agree that ADHD is a medical disorder affecting the several areas of the brain, with the frontal area likely having the greatest involvement. Of significant interest are the areas of the brain that control executive functions necessary for the regulation of behavior, working memory, efficient thinking, and planning and organizing—all necessary for efficient processing of the complex environments of school, home, and playground.

Several theories of the neurobiological pathophysiology of ADHD have been proposed, tested, and supported through neuroimaging, genetics, and studies that examine the neurophysiology and neurochemistry of the brain. While these studies put scientists on the threshold of a consensus regarding the underlying neural deficits, the question of what exactly causes ADHD remains unanswered. Fortunately, the future holds the potential for greater understanding of and changing attitudes about ADHD.

5

Decoding Stress with Neuropsychological Evaluations

I love my job. In my role as consulting neuropsychologist to schools, I have the opportunity help teachers, school psychologists, and social workers think in new ways about learning and behavior. Over the years I have taught in several colleges, training teachers and other professionals to work with children with special needs, and have found this role rewarding and satisfying. Nonetheless, it's my work as a consultant to schools that I find most exciting, for my intervention on the front lines has direct impact on teaching and learning. In this dynamic environment, I am able to offer what are essentially master classes in teaching, with a focus on learning and behavior, delivered to well-trained and committed professionals who are deeply concerned about children. The work is so rewarding because it is so practical. Modeling interactions with students and having the chance to discuss the interaction shortly thereafter often leads to changes in a teacher's perception of a student. This process helps create a road map that teachers and other professionals can use to help students learn and grow in a manner that's commensurate with their ability. This goes a long way toward creating environments that reduce stress for kids with LD and ADHD.

In my clinical practice, I'm fortunate to be able to spend my days working with kids and their parents in the confidential confines of my office. This intimate, deeply personal venture into self-exploration often *rekindles* a spark of hope that even at an early age can already be growing dim. An intensive, comprehensive neuropsychological evaluation should be guided by the yet unanswered questions that both parents and teachers have about a particular child. This process often sheds light on a child's vulnerabilities and strengths in a way that is hard to replicate in any other setting. This sophisticated evaluation process helps equip adults with the understanding and tools that will allow them to support the child in an educated, purposeful, and directed fashion. Most important, my work helps a child achieve better self-understanding as a learner. This is empowering and can affect a child's life in a profound way. A thorough understanding of a child's neurocognitive profile is one of the more important steps in the DE-STRESS model that I present in Chapter Seven.

In the current chapter, I use my perspective as a clinical neuropsychologist to convey to you how the perceptual, processing, and executive functioning weaknesses associated with LD and ADHD make kids with these conditions even more susceptible to stress than other kids. You'll see that it's not really the LD or the ADHD that's the problem—it's the children's *reaction* to their condition. It's their reaction to the environment in which they are educated, and their response to the reactions of others to the behaviors they exhibit *because they don't want to be seen as incompetent.*

LD AND ADHD MAKE STRESS WORSE

It is the very characteristics of LD and ADHD that make kids with these conditions so vulnerable to stress. The perceptual deficits that make it hard for a student with LD to interpret sights and sounds can also make it difficult to understand or read the uncomfortable feelings that accompany stress. The impulsive child with ADHD is less likely to stop and make the stress-fear connection, but instead will jump up and head for the hills at the first hint of challenge. That's why so many kids ask to go the bathroom or the nurse's office when they get backed into a corner by the curriculum. Kids who learn to read their queasy stomachs, their sweaty palms and armpits, their hot flashes or dizziness as signs of stress—these are the kids who stand a better chance of making the connection between stress and the threat of failure.

Think about this. To confident, competent kids, each new learning challenge is an opportunity to get a success fix. The reason that kids without impairments in learning or attention are less stressed than kids with these problems is that they have what it takes to be successful *and they know it*. They have conquered many challenges in their young lives and they know what success feels like. And they want more of that feeling. Sure, these kids might be temporarily thrown off balance by a challenge, but that's just their brain sensing a change in the environment and getting ready to conquer the threat and make it go away. "Another test?" it perceives. "I can handle that!" "A long-term writing project? *Bring it on*."

In contrast, students with learning disabilities or ADHD spend much of their day in environments that ask them to do things that range from difficult to nearly impossible. For kids with LD and ADHD, stress lives in the space between "*I need to*" and "*I don't know how to*." The key to reducing the stress lies in giving a child the tools needed to attain success, and the practice it takes to do that with confidence.

Imagine this scene: A teacher asks the class a question. Declan, a little boy with ADHD, sits in the front row because his IEP says he should have "preferential seating." This distractible little boy has been doodling on his paper, legs coiled under his chair and ceaselessly undulating like snakes. On some level he probably hears the teacher's question, but it does not register with him. His sonar picks up something and alerts him: *"Huh? What?"* Movement on his left and right catches his attention, and he notices that his classmates are eagerly raising their hands. In response to this concrete visual cue, this little impulsive boy's hand shoots up like a rocket, accompanied by repeated, animated shouts of "Oooh! *Oooh!* . . . *Oooh!*" The teacher, delighted to see this particular student taking part in the lesson in such an energized way, says to the class with a smile, "Well, it looks like *somebody* is eager to give us the answer! Yes, Declan?"

You know how it goes from here. Declan mutters, "Uh . . . uh . . . ," looks puzzled, turns beet red. Little chirps of laughter break out all around him. With a gentle but admonishing "Now, *children*," the teacher quiets the class. Declan's hand drops like a rock. He slumps, embarrassed, into his chair. For kids like Declan, this scene replays itself over and over and over again. These kids' frontal lobes just can't override their distractibility or their impulsive nature. As a result, their teachers— despite their good intentions—wind up looking to these kids like pitching machines, spitting out ball after ball that they just can't seem to hit.

So because of his impulsivity and distractibility, Declan gets loads of practice being a failure. In fact, he's become an expert at it. How many times has he looked up from a blank piece of paper on his desk, only to notice that the kids sitting around him have filled *their* papers with creative tales? How many worksheets has he crumbled up in frustration after his pencil won't do what his brain wants it to do?

There are lots of kids like Declan in our schools. How many kids have hurried home the first day of school to make book covers for their schoolbooks, not because they want to keep them clean but because they don't want to be embarrassed by the low-level texts they have been given? How many parents have gone to "Back to School Night" and found it quite easy to recognize their child's paper stapled to the bulletin board? Barely legible handwriting, immature drawings, and multiple erasures serve as the signatures for many kids with learning disabilities.

Many children with LD and ADHD live in fear of failure, and often exhibit behaviors that are counterproductive to learning. Not knowing why they behave as they do, they mistakenly give themselves labels like *stupid* or *dumb* or *retard*, and consequently live down to their degraded self-images. Unless we create learning environments that are matched to students' special needs as well as their individual abilities, we won't break the fear-failure cycle. Until we design classrooms and learning experiences that allow kids to know the joy of accomplishment, to hear the sweet sound of (sincere) praise, and experience the confidence that comes from mastery, these children will continue to suffer. Unless children are *taught* how to work smarter instead of being admonished to work harder, they will languish in a kind of educational Never-Never Land. The tape loops in their heads: "*I will never be successful; I will never amount to much.*" Far too many children with learning disabilities or attention-deficit/ hyperactivity disorder either know or believe that they have limited control over many of the things they are supposed to be able to do every day. This situation creates an incubator for stress. The following sections introduce some students whose personal stories will help me make my point.

THE DECLINE OF SHIRA G.

Eleven-year-old Shira is sitting across from me. I am trying to help her understand the results of the neuropsychological evaluation that I completed with her the week before. We have spent six hours together over the past two weeks, and this is her opportunity to learn what our collaborative effort as co-investigators has yielded. I start by going over the results of the IQ test, the cornerstone of my comprehensive evaluation. I explain that this test (and the many others I had given her) help me understand the ways in which she is smart.

I explain to Shira that her verbal intelligence—probably the most predictive of success in a rigorous academic environment—is extremely high. Attempting to paint a word picture for her, I say: "If we lined up a hundred kids who took this test, only three would have done as well or better than you. All the others would have done less well." I go on, "This testing confirmed for me what I thought when we met two weeks ago and I listened to you tell me about how things were going in school." I show her a graph that shows the gap between most of her scores and those in the average range. "These results tell me that you are a very smart kid." She then lowers her eyes and asks the question that opens the door for me to explain the rest of the evaluation results—the question that so many kids with LD have asked me over the years:

"If I'm so smart, then why do I always feel so stupid?"

It was January of Shira's fifth-grade year. She had been referred to me because she had started to shut down. Her teachers had begun to increase the pace and intensity of the curriculum to prepare Shira and others in her grade for the upcoming challenges of middle school, which would start next fall. Shira had done OK in the earlier grades, in which her strong verbal skills were rewarded and reinforced. She had excellent decoding skills and could read most of what she was presented with, but her comprehension was still weak. After spending many hours on computer-based and live drill, she had memorized her basic math facts. As a result she always did well on standardized achievement tests of computation.

In fifth grade, however, Shira found it very difficult to keep up with the volume of independent reading that was required, falling behind in her assignments and running out of time at night to do her homework well, or do it at all. A conscientious student, she had begun staying up late at night and getting up early in the morning, trying to get everything done. This strategy was robbing her of time other kids were spending on extracurricular activities, as well as depriving her of sleep.

This formerly social and popular student began to make excuses about why she could not spend time with friends. She dropped out of her temple youth group. She became irritable at home, snapping at her parents, needing but then rejecting their efforts to help her. Shira began picking on her younger brother and making fun of him. She began to bite her nails again, a nervous habit she had abandoned some years ago, and had started to twist her hair in her fingers until it pulled out in little clumps. She became a picky eater who sat silently and angrily in restaurants while her family ate their meals. She was losing weight. She complained of stomachaches and didn't want to get out of bed in the morning. As a result, she was often late for school and began to miss many days, telling her mother and father that she felt sick. Not knowing what to do, her parents began to have increasingly intense debates about the right approach to use to help her. This added to the stress level of the entire family.

Alarmed and worried, Mr. and Mrs. G. took their daughter to see her pediatrician, who had known Shira since she was two. The physician was shocked to see that within less than a year, his funny, engaging patient had become a thin, anxious little girl with dark circles under her eyes. As he carried out the physical exam, he asked her how things were going in school. In a quiet, quivering voice, she replied, "OK," but then began to whimper: "I just can't *do* it!" she sobbed. "I am so *dumb!*"

Appropriately worried about this little girl's mental health and what he regarded as stress-induced depression, the pediatrician referred Shira to a therapist in my building. He and Shira hit it off well (a prerequisite to effective therapy), and the counseling and support over the next several months brought Shira some much-needed comfort. Her spirits had lifted, her eating had improved, and she was feeling and looking much healthier. Unfortunately, though, her performance continued to decline in school and attendance continued to be a problem. The therapist thought that Shira was stable enough to undergo testing, and it was at this point that he referred her to me for an evaluation.

Shira grew increasingly interested in learning more about her own learning style as she moved through the tasks I put before her. The testing revealed that she had an underlying learning disability that had not yet been forced into the open by the relatively limited demands of elementary school (and because of the supports that were built into her program, which utilized a team approach). Once she better understood her own learning profile and learned strategies that would allow her to be more successful, Shira told me at a subsequent follow-up visit that she felt she was getting "back in charge of herself." While school continued to be challenging, Shira worked with a tutor and began using the services of the school's learning center. Armed with a new self-understanding and supported by services appropriately matched to her learning style and needs, Shira pulled herself out of a slump and was soon back on the path to success. She continued to experience what she called "peaks and valleys," but said that she was learning how to stay in the high places to keep things in perspective. Having a greater sense of control increased her feelings of confidence, and that reduced the stress that used to plague her. As Shira learned how to manage her LD, her stress lost its controlling role in her life.

MARIA AND THE STRESS-LEARNING CONNECTION

One of the frustrations in my professional career is that sometimes the findings of my evaluations do not trickle down to where the action is: the classroom. This is my opportunity to explain how an intensive evaluation of a student's neuropsychological profile can guide the development of an effective intervention plan, and how important the role of the teacher is in this process.

Maria is an extremely intelligent fifteen-year-old who had become educationally and socially incapacitated by stress by the time I met her. Her story dramatically points out how underlying learning disabilities and poor executive functions can create a source of cognitive friction that virtually shuts down the brain's ability to cope with stress—and what can be done to help a student like this.

Maria's neuropsychological evaluation readily identified her superior verbal abilities. The WISC-IV verbal comprehension score was at the 96th percentile. Other tests of verbal skills confirmed her strength in receptive and expressive language. However, Maria had significant difficulty organizing and using language efficiently. Her executive functioning skills were weak. Despite her superior verbal abilities, her writing revealed rambling thoughts, run-on sentences, and the overuse or misuse of words. She was having much difficulty getting papers or writing-based projects completed within the expected time limits. The very idea of an open-ended writing assignment sent her into a tailspin. Once she fought down her anxiety enough to begin an assignment, she would spend an inordinate amount of time trying to complete it—and was seldom successful.

In the testing profiles of students with learning disabilities, there is often a large difference between verbal skills and visual-perceptual-motor skills, or those skills required for drawing or figuring out shapes and matching visual items. In Maria's case, however, her Perceptual Reasoning score on the WISC-IV fell at the 83rd percentile. Her artistic skills had earned her the praise of others. However (and here's where the detective work comes in), additional testing revealed subtle but significant weaknesses that provided a clue that helped solve the mystery that surrounded her learning difficulties.

When I asked her to copy a complex geometric figure from a model printed on a piece of paper, Maria slowly and carefully constructed it with a degree of perfection that would have made Xerox nervous. However, when I asked her to draw the same design from memory, she looked at me with disbelief. "You gotta be kidding!" she exclaimed, and when I reminded her that we were working as a team to sort out her problems, she anxiously picked up a pencil to begin. Sighing audibly while she worked, she kept saying things like "This is so hard! Can I see that first drawing again?" Working from memory, she created an image in which many of the elements were distorted and others were entirely missing. Pushing it across the desk to me, she said, "This stinks!"

This finding is significant. It demonstrates that while Maria can copy a design from a model (which allows her to make art from a model or a picture in her head), there is a very rapid deterioration in memory for details and their placement. This is often seen in the profiles of anxious students, as anxiety is a great enemy of memory for details. But there's more operating here. Maria's visual-perceptual memory is weak; the resulting poor performance creates anxiety, which further impairs her memory. This is evidence of a very specific learning disability becoming worse under the influence of stress.

I thought that Maria's performance on this drawing task provided a window into her cognitive style, helping to explain her writing. Drawing is not the same as writing, to be sure, but here's the way I interpreted this finding and its impact on writing: Maria might have an idea about what she wants to write about, but she is not sure about the organization and placement of the details. To write well, we have to see the organization of our ideas taking shape in our mind. Maria has a hard time storing ideas in her head in an organized fashion that would allow for efficient retrieval. As a result, she rambles, filling the page with stream-of-consciousness style writing. Superfluous words, phrases, and sentences seem to get their inspiration from the preceding passage and not from any verbal outline in her head.

After we had met for a few times, Maria asked if I'd like to see her "Odyssey," a journal she said she had been keeping since fifth grade. The journal was actually sixteen notebooks, which she brought in a small suitcase. It did not take me long to see that these books contained one continuous tale that flowed onto the pages and from book to book in the way that homemade pasta comes out of a pasta machine. Amazingly, there was no indentation, a giveaway to its lack of organization. It was only one paragraph, but what a paragraph!

The evaluation produced even more evidence of the negative impact of Maria's cognitive style on her performance. She performed at only the 2nd percentile on a task that required her to repeat as many words as she could from a list of ten that I read to her. Her auditory memory seemed to evaporate on this task, even when the lists were read repeatedly. However, she did a great job remembering details from several short passages that I had just read to her. Her performance was much better here because she could use context to help her remember the details.

Additional testing revealed that Maria had difficulty with selective attention. This was very evident on a task on which she had to rapidly shift mental gears. She was given a page filled with color names that were printed in another color ink. For example, the word *blue* was printed in red ink, and she found it hard to name the ink color and not read the word. She performed accurately but very slowly when I asked her to solve simple math problems (for example, $5 - 3$; 2×8) or rapidly read simple sentences (such as "Cows fly in the air") and say if they are true or false.

Maria's performance on several tests like this, confirmed by her own self-appraisal, indicated that she had a lot of difficulty with both behavioral and cognitive flexibility. This rigidity can make adapting to the demands of life and school very challenging.

She retreated to familiar rituals and routines to help assuage the anxiety that welled up in her whenever she had to make rapid decisions or respond to novel situations. She felt restricted by her poor executive-functioning skills and by the stress that this created.

The combination of slow motor speed, cognitive inflexibility, and poor organization helped to explain why writing was very tedious and frustrating for Maria, not to mention being a time sink for teachers who were expected to read and grade her papers! To help her with this problem, I recommended that Maria use a keyboard (and work to improve the speed of her typing) rather than a pen. I also suggested that she use a software program called Inspiration, which prompts a writer to put ideas into a graphic organizer that serves as a visual outline. Then, with a keystroke, the ideas turn into a traditional linear, verbal outline. Inspiration is designed to enhance visual thinking and learning in schools and in the workplace. Students who have difficulty with traditional outlining often find it helpful to see this visual-to-verbal transformation take place before their eyes. For some kids, a picture sometimes really is worth a thousand words. The transformation from visual to verbal can help the writer see whether ideas have the desired relationship to each other. (I actually used this software, which I have frequently recommended for use with students with organizational difficulties, to create the outline for several chapters in this book.) You can get a free trial download of the Inspiration software, as well as of Kidspiration3 (the version designed for kids from Kindergarten through Grade 5), along with information about other great products, at www.inspiration.com.

Maria loved this program. She told me that it was like having an "extra brain" to do the things that she found so difficult. As she gained a greater degree of mastery over organization, she became more comfortable with the task of writing and her anxiety lessened. This did not cure her problem, but it did help her put bookends on her writing.

As you can see, Maria's cognitive profile is complex, and these layers of difficulty have made life extremely tough for her. Prior to the testing and our subsequent discussions about its meaning and what she could do about it, Maria was continually backed into an emotional corner by her own cognitive style—and she was clueless about why this was happening. As a result, she began to avoid tasks that she felt she would not be able to do and buried herself in others that she had mastered long ago, just as a way to allow her to feel good . . . or at least not stupid.

Developing a more accurate understanding of her learning profile and implementing several strategies to help strengthen her vulnerabilities allowed Maria to become more optimistic about her educational future. Maria's teachers, equipped with a new appreciation of the nature of her difficulties, were better able to support her in her efforts to overcome her challenges.

A FRONT ROW SEAT TO THE SAGA OF HUMAN DEVELOPMENT

As a clinical neuropsychologist, I get the opportunity to spend six to eight hours doing interviews and observations, and using a variety of assessment tools that help me better understand a student's neurocognitive functioning. Because I work with kids who range from first or second graders through college or graduate school students, children and young adults of all ages fill my office with their intense emotions and stories of stress, but also with their creativity, their hopes, and their dreams. I get to witness firsthand their courage, their bravado, and their vulnerability.

Doctor Watson . . . hand me the magnifying glass, would you?

When I meet younger kids I tell them, "I'm sort of like a Learning Detective—someone who looks for clues about how kids learn and what gets in the way," and I explain to them that I'm going to need their help in this quest for information about themselves. Most kids like this team approach, which I have found empowers them to act in their own behalf. I believe that engaging kids in this journey of discovery helps them develop a sense of self-advocacy that comes from self-awareness. I saw a cartoon recently that shows a little boy standing up in class imploring his teacher, "Can we hurry up and get to the test?" And he explains why: "My short-term memory is better than my long-term memory." The message of this cartoon is that if we teach kids how they learn (or take tests) best, we have to be prepared to live with them and their newfound self-advocacy. Ah, what a joy that is! In addition to being challenging and stimulating, the work I do with kids is usually fun—and often quite entertaining.

Kids Really Do Say the Darndest Things

A couple of years ago, I met with a fourth grader I'll call Betsy to go over the results of a recent neuropsychological evaluation. Her mother sat in my waiting room while I shared the results of the testing with this engaging little girl at a level I believed she would understand. As I often do, I encouraged this talented youngster to tell me what she had heard me say about her learning style and needs while I sat at my keyboard and typed what was to become a letter to her teacher. From her responses to me, it was clear that Betsy had understood my explanation of her learning style. This was very gratifying for me, and I gave myself a virtual pat on the back. She dutifully dictated her letter to "Dear Mrs. Barnett," and with a satisfied flourish, I handed her the copy that had whirred its way out of the printer on the desk. Out in the waiting room, I told her mom about the letter and its purpose. Betsy's mother's eyes glistened as I praised her daughter's ability to gain new insights from this process of self-evaluation. I said that when kids were able to explain their own learning style and let their teachers know what they needed (and what they would do themselves) to be more successful, most teachers found this personal statement hard to resist. I thanked Betsy for her hard work and said good-bye to mother and daughter.

As soon as I closed my office door, I heard this little girl (who had been such a willing participant in my plan moments before) proclaim (rather loudly): "If that guy thinks I'm gonna show this to my teacher, then *he* needs a shrink." I heard her mother call out her daughter's name as a hushed exclamation, followed by the distinct sound of paper ripping. *"Oh, Betsy!"*

Not to worry, I said to myself, smiling. In the process of dictating that letter, I had heard this little girl very articulately explain her own learning style in a manner that showed she really comprehended the results of the testing that had taken place over the preceding two weeks. Even if Mrs. Barnett never saw the letter, I knew that Betsy understood herself a little better and might feel a bit more in control of her own educational destiny as a result. Perhaps Betsy would get in touch with me near the end of high school, calling to see if I had a copy of "that letter I wrote when I was ten" that she wanted to incorporate into her college essay. I had hit the "save" button, so I knew that I would be able to say yes. (And I also knew that Betsy's mom would be giving Mrs. Barnett a copy of my full report.)

Epilogue: The following fall, Besty's mom called me to tell me about her daughter's transition to fifth grade. She said that Betsy's teacher started the school year by having all the kids write an essay called "How I Learn Best." She asked them to tell her what they had done to solve difficult learning challenges in the past, and what they would like their teacher to do that would make the fifth grade "the best year yet."

Betsy's mom told me how impressed the teacher was with Betsy's self-awareness, and loved it when this eleven-year-old wrote: "I don't think I listen as fast as you talk."

Give It to Me Straight, Doc . . .

When older students come in for an evaluation, they are often motivated to finally find out why they struggle so to do what other kids seem to do with much less effort and much less stress. These kids are tired (literally and figuratively) of spending inordinate amounts of time on homework, often staying up very late or getting up early in the morning to complete assignments. They are angry that whatever free time they might have gets eaten up by their schoolwork. They are fed up with getting C's or D's on an exam after they had "studied their butts off" and "knew the material cold." They feel hurt and confused when a teacher tells them they should be working harder and spending more time in preparation. Middle and high school students may doubt that an evaluation will help them understand why this is happening, and some of them come in kicking and complaining to their parents. Some shed tears of shame when they begin to tell me the story of their efforts, which have too often been in vain, or as they sit silently, lower lip quivering, as they hear their parent recount the tales of sadness and frustration that brought them to my office. However, by the time we get into the first hour of testing, these same kids are often engaged in the task, eager to find out how they did and how this work might help them find more success and happiness in school.

MEET WILLIAM

This seventeen-year-old high school junior was facing the imminent prospect of college admission and was, in his words, "stressing out majorly." When I met William, he told me that no matter how hard he studied and how well he prepared, he was failing every test he encountered. He was certain that he would not be able to go to any college and was "absolutely terrified about upcoming SATs."

William's mother hoped that a neuropsychological evalua-tion would substantiate a request for her son to have extended time on tests, because the daughter of a family friend had gotten a special dispensation based on her test results. As we moved into the initial testing session, William told me that he had mixed feelings about the potential outcome of the testing. "Actually," he confided, "I'm a little worried that having more time will just mean I have more time to get anxious." Despite this concern, William continued to be hopeful that the evaluation might reveal information about himself that might help him understand the source of his stress and give him strategies to deal with it.

I explained to William that some of things I would ask him to do would seem easy and that he might find others more chal-lenging. I assured him that I learned as much from his mistakes as I did from his successes. When he understood that he was providing data for us both to analyze, he was less worried about making errors, and actually began to look forward to my inter-pretations and explanations.

For William, undergoing this evaluation put him under the microscope in a very personalized diagnostic laboratory. At one point, he enthusiastically interjected: "What happened on *that* one [a test of sequential memory] is *exactly* what happens to me in class!" When he did well on other tests, he said, "It's amazing how different I feel when I'm doing stuff like this." In a statement that revealed his incredible insight, William explained: "It's like I have enemies and friends among my assignments. When I'm among my 'friends,' I rock, but when the enemies show up, I put up my defenses. Which means, I basically freeze; I just can't do anything."

"And then . . . ," he added, his voice dropping, "then, the cycle starts. I freeze, I shut down, I start to talk to myself, calling myself a 'loser,' and I just give up."

It's worth taking a closer look at William's performance on several of the tests in the battery I administered to better understand the cause of the stress that immobilizes and demoralizes this young man. On the Tests of Word Reading Efficiency (TOWRE), William's ability to read as many "real" words (sight words) as possible in forty-five seconds fell at only the 7th percentile. His reading was accurate—he didn't miss any—but it was excruciatingly slow. At his age, he's supposed to know these words on sight, with no need for conscious analysis, but he has to decipher each one. His performance on the Phonemic Decoding Efficiency task (reading made-up words) fell at the 16th percentile. This score revealed a lingering weakness in the phonemic analysis (decoding) of unknown words. For example, when William was presented with the nonsense word *trober*, he read that as tumber. Most revealing, *poth* was read as *both*. When required to use his sound-symbol association skills to read these made-up words, he did poorly despite years of instruction. He inserted, changed, or deleted letters; the p-for-b inversion is very uncommon among students William's age. No wonder school (and all the reading that's involved) is so stressful! Have you ever tried to read a menu in a Latin American country by using the Spanish that you studied for a year in middle school?

On the Gray Oral Reading Tests (GORT), William was asked to read a series of progressively more difficult passages aloud and then answer five comprehension questions about the selection. His scores fell in the average range, but a neuropsychologist learns early on not to be too dependent on scores and is always on the lookout for clues to solving the mystery. What is not reflected in William's GORT scores was the number of times he repeated the first syllable of a word—sometimes two or three times—to connect with it—to get clues from it. He ultimately gets the word right, but because of his weak sound-symbol association skills, he needs to take a lot of time to do it. Not only does the need to reread slow him down, it also disrupts the flow of his reading (which in turn undercuts his understanding of the passage). He was only able to correctly answer two of the three questions asked about the ninth-grade passage. He got three of the five questions correct after reading the tenth-grade passage, but could only get two of five correct on an eleventh-grade passage. These variable test results start to paint a clearer picture of the cause of this young man's anguish.

I also gave him the Nelson-Denny Reading Test, using the standard timed administration. This is a test of vocabulary, comprehension, and reading rate. William missed only two vocabulary items of the ones he attempted. However, he had to read and reread the multiple-choice answers, and this slowed down his performance appreciably. His slow performance lowered his score, which suggested that his vocabulary was not very strong. But his superior scores on the WAIS-IV (Adult IQ test) tell a different story.

William's reading *comprehension* score on the Nelson-Denny falls at the 22nd percentile. Again, this is much lower than we would expect from a student with such a strong verbal profile. There is also more evidence that his comprehension suffers from his slow rate of reading (7th percentile) as well as weak decoding skills, as noted in the discussion of his GORT results. Having to restart words (and it's likely this is happening on the Nelson Denny in the same way as it was on the GORT) takes time. Slow and inefficient decoding of unfamiliar words slows down reading, requires rereading to gain meaning from context, and, unsurprisingly, has a deleterious impact on comprehension. As a result, William's *total* reading score on the Nelson-Denny falls only at the 14th percentile overall. It is no wonder that he has to spend much more time than his classmates do on reading-intensive assignments. And it's no wonder that he questions his own intelligence.

As with the other students I introduce in this chapter, an explanation of the results of this testing helped William understand why he didn't feel as smart as his classmates, despite impressive evidence to the contrary. Even though the interpretation was helpful to him, as he listened to my analysis of the test results, I could see that his eyes were brimming with tears—tears of relief, mixed with tears of disappointment about not knowing this before, and with tears of anger for having beaten himself up so many times about being dumb. For me, this emotional reaction has come to be an expected but nonetheless sad consequence of giving kids the news. But it's both bad news and good news, for solving the mystery that lies beneath years of frustration can be liberating. It can lead a student down a path of greater success. And together with his parents, William was able to move on—to look ahead with a greater sense of optimism and hope.

In the recommendations section of William's report, I made several suggestions about what teachers and other specialists could do to help him improve his reading skills and his speed of responding. They know a lot about how to do this—that's their specialty. With a better understanding of what was before an invisible disability, they could fill the prescription I had written. However, my most important recommendation reflected the theme of this book: To help William maintain a sense of optimism by teaching him how to attain greater mastery over his reading difficulties.

I also wrote about how to help him deal with the reality that he might always be challenged by reading, and that there were strategies that he could use to help him bypass or lessen some of the struggles. For example, the testing had also shown that William could understand what he had heard. His listening comprehension was clearly an asset in his neuropsychological profile and could be put to good use. His teachers were familiar with the "talking books" provided by Recording for the Blind & Dyslexic (RFBD) and could use them to bring knowledge into William's brain through the spoken word, bypassing his weaker sound-symbol association skills and using his much stronger listening ability.

Recording for the Blind & Dyslexic (www.rfbd.org) is a national nonprofit organization with the largest textbook library of accessible education materials available on the Web. This site offers a free download of the ReadHear software player for Macintosh and Windows users, which makes pleasure reading and educational materials more accessible for people with learning differences.

Based on the fact that William had had a lot of experience devaluing his own efforts and shutting down in response to his frustration, I wrote in his report:

> William needs to develop a better understanding
> of his own learning disability. While the process
> of self-understanding was initiated by this
> evaluation, he has to continue to be encouraged
> to examine his errors, and generate strategies to
> help him minimize them. If his first mental
> response is "I can't," quite simply, he won't. He
> should be helped to confront new challenges by
> greeting them instead with "this might be hard
> for me, but I know what I can do to master it."

FINE-TUNING THE STRESS/LD/ADHD HYPOTHESIS

Don't assume that a student understands stress. Only when a parent or teacher knows that a child correctly interprets the bodily sensations and feelings associated with stress, and has at least a basic understanding of learning or attention difficulties, can a connection be made between the two. It's hard to overcome stress if you don't really know what it is. Some children with LD or ADHD need to be actively taught about the symptoms of stress. A unit in a health class, taught to all children, is the most natural way to expose kids to stress and its impact on them. Students can be encouraged to talk about when they feel stressed and how they know it. This can help the student with special needs understand that stress is a normal reaction for all kids.

The importance of a differential diagnosis. In some students, the ADHD or LD may mask a serious underlying anxiety disorder. In other words, if parents and professionals automatically attribute the signs of stress to the learning and attention difficulties because the latter are so present and obvious, they may miss or misdiagnose an underlying generalized anxiety disorder (GAD). GAD is an emotional disorder in which the brain generates chronic and exaggerated worry and tension that seem to have no substantial cause. Adults who have GAD often worry excessively about health, money, family, or work, or they might continually anticipate disaster. Depending on the developmental level of children, they can worry about anything you can think of. We're not talking about the mild worries experienced by all kids, but a level of excessive preoccupation that impedes learning and affects social experiences, relationships, and health.

The family that frets together . . . In the same way that there are adults who seem to be excessively worried about everything in life, there are also children who view even the smallest event with a general wariness or sense of foreboding. Sometimes, these adults and children are even related! If one or both parents are negatively impacted by stress, their child might inherit or learn this tendency. While there is a strong genetic predisposition, children are sometimes the first in their family to exhibit symptoms of a more generalized stress disorder. Then the specialists working with a child need to make a "what came first" decision. Is it the anxiety and stress that caused the primary problem or is it the LD or ADHD that created the stress?

If anxiety is the primary cause of a student's difficulty in school and in life, then therapy and perhaps medication may be the first line of attack. If it's the LD and ADHD that create the stress, then the focus for intervention needs to be on reducing the negative impact of these conditions.

It's important to point out that all three of these conditions can coexist in the same person, and any intervention must address the learning, attentional, and emotional components simultaneously. It's possible that high anxiety may actually mask LD or ADHD. Students who worry a lot often find it difficult to focus for very long on anything—including schoolwork. What's initially regarded as ADHD may actually be the inattention caused by internalized worries rather than the distractibility and intermittent attention that has its roots in a neurologically based attention deficit. It's important to rule out anxiety as the underlying disorder, and this generally requires an evaluation by a child psychiatrist or a clinical psychologist who is familiar with this condition.

A *note of caution:* If the learning or attention issues that created the stress in the first place are being addressed adequately, but stress lingers, any reputable program that's designed to help children identify and reduce stress can be helpful for children with LD and ADHD. If kids understand how *their* LD or ADHD make certain things in school particularly challenging, and if they are in environments that give them multiple opportunities to be competent and attain mastery, then programs that help reduce any anxiety that still exists can certainly be helpful. If the roots of the stress lie in undiagnosed or misunderstood LD or ADHD, or if the stress festers in an environment that does not address the child's need to feel some sense of control over learning, simple stress-reduction programs are not the answer. While these programs will probably do no harm, they are not the right medicine for what ails these kids.

STRESS WITH AN ACCENT

Special consideration for English language learning (ELL) or bilingual students and students from other cultures is often in order. Students from different language or cultural communities who happen to have ADHD or LD are more likely to manifest symptoms of stress than students who have LD or ADHD without the added cultural tension. A diagnostic evaluation by a bilingual diagnostician who is familiar with LD and ADHD, as well as its cultural nuances, must be provided to students who fall in this category.

I am reminded of Cruz, a ten-year-old whose family had immigrated to the United States from the Dominican Republic. An evaluation by the bilingual school psychologist showed that Cruz was challenged by learning disabilities in both English and Spanish. His role as family translator, which included putting him in a position of interpreting messages from the school to his parents, only made the situation worse. The stress caused by his difficulty performing in school, as well as his difficulties processing both languages, gave few opportunities for him to experience the sense of mastery that builds students up from the inside out. As a result, he began to shut down academically and act up behaviorally. Both responses were predictable and understandable ways to avoid the stress created by tasks over which Cruz had little or no control.

His subsequent movement to a small, specialized LD class taught by a bilingual teacher resulted in a significant improvement in both his learning and his behavior. During this time, he learned about why he had difficulties in both English and Spanish, and was engaged in a plan to improve his performance in both. Within in a few months, Cruz was able (and eager) to return to an integrated classroom, in which he felt increasingly more competent and more confident. His language-processing skills were still weak, and he received continued specialized service in a pull-out model, but his emotional reactivity subsided. Improved behavior helped Cruz to rebuild his reputation in the building, and he gained status in the school (and in his proud family) for his accomplishments. His teachers enjoyed working with him and other kids were no longer frightened by his frustrated outbursts.

I hope that this chapter has helped you understand and appreciate the value of a neuropsychological evaluation understanding the causes of stress experienced by students with LD and ADHD. In Chapter Six, I describe the phenomenon that I call "Saving FASE," offering you some very concrete ways to break the cycle of Fear, Avoidance, Stress, and Escape that so often characterizes the lives of these students.

PART THREE

How Kids "Save FASE" and DE-STRESS

6

Nowhere to Hide

How Negative Behaviors Help Kids "Save FASE"

Chapter Two outlined the ways stress affects thinking and learning, and how successful experiences build positive memories. It's this foundation of confidence that gives children the courage and optimism to delve into new, unfamiliar terrain with a sense of excitement. The belief that they have what it takes to master the task put before them allows them to take the risks involved in learning new things. This is the spirit we'd like to see in all kids, but many of them—the ones about whom this book was written—instead deplete valuable cognitive resources trying to *avoid* these challenges.

WHAT IS FASE?

This chapter examines the cycle of Fear, Avoidance, Stress, and Escape that characterizes the reaction many kids with LD and ADHD exhibit when they are confronted by tasks that they perceive as beyond their ability to master or control. I hope that my exploration of this phenomenon helps you understand that many of the behaviors that seem negative or bad are actually the self-protective strategies children employ, either consciously or unconsciously, to hide their incompetence. The first letters of the words in this cycle create the acronym FASE, and I refer to the protective but maladaptive behaviors these kids exhibit as "Saving FASE."

When students with ADHD and LD who are familiar with failure are exposed to tasks, or directions, or even environments that contain threats to their self-image, they are, to put it simply—*scared*. The Fear component of Saving FASE is activated, much as the breaking of a twig in the snow puts a jittery rabbit on high alert in the forest. Frightened animals (including humans) try to avoid fearful situations. "That might hurt me," they say. "I need to protect myself."

That explains the Avoidance component of Saving FASE. The first duty of any brain is to protect itself and the body that carries it around. It is fear that tells the squid to pump black ink into the water. The human brain, not able to create a watery smoke screen in which to hide, calls out to the child: "Look out!" it says. "Avoid those eyes!" "Put your head down on the desk!" "Go sharpen your pencil!" "Dump stuff out of your desk." If these minimally evasive strategies don't work, the brain ups the ante— the student who is scared and can't avoid by diverting attention gets more self-protective messages—all intended to avoid the fear-invoking stimulus. "Puff yourself up and make yourself look bigger, tougher!" says the brain.

"Sneer! *Snarl!!*" "Tell the teacher to take a hike; swear under your breath!" "Do something!—do *anything!!*" Teachers see this negative behavior and often interpret it as oppositional. Repeated episodes like this can ultimately (and extremely inappropriately) lead to a formal diagnosis of oppositional defiant disorder. Disorder? *Really?* No. No! *No!!*

The savvy teacher asks: "Why in the world would this student be acting this way? This is a nice kid. A capable student, I think . . . *what's going on here?*" Teachers can actually diagnose the cause of this behavior by reading the feeling that it generates in *them*. For example, they might feel hurt by the student's language or rude behavior. It's likely that they are frustrated and disappointed that they can't reach this student. They might even feel that this student is preventing them from doing the job they are very good at—teaching.

Say that *again?* Preventing them from doing their job? *Bingo!* That's *it!* If we look closely, the behavior of students under siege actually has the function of controlling their teachers, effectively stopping them in their tracks. Teachers, after all, are the agent of this fear, are they not? In the student's mind, if the teacher goes away, so does the threat. "I can be safe if I just get the teacher to retreat!" The best way to do this is avoidance: resisting, saying no, saying "I won't." And never that "I can't."

What's the takeaway lesson here? *It's this:* If you're a teacher and a student's behavior makes you feel like you can't do the job you were trained and hired to do, this may be an indication that the student is trying to control the situation you're both in. Control? *Control?* Yes! Don't you remember? The best way to combat stress is to gain control of the situation. Isn't that just what your negative (OK . . . oppositional) student is doing here?

THE REMEDY

So what do you need to do? You need to build up a child's competence and confidence, so that Saving FASE is no longer necessary. In Chapter Seven, I provide more detail on the DE-STRESS model, which contains abundant strategies to help you turn this situation around. At this point, let me simply say that the solution is to give the student the opportunity to be in control—in a manner that is acceptable to you—while staying on mission.

"Come *on*, Doc!" you may be thinking. Still an unbeliever? OK. Let's deconstruct this a little more. Say that you, the teacher, have misread the student's behavior. You are, as they say, teed off. You just don't get it. You interpret the student's resistance not as an avoidance technique to Save FASE but as *oppositional*.

You are upset. You dig in your heels and ramp up your demands. *"This is something that you have to do, young man. You are the student and I am the teacher."* You think to yourself: *"If you don't let me teach you, then, just what am I? (Chopped liver??)"*

If the scene plays out this way, and the teacher restates the demands on the student or suggests that it's necessary to step up to the plate here and do what's expected—guess what happens to the student who can't? (Or thinks that's the case?) This student, this generally likeable and you believe capable student, is backed into a corner, painted in by impossible demands. The interaction has created a situation in which the student is confronted with a task (or a series of tasks) that in reality or in mind (either is an equally potent toxin) will lead to failure. Agreement even to *try* what you are suggesting will be a disaster. This is familiar terrain to this kid, who has been trapped at this intersection of "I can't" and "I really think you can" thousands of times. The vivid perception that "I will (again) be a failure—no matter what this teacher says" puts the kid in an "I can't" state of mind, in a "you will" kind of world. Folks, this is the absolute *definition* of stress. This is where the S part of the Saving FASE reaction shifts into gear. Neurochemicals flow, and after a while, the student's brain screams out: "I can't take this anymore!" This is when the brain musters all its resources to get this kid out of trouble. Neurochemistry switches into stress mode and takes the driver's seat.

What's a kid under inescapable, unrelenting stress to do? Get the heck out of there, that's what! To paraphrase Cole Porter: *"Birds do it, bees do it—even educated fleas do it!"* When they're stressed, they *skedaddle.* This explains the Escape part of Saving FASE. Avoidance turns to "where's the exit?" The problem is, that as the title of this book suggests, these kids have nowhere to go. They can't run and they can't hide. So what happens now? Now the fear overcomes the student. The stress level is simply too hard to take. Evasive avoidance strategies have not been effective.

So . . . the reaction escalates. No heads down this time; no averted eyes; no comic distractions. The only course left to this organism under attack is to repel—even repulse—the teacher: "*F-you, I'm not going to do this S_ _ _!*" Display items are ripped from the bulletin board. A chair is pushed back in anger. A desk is toppled, throwing the whole class into a panic. The teacher's desk is wiped clean of papers and personal belongings in one angry sweep of a forearm. Things are in chaos. The student appears out of control. Restraints are considered . . . a call to 911. An ambulance with flashing lights. A parent is called and is now in tears. A student is, yet again defeated . . .

And to think: all this could have been avoided.

PUTTING THINGS IN PERSPECTIVE

Let's back up a minute and take the long view here. Certainly not all misbehavior can be explained by stress. There are a lot of ways to interpret the unmotivated, oppositional, or even defiant behavior that some students display at home and school. They might be angry or they might be depressed. Some kids might even be trying to look dumb or look bad to fit in (or get excluded from) a particular social group. (We don't often hear the words *academically gifted* and *juvenile delinquent* in the same sentence.)

However, my interactions with teachers, parents, and kids with LD and ADHD over the past three decades has helped me come to regard the misbehavior of these students in a different way. Despite average to above-average intelligence, many of *these kids act up or act out to hide from shame and embarrassment.* I want to help parents and teachers understand that the apparent lack of motivation, the opposition, or even the defiance exhibited by some students with learning or attention difficulties is a way to avoid having their flaws found out. It's their *camouflage.* It's the suit they put on to hide their true perception of themselves—that they are dumb or stupid. The more stress these kids feel, the more camo they need. Sometimes their self-protection needs are so significant that they don armor! Psychological flak jackets, if you will. As a result, what you see are "lean, mean, fighting machines" protecting the most valuable asset that exists—themselves!

Humans naturally feel stressed when they've been thrown off balance by unexpected events. It's nature's way of getting us ready to handle threats to our safety. This is a good thing; it helps protect us. We combat stress by doing something to reduce the stress or get rid of the stressor. When we encounter a physical threat—one that we can see—we do this by scaring it away, by physically overpowering it, or by outsmarting it. In that way, we gain a sense of control that puts us back into a state of balance or equilibrium. What I hope to show you in this book is how to do that on a day-to-day basis, in the classroom, where the student with LD or ADHD feels most vulnerable. But first, let's see how a teenager who's alone in a mountain wilderness takes control of the situation and protects himself in a dangerous environment. There are lessons to be learned in the out-of-doors.

Brendan Braves the Elements

Brendan's on a camping trip with his scout troop. He has camped many times with his family and his scout buddies, and he's at home in the wilderness. This adventurous twelve-year-old is eager to face the challenges of the "solo survival" experience. During this much-anticipated event, all the boys get to pick a remote spot to pitch their pup tents and make their own meals with a limited selection of supplies and equipment. Brendan will be on his own for two days and two nights, out of contact with the other boys and with his troop leaders. He sets up his tent, digs a rain gutter around the perimeter, and hangs his food supplies from a tree, as he has been taught. He's getting tired, and he's hungry. After gathering twigs and starting a campfire, he's ready to prepare his dinner. When he reaches up for the food bag, he jumps back when it starts to move. As he trips backward over some rocks, he sees two adult gray squirrels scamper noisily out of the food bag, exposing shreds of paper. As he anxiously peers into the bag, he sees that everything edible has been eaten by the squirrels. As a chilly breeze blows through the tall pines, and darkening clouds cast deep shadows in the forest, Brendan feels a fleeting sense of panic come over him. He sits down for a few minutes to consider his predicament, then pulls himself up and goes into action. Two days later, when he rejoins his fellow scouts and the troop leaders, he's excited to share his story of survival in the wilderness.

When Brendan's deep in the woods, facing two lonely, wet, cold, and hungry days—he summons both his courage and his resourcefulness and begins to take steps that will reduce the stress-producing threat. He knows how to identify nutritious berries, and dig for and cook edible roots and mushrooms. Why, he can probably even capture and cook one of those squirrels who made off with his cache of food. Wouldn't that be sweet revenge?! A problem turned into protein. In the forest, Brendan copes with stress because he has indeed followed the motto of the Boy Scouts, which has been internalized by millions of scouts around the world since 1907—"Be Prepared."

In *Scouting for Boys* (1908), Robert Baden-Powell, the founder of the scouting movement, talked about being prepared in two ways. He explained, "To be prepared in mind means having thought out beforehand an accident or situation that might occur, so that you know the right thing to do at the right moment, and are willing to do it."

"To be prepared in body," Baden-Powell continued, "involves making yourself strong and active and able to do the right thing at the right moment." Good advice for boys (and girls!) in the woods.

If we're confronted with situations that we can't conquer through concrete action—if the problem that presents itself is more of a silent or invisible threat—it's much more difficult to combat. In the deep woods, Brendan the Scout is the master of his destiny. But Brendan the Student faces daily challenges in school that are difficult for him to overcome. He has dyslexia. He's almost thirteen years old and reads at a fourth-grade level. In the vignette below, we see Brendan a week after his camping trip, this time . . . back at school.

Brendan in the Classroom

Brendan's sitting with his twenty-four classmates. He's feeling tired and unhappy—as he does most days in school. His social studies teacher has just handed out a packet of reading materials that's the prelude to a large independent project that will be due in three weeks. Brendan sighs and reaches around to the back of his chair, eager to bury this sheaf of papers deep in the "black hole" of his backpack. Just then, the teacher says, "Pick a partner, read the directions on page one and the five pages that follow, and then brainstorm about how you plan to organize and execute your independent study." Brendan freezes. Then he looks around in a panic. He desperately hopes that no one will seek him out as a study partner, but realizes that if that happens, his teacher will pair him with some other left-over kid. His stomach ties up in knots at the thought of reading with a classmate. His brain replays visions of other times he has been unable to keep up with the pace of other kids, getting stuck on so many words he loses track of the meaning of the sentence. He gets a sick feeling in the pit of his stomach. He gets up and heads for the door. "Where are you going, Brendan?" asks his teacher. "To the bathroom," he answers in an embarrassed, frantic whisper. "Can't you wait until after we get started on this? I don't want you to miss the beginning," replies the teacher. Brendan shakes his head and leaves.

He comes back to class just before the bell rings for the next period.

With the scout motto in mind, contrast the images of Brendan the Scout and Brendan the Student. Among the dark and towering pines, this boy was in his element. A scout since he was a Cub, Brendan had prepared for several years now for the situation in which he found himself in the wilderness, and he knew he would be OK. He was mentally prepared to know what to do, and he was physically able to do what needed to be done. No need to Save FASE in the forest.

In the classroom, it was a different story. In full view of his peers and a teacher he respects, Brendan faces a psychological threat, knowing that he will read slowly and poorly, and will have to face the prospect of shame and embarrassment. He, like his woodland alter ego, had prepared long and hard for this challenge—but despite all his efforts, he was neither ready nor able to face this problem. And this was not the first time. Brendan has been at this dangerous intersection many times. His fear fuels anxiety, and he can predict the outcome with unerring accuracy: He will try, and he will fail, and he will feel worse than he felt before.

In addition to practicing reading since before kindergarten, Brendan was also practicing another survival skill—the art of escape. The saying "When the going gets tough, the tough get going" was in Brendan's case a literal reality. A perfect personal anthem for Brendan might have been that song made popular by the Animals in 1965: "We've Gotta Get Outa This Place!"

While Mrs. Blue Jay and Cesar, introduced in Chapter Three, might lash out as a response to threat, the first response of most species is to not engage in conflict but to flee or take cover. A nonhuman animal that is threatened in the wild can fly away, run under a bush or into a cave, or use camouflage as a disguise. But for Brendan and so many kids like him who experience inescapable stress in school, it's just as Martha and the Vandellas put into verse. For these kids, there's truly *"Nowhere to run, baby . . . nowhere to hide."*

So What Should We Do?

I talked about the value of a comprehensive diagnostic evaluation in Chapter Five. Brendan certainly needs to have a thorough evaluation of his cognitive and learning style. He needs to understand that because he has a neurologically based learning disability, he may never become an excellent reader. He also needs to learn that children (and adults) with severe learning disabilities can improve their skills with proper intervention. Brendan can become a better reader, and more important, feel better about himself, if he has a clear understanding of his learning disability and develops a sense of control over his own progress as a reader. He will not have to live in fear and shame if he is provided with a systematically taught, specialized approach to reading instruction that has been shown to be successful for students with dyslexia.

Kids like Brendan need teachers who understand that all human behavior sends a message. Teachers who are tuned in to the cycle of Fear, Avoidance, Stress, and Escape understand exactly what Saving FASE means—and they react not to the behavior but to the underlying cause of the behavior. They see oppositional behavior, absences, trips to the nurse, and coming late or unprepared to class for what they are: attempts to avoid the shame of having to do what you can't do easily or well in front of a lot of kids who can.

Unmotivated? Oppositional? Probably Not!

I invite you to sit in on a conference I had with Emma's teachers. Listen to the conversation, as these concerned professionals try to get a handle on Emma's difficulties:

"I'm so worried!" exclaimed one of the teachers sitting across from me at a clinical consultation at a local elementary school. *"We thought maybe Emma was having seizures! We actually waved a hand in front of her face! She just sits there, staring out into space and does absolutely nothing. We ask her what's wrong. We tell her that we know she can do the work. We offer to write the story down if she will just dictate it to us. We walk away, thinking she might 'need space.' But then we come back, and she hasn't put pen to paper. We're frustrated. We're feeling like we aren't doing our job!"*

Another teacher looks at me with a sheepish smile: *"I'll admit it,"* she says. *"We sometimes bribe her. The saddest thing is that we know she can do the work—Emma's a very smart little girl. It breaks our hearts."*

Emma, a bright eight-year-old who is a whiz at math computation, has a nonverbal learning disability. I had carried out a comprehensive neuropsychological evaluation of her a few months earlier, and it was clear that despite her obvious intelligence, she had a significant deficit in executive functioning. Like many kids with NVLD, she can't organize her thoughts well enough to create a story in her head that she's going to then write down. Other kids are helped by writing an outline before starting to write the story, but Emma can't do that, either. It just doesn't make sense to her. The thought of doing an outline overwhelms her with debilitating anxiety. What frustrates her teachers so much is that she can write incredibly well—when she chooses the topic. She's been writing a story that reveals her strong vocabulary and her complex sentences. But Emma's story is a rambling, disconnected discourse about unicorns, with which she has had an almost obsessive preoccupation since the first soft, cuddly stuffed one was placed in her crib. She has a collection of over seventy-five of these mythical creatures, made out of every substance known to science, and she owns just about every book or CD ever created having to do with unicorns. Needless to say, her favorite song, which she knew by heart and sang incessantly from a very young age (and sweetly for me in my office during a break from testing), was the *Unicorn Song*, based on a poem by children's author Shel Silverstein and popularized by the Irish Rovers in the late sixties.

The unicorn, in all its incarnations, had become for Emma, her *binkie*—the all-comforting representation of calmness and inner peace. She wouldn't have maintained her love affair with this single-horned creature had she not needed it. The Unicorn was her yoga; it was her Valium.

If Emma's teachers asked her to write a story (or anything that had more than a sentence in it) about a topic they chose, she would freeze like a deer (or a unicorn, I guess) in the head-lights. Even if her teachers told her that a unicorn could be the protagonist in the story they asked her to write, Emma resisted because she had to be in control of the plot to avoid the anxiety that came from creating someone else's story in her head.

Emma is a child who can't hold and organize thoughts, words, or images in her mind. The neuropsychological testing revealed significant deficits in auditory memory for stories told to her, and a very weak visual sequential memory (remembering a series of images that were shown and then taken away). When she was asked to copy a complex figure, she could do it pretty well from a model. When the model was taken away, the image "went up in smoke" and she could only re-create a couple of elements that she had seen (and copied) in the original. This situation—being asked to do something that she couldn't do well—created a level of anxiety that caused Emma to scoop up her purple "Uni" and flee my testing room to seek the company of her mother and the comfort of—you guessed it—several more unicorns that were sitting with her mother in my waiting room.

Although Emma's teachers tried to get her to visualize a story unfolding, she was unable to project an image of an object or scene on the "theater screen in her brain." In fact, she was so anxious that she couldn't even imagine the *screen*. When Emma's teachers and I discussed her progress in a staff consultation, they had a collective "aha" moment when they understood that her neurocognitive style created anxiety that caused her to shut down. They were able reframe their perceptions of this young girl. Her behavior, they now understood, was not oppositional, nor was it due to a lack of motivation. It was her effort to Save FASE.

Emma's teachers tried new approaches with her, based on the hypothesis that successful experiences reduced stress and helped to free up a mind frozen by fear. They gave her small tasks to do that were related to a larger goal. They built her confidence in little increments. They only introduced higher-level skills after she had clearly mastered lower-level tasks. They related the new challenge to the previous task, and helped to put her limbic system into an "I can" mode as opposed to a "no way" mode. The use of this careful approach, which was reinforced at home by her parents, meant that things started to get better for Emma.

As these teachers saw Emma doing things that they believed she could do, it increased their sense of satisfaction and enjoyment in teaching. This had a positive circular effect. Emma's successes reinforced the wisdom of the approaches the teachers had implemented, and they felt greater confidence in their ability to get through to her. This increased *their* feeling of control, an important component in stress management for kids—and, as it turns out, for their teachers.

Is There a Happy Ending to Emma's Story?

There is progress. Things got a little better for Emma after I explained the results of the testing with her. It's important for kids to understand what's wrong with them, or they tend to give themselves pejorative labels like "retard." Emma was a very intelligent little girl. She was able to see that her problem had a cause, and she wanted to do everything she could to make it better.

This self-awareness helped her believe that it might actually be possible to get better.

Emma tried a meditation class for kids, but that didn't work because there was too much quiet downtime for her, which she filled in with obsessive thoughts and worries. Her parents wisely enrolled her in an Irish step-dancing class, which was a great match. Her lifelong relationship with the Irish Rovers had left her with a very favorable impression of Irish tunes. Her amygdala and hippocampus loved the music, and Emma was very receptive to its lilt and to the buoyant movement of the dances. The intensive, repetitive physical activity helped to pump up her endorphins, leading to an improvement in her mood and a lessening of anxiety. In addition, her social status was enhanced by her improved stage presence, which carried over to social situations at school and in the community. Emma took part in the school talent show, and the uniqueness of this activity and her dancing skill put her in a new light. In the past, she had been treated poorly (some might say bullied) by some less-than-compassionate classmates, and now she was admired by many for her talents.

Meanwhile, Back in the Classroom . . .

You're probably wondering about Emma's problems with writing. Her very wise teachers started having the kids in the class cut out pictures from a magazine that related to a central theme. This made concepts more visual and more concrete, which met not only Emma's learning style but also that of many other kids. Teachers paired Emma with other kids who had broader interests, and she began to engage in conversations about topics that went well beyond unicorns (which most of the other kids had grown weary of). The magazine pictures and clip art from the computer were then made into a large collage, about which the kids, in writing teams, brainstormed ideas. They used the Inspiration software I described in Chapter Five, which allowed them to move ideas from linear outline form to a graphic representation with a keystroke. They then turned their writing into a PowerPoint presentation (which also helped with the organization of the ideas) and presented them to the rest of the class. Emma flourished in this new medium, and became the PowerPoint technical expert for other kids (and their appreciative teachers). Ultimately, she was able to share her excitement about "being able to write like the other kids."

Emma not only "Saved FASE" but now enjoys a richer academic and social life. She is still anxious, and new ambiguous situations make her very tense. Her parents are planning to talk to her pediatrician about a trial dose of anti-anxiety medication to help her cope with periods of excessive worry. This way, she will be able to have more successful experiences that will increase her confidence and her willingness to try new things.

WHAT'S NEXT?

In this chapter, I suggest that in order to reduce the negative impact of stress kids need to overcome their disorder and gain some sense of control over their academic lives. I've included some examples of what parents and teachers have done to help a child understand and manage the anxiety that gets in the way of learning and social life. I've shown how many of the negative behaviors exhibited by students are but the tip of the iceberg; visible hints of a much deeper, darker threat to self-esteem and success that lies below the surface.

By now, it's clear that stress happens when we don't have control over threatening events. If threats are headed our way, we want to avoid them or subdue them. Our perceptions and reactions are mediated by the intricate flow of impulses along neurons, and the subsequent regulation of neurochemicals that control our reactions. The good news is that there's an important flip side to this neurobiological phenomenon. While negative experiences can trigger a rapid retreat, the stress reaction can be chemically neutralized by the pleasurable feelings that come from success.

This makes it reasonable to hope that appropriate interventions can prevent the need to Save FASE and stop and even reverse the damaging cycle of stress. In Chapter Eight, I present the DE-STRESS model, which tells you exactly how to do that. Parents and teachers will learn what to do and what to say to break the cycle of Fear, Anxiety, Stress, and Escape and replace it with self-understanding, self-advocacy, and success. Pour yourself another mug of herbal tea and read on . . .

7

From Distress to DE-STRESS

Breaking the FASE Cycle and Putting Kids on the Path to Competence

Chapter Six described how a child with LD or ADHD might exhibit behaviors that, while generally regarded as negative and counterproductive to learning, serve a very important purpose. By acting out or acting in, these kids are trying to "Save FASE." When viewed from the perspective of the protective function of the stress response, these behaviors can be seen as expected and understandable efforts to protect the child from shame or embarrassment.

Throughout the book, I've introduced several students whose behaviors demonstrate the negative impact of stress. Some of these kids were able to change course in a way that put them on a path toward increased success and better mental health. In many of these stories, insightful and creative teachers, parents, and clinicians worked together to create appropriate environments for the students. Now I'd like to suggest a method for doing this in a conscious, thoughtful way.

In this chapter, I introduce the acronym DE-STRESS to formalize and describe a model for intervention that is based on my many years of clinical practice and experience in the classroom. It's an approach that is supported by research on best practices in education, psychology, and neuroscience. This model has been helpful to countless parents and teachers, who have used it to break the cycle of Fear, Anxiety, Stress, and Escape (FASE) that has prevented so many kids with LD and ADHD from reaching their full potential. I am pleased to have the opportunity to share it with you.

I've infused my presentation of the DE-STRESS model with lots of practical advice, to let you see how the ideas can be put to immediate use. In this chapter, you'll learn why the *process* students use is more important than any *product* they may create, and how teachers, parents, and kids can learn to appreciate that fact, even in schools that sit in the ominous shadow of large-scale standardized testing. I'll tell you exactly what to say when a child says, "My work sucks!" (and it *does*). Among other helpful strategies, you'll learn how to teach students how to trust your appraisal of their work, and more important, how to honestly evaluate their own efforts.

HOPE, LOVE, AND HAPPINESS CAN CHANGE THE BRAIN

> "Behaviors and thoughts that relate to hope, love
> and happiness can change the brain—just as fear,
> stress and anxiety can change it. It's completely
> symmetrical."
> —*Dr. Eric Kandel, Nobel Laureate and Professor*
> *of Neuroscience at Columbia University,*
> *in Neuron, September 2008*

As a prelude to this very practical advice, I want to first make sure that you believe that it's all worth doing. Let me share a bit more brain science to show you why I'm so confident that this negative cycle can be broken, and to help explain why the DE-STRESS model works so well.

When parents and others who care about kids with LD and ADHD learn that chronic stress can change the way brains work and how that impedes memory and learning, they are appropriately alarmed. They immediately want to know if this damage to the brain can be stopped, and if it can be reversed. The answer: yes and yes. How do we know? Mice.

Using sophisticated research methods, neuroscience has found that if humans are anything at all like rodents (and it turns out to be true), we have reason to be hopeful. Dr. Eric Kandel, often described as a "rock star" of neuroscience, has, along with his colleagues, carried out research on mice that has very positive implications for humans. Consider, if you will, just a few of Dr. Kandel's findings.

"Learned Safety" Trumps "Behavioral Despair"

Kandel and his associates use the term "learned safety" to refer to the process by which mice are exposed to some calming sound while they are in a nonthreatening environment (say, cavorting in a mouse playground). During this training, the experimental mice learn to associate a particular tone, made by a sound-generating machine, with the safety of the environment. In this way, the sound telegraphs a message to the mice: "Everything is copacetic. You can chill out, little rodents."

In Kandel's experiments, a bunch of mice, some with the safety conditioning and some without it, are then exposed to the fear-inducing situation of being forced to swim in deep water (well, deep for a mouse, anyway). A mouse's brain responds to a physical or psychological threat pretty much the same way a human brain does. It goes on alert and devotes all of its resources to helping get its owner out of trouble. In case you have not experienced this firsthand, when mice are forced into water over their heads, their natural reaction is to freak out and become immobile. Overcome by the threat of drowning, all of Kandel's wet mice froze—and the unconditioned ones stayed that way. With both their spirits and their lungs quite dampened by the experience, one by one, they drowned. Essentially, they gave up hope. Kandel and his colleagues have labeled this reaction "behavioral despair."

The Romans apparently understood this phenomenon a long time ago, when they chiseled out the phrase, *Sedit qui timuit ne non succederet:* "He who feared he would not succeed sat still."

Something quite different happened to the mice that had been safety-conditioned. When the familiar calming tone was turned on, their fear was significantly reduced; they were less immobile. They calmed down, got their little mouse wits about them, and started to swim toward safety.

The Story's Not Over Yet

The safety-conditioned mice did not, it turns out, have the last laugh, but they were able to make a great contribution to science. Dr. Kandel, to use the prevalent euphemism in the field, "sacrificed" the surviving rodents. With what must have been an incredibly tiny scalpel, he dissected the brains of both groups, looking for differences that would identify the area that was affected by the fear experience and by the safety training. By comparing the neurons of the trained mice with those of non-trained mice, the researchers found that learned safety allowed more cells to survive in an area of the hippocampus called the *dentate gyrus.* In other words, learned safety prevented the loss of brain cells that was noted in the super-stressed, waterlogged mice.

And How About This?

The same researchers used x-irradiation (x-rays) to destroy the dentate gyrus and prevent it from generating new neurons.

(Ouch!) Then they put these mice to the same tone-and-swim test described earlier. And, what do you think they found? First of all, the mice that had had their brains zapped by x-rays learned absolutely nothing about safety after a day of training. As expected, brain damage impaired learning. In contrast, the control mice that had gotten some fake x-rays (that is, they saw the same equipment and heard the same sounds, but did not actually get zapped) learned safety fairly quickly. However, after an additional two days of training, *both* the x-rayed mice and sham mice (not x-rayed) showed less freezing in the deep water when they heard the safety signal.

What does this all mean? It means that mice with neurologically impaired brains—even though it them took a little more time (*read that as special education*)—could acquire learned safety.

In contrast (and get *this!*), learning to be scared was not affected by the x-ray-induced brain damage. In other words, while *safety* learning was made more difficult by brain damage, both the brain-damaged mice and non-brain-damaged mice required the same amount of time to learn what scared the *shipoopy* out of them. The takeaway lesson: Fear is easy to learn, but learning to be safe in the face of fear takes longer. As Matt Damon once famously said in the movie *Good Will Hunting:* "How do you like *them* apples?"

Of Mice and Men (and Women) Whether you're born *Homo sapiens* or *Mus musculus*, a little stress can enhance learning and memory. However, when practicing things over and over again in a nervous state, your brain can create an association between the negative feelings and the memory of the event itself. This is *learned anxiety*, or learned fear. It happens to kids in school who can't succeed, and it happens to you. Think about when you first tried to drive a stick-shift car, or ski, or knit, or swim—and it didn't go well! How much money would it take to get you to do that activity again? *Right.* Learned anxiety is not always selective; it generalizes to other tasks as well. Fears translate into stress when we face tasks that look like, smell like, or sound like the original bad experience. (Think readin', writin', and 'rithmetic.)

Of Mice on Meds Here's a little more juicy information. Kandel's researchers wanted to see how the safety training compared with a little antidepressant medication. So they gave some mice the safety training and gave some others a tiny dose of Prozac (fluoxetine). Guess what? Compared to the control mice (those that had no training *or* drugs), the antidepressant mice and the safety-trained mice did equally well on the forced swimming task. Another group of mice who got *both* the medication and the training showed less immobility (freezing) in the water than any of the other mice. So this all suggests that training mice how to protect themselves from the ill-effects of stressful events was just about as effective as antidepressant medications, and a combination of both treatments worked *even better.*

What can all this teach us about human children who are besieged by a steady stream of anxiety-inducing stressors generated by the experience of schooling? It may take a little leap of faith to apply this research to kids, but the implications seem clear to me. The animal research of Dr. Kandel and others has demonstrated that learned safety is a critical element in combating chronic stress. Yes, his subjects were little mice and not little kids, but remember that it was rodents who helped make B. F. Skinner (the father of behavioral psychology) famous, and it was lab rats who helped demonstrate the effectiveness of methylphenidate (Ritalin, Concerta, and others) and countless other drugs that many humans use. I'm not pushing the use of medication here, although there are many prescription drugs that have been shown to be effective in managing attention, lessening anxiety, and lifting depression. Instead, I am focusing on the things can be done at home, in the classroom, and in the community that constitute safety training for kids.

In the pages that follow, I present a model that will help you inoculate children with ADHD and LD against stress, to give them virtual flotation vests that can help them cope with the metaphorical deep water that they encounter so often. As you read on, you will learn some simple, effective, and inexpensive ways to work with these students so they will not become immobilized when they are stressed, but will instead swim to safety.

TAKING KIDS FROM DISTRESS TO DE-STRESS: A MODEL FOR CHANGE

Here is an overview of the DE-STRESS acronym to give you a quick idea of what's in the model. I follow this with an in-depth discussion of each of the elements, so that you'll be able to examine and modify your behavior in ways that will improve student self-esteem, self-advocacy, and self-understanding. Implementing the strategies contained in this section will help children and adolescents recognize and combat unproductive, unhealthy stress, putting them on the road to success. These are the steps of the DE-STRESS model and what each involves:

- *Define:* Analyzing and understanding a student's learning profile. Diagnosing and defining LD and ADHD and the impact they have on academic, behavioral, social, and emotional performance.
- *Educate:* Showing the child how to answer the question, *How does LD or ADHD impact my schoolwork and my life?* Educating those who work with or live with this child about the child's individual learning style and needs.

- *Speculate:* Helping kids learn to look ahead; to anticipate the problems they might encounter as they face new challenges. Encouraging them to identify the assets they bring to each task, along with the additional supports they might need from other people to be successful.

- *Teach:* Teaching students the strategies, techniques, and approaches that will maximize success and minimize frustration and failure. Teaching them how to recognize and manage stress, along with the skills of honest self-appraisal and how to learn from and repair errors.

- *Reduce Threat:* Creating learning and social environments that reduce, remove, or neutralize the risk. Teaching children how to recognize and deactivate "stress triggers."

- *Exercise:* Building in opportunities for regular and rigorous physical activity, which is known to enhance brain power and reduce stress. Also, recognizing the importance of proper nutrition and hydration.

- *Success:* Providing abundant opportunities to display mastery and experience success. Teaching students to replace the language of self-doubt and fear with the language of confidence, and using the language of success at home and in the classroom.

- *Strategize:* Using what you and the child have learned about minimizing and managing stress, and about the relationship of stress to LD and ADHD, to plan for a future in which continued success is likely.

In the following in-depth explanation of the components of this model, I describe what I think we need to do *for* these kids, *to* these kids, and *with* these kids to eliminate the need for them to run away from stress.

Note: The order in which these appear is intentional and meant to imply sequential steps, but Reduce Threat, Exercise, and Success can be implemented throughout the process.

Ready? *"Gimme a D!"*

Define

As adults living or working with kids who have LD and ADHD, we need to have a clear idea about how children learn. We need to *define* the problem. If your car's not running smoothly, you can drive it into the shop, have the mechanic hook up some wires, and let the on-board computer show what's wrong and what to do about it. Physicians use x-rays, scans, and blood and urine analysis as objective ways to find out how people's bodies are doing. It would be wonderful if we could hook kids up to computers or give them lab tests that would generate a prescription for success. Since we don't (at least not yet, or inexpensively and on a large scale), we have to rely on formal and informal assessment as a first step in developing an understanding of what makes a student tick (or get ticked off).

The Role of Testing in Defining the Problem A wide variety of formal tests have been designed to show how students perceive and interpret various kinds of information, analyze data, store and retrieve what they see and hear, or make connections between symbols or ideas. These instruments also provide clues about how well children can attend to different kinds of stimuli or how well they can organize material they see or hear. There are tests for just about any human behavior or trait that you'd care to measure.

While it's not within the scope of this book to explain all the tests used in the assessment of LD and ADHD, I have mentioned a few frequently used evaluation tools in the stories about different students I have presented in this book. Suffice it to say that the science of assessment is more refined than ever before in the history of testing, and evaluations carried out by trained professionals can add much to the understanding of a child with these conditions.

That said, the secret to testing is *not* the test; it's the assessment process. Tests sample small bits of data about a child, often under conditions that are not much like a classroom. A formal evaluation describes how a child is doing *now,* on *these* tests, in *this* setting, with *this* evaluator. The tests may not explain the problem that initiated the referral; in some cases, a formal evaluation can't produce evidence that the problem even *exists*.

Take the example of a very bright student who consistently bombs all reading comprehension tests that are given in large rooms with lots of other kids. However, the same child can answer every question, solve every puzzle, and ace every task presented as part of a comprehensive neuropsychological evaluation. All that time and all that money spent on testing, and the problem does not appear! It's like taking your car in for repair and the mechanic writes on the bill (next to a charge for time spent): "Could not replicate problem identified by owner." Yet in both cases, the problem exists—it's real. The child wouldn't be sitting at the testing table if it weren't. The instruments used to diagnose the problem may just not capture the essence of the problem.

This is not to say that an extensive evaluation has no value. In the situation I just mentioned, a comprehensive neuropsychological evaluation clarified and quantified this student's strengths, and ruled out many factors that *might have been* causing the problem. In this case, a discussion of the results of the testing led the evaluator to conclude that the problem was related to very specific test anxiety. The process of assessment got this student and the team of teachers thinking about what can be done to help get over this important hurdle. I'll say more about a very effective and simple technique to deal with this in the Teach section of the DE-STRESS model.

Because tests (and testers) are fallible, and test results are subject to the influences of a variety of factors such as the timing of the test or the health and attitude of the student, defining a student's problem has to be a multifaceted team process that looks forward as well as backward. A thorough evaluation, therefore, has to consider observations and testing that may have been carried out in the past. This is like your doctor looking at an old x-ray and finding evidence of a hairline fracture that had been missed in the past but helps to explain your current pain. To hear evaluators say they don't like to be prejudiced by previous testing drives me bananas. This is like the guys in *CSI* saying they don't need to go to the crime scene! In both cases, you may find nothing, but you *have* to look. In children, we're looking for emerging patterns, not just taking a snapshot of current performance.

A thorough evaluation has to compare and contrast information, not only from different time periods in a child's life but also between and among different evaluators and observers. For example, one parent often fills out a Conners Rating Scales-Revised (often simply called "a Conners"), or a Behavioral Rating Inventory of Executive Function (called "a BRIEF"). What does the *other* parent have to say about the traits that are rated on these popular instruments? What do the *grandparents* have to say? (Perhaps that's another book!) The French teacher may give a different rating from, say, the football coach. One report does not cancel out another; each adds a layer of complexity and helps us understand how a child does in different settings, on different tasks. Remember, we're looking for evidence of strength, and we're trying to create a profile, not a score.

The Importance of Defining Strengths All children do *something* well, or at least better than they do other things. Like many of my colleagues, I am a practitioner of what I call "asset-based assessment." That means that in addition to identifying the vulnerable spots in students' profiles, we're intent on finding out about the strengths they bring to different tasks or situations. We can learn much about how to create successful futures by examining what kids do well now. As a part of my diagnostic interview, I ask kids: "If I were to hire you to do something for me that you can do very well, for which I would pay you a reasonably large amount of money, and about which I wouldn't have to worry very much—what would that be?" The responses to this question vary, and are quite revealing. Very often, kids with learning or attention difficulties name something outside of school—things like lawn care, or Legos, or art, or rap. Then I ask the parents what skill they would nominate. In some cases, they agree with their kids' self-appraisal, adding a personal story that confirms the asset, like a time the child fixed a toaster oven or painted a mural on the wall of the church, or built a canoe with a grandparent.

These delightful stories of success are often in direct contrast to the tales these kids and parents tell about school. Some kids can't think of an answer, or are too shy to respond. In those cases, parents may describe an asset. Some kids listen warily as parents describe what they think are their child's strengths. Sometimes kids say "Oh, yeah—*that*." Other times, kids discount their parents' evaluation or reject it altogether, saying things like: "I'm not good at that!" or "Anybody could do *that*." More often, though, children beam with pride when their parents identify a skill. This simple exercise tells me volumes about what kids can do well and how they and their parents feel about it. And it reminds me of how seldom in these kids' lives they hear positive feedback. How long would you work without a paycheck? And if others around you were getting an envelope every payday filled with more cash than you were getting, wouldn't you start to worry about the quality of your work? Question your own talents?

Defining the Emotional Side of Things We do know that students who do not do well in school despite trying very hard get down on themselves. Some get "situationally sad" because of a life event, and others become clinically depressed. It's necessary, then, to include an assessment of a child's emotional state as part of a comprehensive evaluation. When emotional features figure prominently in a child's life, it may be necessary to request an evaluation by a psychiatrist, a medical doctor who is trained in the evaluation and treatment of emotional problems and mental disorders. Many times, conversations with school psychologists, social workers, or guidance counselors may tell us what we need to know. The most valid information often comes directly from the child; disclosures that are more likely to be shared in a relationship that's built on trust and mutual respect. Whichever mental health specialist has such a positive connection to a child is in the best position to assess this important area of that student's life.

In my view, there is no formal instrument that can accurately measure the impact of academic success or failure on a child's self-esteem. We have various rating scales at our disposal that purport to measure self-esteem, but most of these just give children and their parents the chance to confirm that a child is displaying behaviors that *reflect* self-esteem. These are mirrors more than they are diagnostic tools. Nonetheless, they have value. If the purpose of the evaluation is to create a program or an environment in which the child feels a greater sense of control through competence, such rating scales might provide some pre-intervention data against which to measure emotional growth.

Also, we do not yet have a readily available test to measure the effect of stress on the brain. We *are* able to measure cortisol levels in saliva. Research shows that when stress goes up, cortisol goes up, and we know that excessive cortisol can have a negative impact on brain function. Unfortunately, cortisol levels are generally only measured when kids are involved in research projects. This is true too of the use of brain-imaging techniques, even though they are able to identify brain changes that have a negative impact on learning. Perhaps someday in the future, *"where no man has gone before,"* we will have such tools at our ready disposal. For now, we have no "Bones" McCoy in a Space Fleet uniform to run a hand-held scanner over the brains of our kids.

The Defining Moment You'll note that the "D" in DE-STRESS stands for *define,* not *diagnose.* While it's always great when we have enough data to lead us to a diagnostic conclusion with confidence, formal diagnosis in and of itself is of limited value. We may need a diagnosis to qualify a child for special services or to satisfy insurance company requirements. A diagnosis may only name a problem but not describe it. Without a diagnostic *formulation*—a very firm idea about what's getting in the way of learning—it's virtually impossible to plan an effective intervention program. To fully define a child's profile, we have to make sure that all sources of data are laid on the table for our review, and that we translate our collective information in a form that all of us—the professionals, parents, and most of all, the student—can understand. This challenging task is much like having a group of people working together on a large, complex jigsaw puzzle without a completed picture on the box to go by. We have to fill in as many pieces as we can to get to that Aha! moment, when the intended figure or scene (or in our case, solution) comes into view. This is a prerequisite to what we have to do next—*Educate*—the second component of the DE-STRESS model.

Educate

Once adults understand a learning disability or the nature of a child's ADHD, somebody has to explain it to the child in a nonthreatening, developmentally appropriate way. Unlike mice, children can't fully benefit from safety training until they understand the problem. Kandel's research showed that the positive emotions that come from pairing a tone with a pleasant environment improve learning capabilities in mice. This may work in rodents, but it's not sufficient in kids.

Don't Keep Kids in the Dark To become self-advocates, children have to be educated about the findings and the implications of the testing they've been a part of. One of the things that amazes me is the number of kids who have (willingly or unwillingly) given hours of their time to be evaluated by a variety of talented professionals, and yet who have never had the results of the testing explained to them. They may have heard from a parent that "Dr. B. said you're very smart." Or "it looks like you learn better through your ears than through your eyes," or even "your language skills are much better than your visual skills," but to build a foundation of understanding that leads to competence and the reduction of stress, these oversimplified explanations are far from adequate.

If you had just had an examination by an orthopedist who told you, "Yep, you broke something—we're just gonna cast you right up!" Would you demand a better explanation? Might you be oppositional? Would you look for the exit to the examination room? *You bet you would.* Yet we have thousands, maybe millions, of kids who have no clue about the results of their testing. This is a gap that needs to be filled if we're going to reduce the stress that kids with ADHD and LD feel every day. We want kids to be self-aware so that they can be engaged in their own learning—so that they can take control of their own learning. Self-understanding will help them own their success and understand (and learn from and repair) their failed attempts.

Self-Education 101 and 201 Education about LD and ADHD can be thought of on two levels. The first and most important consists of the lessons the individual student learns about himself or herself. The timing and level of these lessons is extremely important. When parents ask me when and what they should tell their kids about their conditions, I generally give them the same advice I give to parents who want to know how and when to talk to their kids about sex: *Use a positive tone, talk at a level that's age-appropriate, use as little language as is needed to cover the topic, and read your child's reaction to know how the information is being received and when you've said enough.* Do this with the understanding that this conversation will most likely happen again—if not with you, then with someone else—at different times in the child's life.

Because we're talking about students who most likely have language-based learning disabilities, the use of visuals (like graphs of scores or actual examples of the types of materials that a given child might find challenging) and clear, direct language is imperative when teaching children about themselves. For distractible children, the lesson has to be brief and concrete. Asking children to repeat what they have heard can *create* stress rather than reduce it, since the demand may be regarded as yet another test of ability (or further proof of disability). Kids like to look and feel smart around their parents, and they are not necessarily at their best when personal weaknesses are being discussed. A teacher, psychologist, or other specialist may be enlisted to provide this information to parents and child simultaneously, or to the parents first and then to the child alone. Deciding the best way to do this depends on the child's age and personality, comfort level when talking to adults, and relationship with the specialist.

To Read or Not to Read? Some older students may want to read the entire evaluation report. This may not be advisable, since the report may contain family information that is not known by the child, or quotes from teachers or parents that might be misperceived or misunderstood by the student. If I'm writing a report about a student in high school or college, I assume that the adolescent or young adult may be reading the report, and try to think about that student as part of the audience for whom I'm writing. In other situations, I may write a "Junior Executive summary" of the report, created especially for student consumption. Teachers and parents often value having a copy of this abbreviated version of the report too, after they've read the entire report or had it explained to them. It helps them focus on the salient features and not get bogged down by language and terms that might be very familiar to the evaluator, but may be like a foreign language to them.

Self-Education 202 In addition to personalized, individual explanation, educating students about their condition can also be done on a meta-level. This involves exposing a child to sources of information about LD or ADHD that are designed to explain the condition to the general public, and to children, specifically. There are many great resources for information about how to teach kids about a learning disability or ADHD. These include, but are certainly not limited to: ldaamerica.org; www.ldonline.org; www.interdys.org; www.chadd.org; and www.insideADHD.org. There are also many wonderful books that have been written to help kids at different levels understand these and other conditions that affect learning. You can ask your town or school librarian for suggestions.

Writing about the condition can be instructive and also very therapeutic. Some students may feel secure enough to write a paper for school about their condition (and how they have overcome it). The heartwarming tale of self-discovery and self-advocacy leading to success has often found its way into the essays of many young college applicants with LD or ADHD. The journey to self-advocacy is hastened when we teach students how to independently assess the factors that might get in the way of their learning and also those that might help them do well, whether they write about them, talk about them, or think about them. Remember that forcing (or even encouraging) students to describe their own learning or attentional problems before they're ready to do that, or in a medium in which they do not feel competent, can back them into a stress-filled corner.

The next section of the DE-STRESS model tells you how to help kids look ahead and pave their own roads to success.

Speculate

The word *speculate* comes from the Latin root, *speculari*: to observe. I use it here to remind us of the need to observe or look *ahead* and think about what challenges, opportunities, barriers, or rewards might lie in the educational path of students, and to use those factors to help give focus to our work. It's also important to teach students how to do this—how to anticipate and get ready for the next event. Let me share a personal story that may help you understand why this concept is so important to me.

Get Ready, Get Set, Go! My wife and I love to travel. Sometimes we go on our own as a couple, planning the trip ourselves. Because we enjoy meeting others from all over the world who value new experiences and being in the outdoors, we prefer to join different small groups of people on trips planned by a hiking and touring company that specializes in adventure travel. No matter which company we use, it always sends us a lot of material in advance to help us think ahead and get ready for the trip. Along with a very specific list of supplies and clothing we'll need, we receive a letter of introduction from the guide who will escort us on our excursion—including reminders about all the exciting adventures that lie ahead, as well as some of the challenges we might encounter on our trip. Because some of our journeys take us to the edge of civilization, away from certain amenities and far from ready access to medical care, we have to prepare for the unpredictable. Depending on where we're headed, this list of possible impediments might range from intermittent electricity ("bring flashlights and extra batteries") to biting or stinging insects ("sprays or lotions") to rocky or dangerous terrain ("hiking boots and walking sticks highly recommended") or rapidly shifting extremes of climate ("layer, layer, layer!"). These comments help us to speculate—to think ahead not only about the challenges that we might face, but more important, about how to prepare to meet these challenges. ("Climbing up and down the stairs in your office building instead of taking the elevator will be an excellent way to prepare your leg muscles for the steep, narrow paths that we'll be using.")

We are happy to have the suggestions of the guide, who has much experience leading trips through the less-traveled areas of the country we're visiting. This exercise in preparedness also helps us when we plan our solo trips. You can't always know what unseen challenges you may confront while traveling far from the comfort and familiarity of your home, but thinking about this in advance and preparing for as many contingencies as you can (without going bonkers about it) brings a little peace of mind. (*Note:* This is not the kind of travel for highly anxious people. With all due respect—cruise ships are a very sensible alternative.)

Whatever your mode of transportation or your destination, proper planning can make or break a trip. Thinking ahead helps keep your stress meter at "Very Exciting" (which means you are good to go) and keeps it from sliding into the Red No-Go Zone! (Heli-skiing in the Alps, anyone?) Well, anyway, while my intrepid spouse and I were trekking in Nepal last year, I thought about how this applies to kids with LD and ADHD in the classroom, and how teachers can use all this. (*Seriously!* It was a long hike.)

Introducing the (Himalayan-inspired) Impediment/Asset Inventory
Teachers can help students overcome stress by teaching them *how* to speculate. This involves the ability to identify the impediments they might encounter in doing a certain task, the resources they need to make the journey successful, and how to get what they don't have but need to achieve success. Once the teacher explains an assignment to the students, but before they take even one step in the direction of completing the tasks that have been laid out for them, the teacher should pose several questions that can help kids increase their level of preparedness. Formally, I refer to this method as the Impediment/Asset Inventory (IAI). When I use this with students, I call it the "Aye, Aye" method, which is how you might pronounce the word IAI. For me, that affirmative mnemonic reinforces the "can-do" theme of this book. Here are the *Aye, Aye* questions, followed by some thoughts about how the assessment might play out in the classroom and what you can do to increase the effectiveness of the strategy.

1. HURDLES: What's going to get in the way of you doing this work?

2. HELPERS: What's going to increase your chances for success?

3. SUPPLIES AND EQUIPMENT: What are you taking with you?

Question 1: HURDLES: what's going to get in the way of you doing this work? The answers to this question about potential impediments to learning, which I refer to as *hurdles*, are as varied as the students who answer them. Some kids might find the question easy to answer. One may say, "I hate social studies." Another may respond: "I've never been good at this." Still another: "My parents are planning my sister's graduation and they won't have time to help me with this." Others, who are fortunate enough to know their own learning style preferences, might say, "This requires me to create an outline in advance. I have a hard time thinking about things in such an organized way."

Other students, especially those who are not used to being asked such questions, may remain silent, indicating that they may be shy or they haven't a clue how to answer. The teacher may have to jump-start a student's thinking by suggesting a list of "things that have gotten in the way of other students I've taught," such as these:

- Competing events (family activities, friends calling, IM-ing, new video game . . .)
- Lack of adequate place to study
- Inadequate prior preparation or skills
- A negative attitude ("This is not necessary"; "I can't do math"; "I'll never need to know this")
- Health factors ("I'm sick"; "I'm tired"; "I'm *going* to be sick and tired")

Priming the pump this way helps students generate a personalized list of the potential barriers to success. Students might also be encouraged to ask their parents (or former teachers) about how *they* would answer this question. (*"Knowing me as you do, what do you think might derail me?"*)

A classroom discussion about impediments helps kids see the range of things that might get in the way for other kids. The teacher might tell a story of a personal challenge, and what got in the way of success at that time. Showing a movie about some adventure or reading a book about a challenge faced by other kids might also serve as a catalyst for self-disclosure. These open discussions about impediments to goals helps normalize the phenomenon; other people have hurdles, too.

Step into my office, please. For kids who are not ready or able to share information about their LD or ADHD publicly, teachers can have a private conference at which they can help students predict how their learning or attention difficulties might have a negative impact on their performance. When it comes time to identify personal assets, the teacher can, in this confidential discussion, help the child see how the presence of a particular condition might actually increase the likelihood of success. For example, a creative child with impulsive behavior might be a real whiz at a brainstorming activity that focuses on the rapid generation of ideas, all of which are valued and none of which will be judged—a perfect fit for a kid with ADHD.

Question 2: HELPERS: what's going to increase your chances for success? Conversely, teachers have to teach students to identify what I call *helpers*. In other words, what's going to make it more likely that you will be able to do this, and do this well?

Students may say things like this:

- I have confidence in my ability.
- I feel competent in this skill.
- I am committed to learning this because . . .
- I have the necessary resources to complete this task, such as materials, sources of information, people supports: parents, tutor, other kids.

Here again, the teacher may have to seed the responses with real or hypothetical responses of others. Of course, the idea here is to have students do a reality check on both the factors that make success more likely and those that might get in the way.

Question 3: SUPPLIES AND EQUIPMENT: what are you taking with you? The process of breaking the stress-fear cycle doesn't stop with the assessment of *hurdles* and *helpers*. Now we have to help students do an inventory of the *supplies and equipment* they need to make the journey into new learning, prompted by a two-part question from the teacher. The first part is: *"What skills, talents, or experiences do you already have that will help you achieve this goal?"* The teacher asks the students to write down (or check off on a prepared checklist) the things that they bring to this learning adventure. This list might include concrete things ("I could use my Legos to build this") or more abstract personal assets ("I'm a hard worker, although it may not always pay off"; "I know something about this because we did a unit last year"; "My mom's an accountant, so she can help me"; "This is related to something I have to do in another class, so doing this will save me some time on that assignment"; "I think I might be able to use this for my college application essay, so I'm a little more motivated than usual").

The second part of the question the teacher asks at this point is: *"What else do you need to successfully make this journey, and where can you find it?"* For example, the students will be asked to create a list of "things I need from my parents or my teachers." Items on the parent list might include things like *time* (to help me), *money* (for supplies), or *transportation* (to buy the supplies or go to the library). The list for teachers might include workload adjustments: "I need my English teacher to cut me some slack on the big project for that class, because *this* one is so huge." "Since so much writing is involved in this, maybe I could get some extra credit in my English class." (Now, that's the kind of language that's music to my ears!)

Teach

To combat stress, we need to know how to relax. Kids don't learn how to relax all by themselves. This doesn't happen automatically, even for adults. If it did, there wouldn't be so many adult yoga classes! Teachers, guidance counselors, or occupational therapists and parents need to actually *teach* children (of all ages) how to get themselves into a physical state of being relaxed. Some children are so agitated that even if they know how to relax, they can't do it. If you think about it, when you're upset is the hardest time to calm down! Other kids can't calm down or relax because they don't know what the state of relaxation feels like.

Consider this vignette:

Roxanne: [agitated and loudly] I can't stand this freakin' book!

Teacher: "Roxanne, you need to take it easy. Just calm down! Try to relax. You need to finish your reading.

Roxanne: [to herself] Right—easy for you to say, teacher. But very hard for me to do. What do you mean *calm down?* I feel like my head is going to explode.

Teacher: [seeing no response] Well, if you can't settle down, maybe a trip to the office will help you!

Roxanne doesn't have the skill to take herself from distress to de-stress. She needs a guide. While that trip to the office might put her under the care of a sensitive, trained guidance counselor who can talk her down and help her practice the skills of self-calming, this kind of reaction on the part of the teacher does not usually carry that intent. It usually conveys the message, "You're doing something wrong and you need to stop it." That's like telling a hungry person to stop being hungry. Roxanne, like the famished person, needs to be shown how and where to get what she needs. No one can just get un-hungry; no one can just get de-stressed.

Baby Talk During his work in an intensive care unit, pediatrician Dr. William Sammons observed that some infants were able to tolerate stress better than others. He subsequently wrote *The Self-Calmed Baby*, in which he offers suggestions for new parents about how to allow their children to learn what it feels like to be stressed by not responding immediately (or preemptively) to their discomfort. In Dr. Sammons's view, allowing young children to tolerate discomfort early in life better prepares them to handle stressful events in the future. Assuming that their basic needs for food, water, love, cleanliness, and warmth are consistently met, children will learn that with the passage of a little time, help will come. This knowledge that things will work out helps relieve stress and allows them to self-calm—a coping skill that lasts a lifetime.

I mention this book about infants here because Dr. Sammons's central theme supports an important point I'm making in this book: The degree of dependence or independence can be influenced by the level of control children feel they have in their environment. Dr. Sammons posits that those feelings of competence begin in infancy. In his book, he says that if a parent anticipates a child's every need and tries to meet it (for example, by feeding or cuddling after every bit of fussing), that pre-emptive intervention prevents a child from experiencing discomfort and learning how to live with it.

While Dr. Sammons's approach has generated some controversy, especially among parents who can't stand to hear a baby crying, his premise makes sense in our discussion. If adults working with students with LD and ADHD anticipate their discomfort and automatically try to take away that which discomforts, they remove the opportunity to learn to deal with adversity. If a parent, teacher, or instructional aide gives students the answers, prepares them too much for stress-filled transitions, does their homework for them, or makes the work easier when it need not be modified, then the students cannot learn to deal successfully with the many challenges they will face through-out their lives. I have often heard from kids with LD or ADHD: "I may get A's and B's, but that would have never happened without a personal attendant. My aide [or my parent] should get the report card, not me." While *The Self-Calmed Baby* focused on infants, Dr. Sammons's philosophy can be applied to kids in elementary, middle, and even high school. It's never too late to teach students how to take care of themselves by teaching them how to relax, how to wait without worrying, and how to face challenges without becoming anxious even if they weren't exposed to self-soothing lessons as infants. To learn these things, students must have the chance to encounter the challenge. They must be afforded what the disability rights activists Burton Blatt and Wolf Wolfensberger called "the dignity of risk."

Teach Simple Techniques to Reduce Worry I encourage teachers who are trying to help students with specific test anxiety to employ a simple but effective technique that involves having all the students in the class spend ten minutes before an exam writing about their thoughts and feelings. According to recent research carried out at the Human Performance Lab at the University of Chicago, this technique frees up brainpower that was previously occupied by worries about the testing, result-ing in significant improvement in test results of anxious students.

Although this research did not specifically examine the performance of students with LD or ADHD, what we know about brain science tells us that these students are at risk for elevated exam-related stress. Further research would be necessary to confirm the usefulness of this emotive writing technique, but it would probably be very effective for students who do have either or both of these conditions. It just makes sense. That is, of course, unless the student has a writing disability. Then the intervention itself might produce its own kind of anxiety. I have often recommended that teachers ask kids with writing disabilities to simply think about their worries, and then teach them how to generate internalized, positive statements to counteract their fears before starting the task. After all, successful athletes practice this kind of positive self-talk to "get game." Why not kids with LD?

Change the Paradigm, Change the Program The Teach component of the DE-STRESS model involves more than teaching students how to recognize stress and see its relationship to their disability. It also refers to creating an environment that allows teachers to teach. Let me explain. Effective teaching is continuous and connected; effective learning is cumulative. However, much of the education provided to students with LD and ADHD is fragmented and disconnected because their day is interrupted many times by the various special educational services that are supposed to help them. Chapter Eight focuses on what teachers and administrators can do to create environments that reduce stress, but the issue of discontinuous education for students with ADHD and LD, which is often acknowledged but infrequently modified, merits special attention here. I think you'll see what I mean as you read on.

Helping Kids Get with the Flow Mihaly Csikszentmihalyi (MEE-hye CHEEK-sent-mə-HYE-ee) is a Hungarian psychology professor. A prolific author, he wrote a book called *Flow: The Psychology of Optimal Experience* in which he described the following optimal mind-body states for learning. If you read this with kids with LD and ADHD in mind, you'll see why I'm concerned. Csikszentmihalyi said that students learn most efficiently and effectively when these three things take place:

- They are appropriately challenged by a personally relevant, intrinsically motivating task.

- They are operating under a state of low stress (not *no* stress), in a state of general relaxation.

- They are immersed in a "flow" state in which their attention is on learning and doing.

Csikszentmihalyi defines *flow* as a state in which skills, attention, environment, and will are all matched up with the task. A teacher who wants to help kids feel successful and *not stress-full* may ask: *How do I create a learning environment that meets these criteria? Is it possible to do this for students with special needs?*

Going with the Flow For one thing, it's difficult to get students in a state of flow if their day is continually disrupted by therapists who come to their regular classroom to pull them out for some specialized service, such as speech and language therapy or a pragmatics group (helping kids to navigate difficult social interactions and communication). While their special interventions are certainly necessary and helpful, these ancillary service providers may not be able to arrange their schedules to come into a class at a time of natural transition. Witness a worst-case scenario: The eighth-grade English class has just gotten started, and they're discussing the role of flatulence in Chaucer's *Canterbury Tales*. Jason is loving it; he's more energized than he has been in weeks, and he's engaged, interested, and motivated. Farts do that to kids. The speech and language pathologist appears at the door. The entire class looks up. The SLP says, "Jason, it's time for social *prags* [social pragmatics—training the art of social communication]. Let's go."

Unfortunately this scene is replicated over and over again in every grade, in every school in the country. The therapy, which is undeniably important to Jason, becomes a disruption in his life. It creates discontinuous education. Jason goes with the speech and language therapist and misses a critical part of the lesson. The specialist takes him out, and they work for a half an hour. He then finds his way back to class and when he gets back is so far out of the loop that he flops into his seat and sits, disconnected, through the last ten minutes of class.

Take Two Let's replay that tape and see how the scene could have worked out. In a program that provides "inclusive services," the speech and language pathologist plays a different role. She approaches the classroom. She looks through the glass panel in the door. Waiting for a nonverbal signal from the classroom teacher that there is a natural breaking point, she enters the room. "Hi, Mrs. Goldman!" "Great to see you!" says the teacher. "Looks like you're doing something really interesting," says the speech and language pathologist. The teacher responds by calling on the student who is the intended recipient of the therapy: "Jason, why don't you tell Mrs. Goldman what we've been talking about, and remember to use the *scientific* word!" At this point, Mrs. Goldman is brought into the classroom discussion and becomes a part of the lesson. Is she able to study the social communication that's going on about his provocative lesson? You bet! Is she able to give kids (not only Jason) suggestions about how to communicate in the context of the classroom discussion? Sure. Is she able to model pro-social communication via her interaction with the students and with the classroom teacher? Absolutely! And she does this in a naturalistic setting, with much more impact than she would have had by pulling Jason out for individual therapy that's supposed to teach him how to communicate in a group setting.

Call it "educatus interruptus." (I made that phrase up, but you may get the implication.) Discontinuous education is an artifact of so-called pullout services for kids with LD and ADHD. Yanking a child out of a lesson in progress eliminates important opportunities for the child to develop mastery over the subject matter being presented and over the social connectedness that's a part of the activity. It turns education into a sort of Swiss cheese; depending on where you slice it, the hidden holes show up in different places. In the same vein, mastery seldom occurs in the private lessons for speech or occupational or physical therapy, because there's just not enough time. When you've got one alone, ask any OT or PT how satisfied they are with the progress made by kids who are getting pullout services as specified in an IEP.

Furthermore, the specialized skills that are learned outside the classroom are rarely reinforced through practice. They are left to chance. It's unlikely that a child would learn to play violin using this approach. Pulling a student out for isolated training in the social use of language has less likelihood of being translated into everyday performance than if the intervention is provided in the context of the natural communication that goes on in the classroom. I sincerely believe that schools that practice what have been called "inclusive" or "integrated" therapies tend to do a better job with educating kids with special needs. This approach involves co-planning and team-teaching by the specialist and the classroom teacher, and modifications of activities so they will in fact be more inclusive. But I think it's worth it.

It doesn't break the flow, and it keeps kids in the know.

Don't Break the Flow; Keep Kids in the Know By keeping a child in a classroom, exposed to activities that are designed to carry out the objectives listed in an IEP, the beat goes on—flow happens, and IEP goals are better met. The good news is that many schools are able to provide this kind of service. Other schools actually begin creating the master schedule by first putting in the specialists' time and building the rest of the day *around them!* How forward thinking. How smart. How good for kids. And think of the positive impact on staff performance that comes from having two or more specialists work as a team at the same time, in the same space. In my view, that's far superior to after-school workshops for teachers on "how to work together collaboratively."

Don't Be So Quick to Lower the Bar Speaking of people other than teachers who work with kids with special needs, let me share another concern I have about how we sometimes teach these students. This is a thorny issue, but I think it needs to be put on the table for discussion. It's often the case that the children with the greatest special needs spend a good part of their day with the person who is, at least by virtue of formal training, the least qualified to work with them. Sometimes, if the LD or ADHD is severe, these students receive a lot of one-to-one instruction from classroom aides who are not trained as special educators, many of whom are not certified teachers. Sometimes the support they provide is delivered in the back of a class in which a student is theoretically participating, with the aide sitting next to or near the student, moving in and out of direct service as the need exists. There are a couple of unintended consequences to this practice of assigning personal aides. One is that some students are isolated from the rest of the class, and spend little time with typical classmates, even though they can be said to be "included in a regular classroom." This reality deprives these students of the chance to learn from and with other students who would have much to teach them, and who would have much to learn from them.

The other situation that's problematic for me is that in some cases, when undertrained people work with kids with special needs, they have a tendency to make things easier for the students when they perceive that the stress level is rising. They may modify materials unnecessarily when a child moans that it's too hard, provide too much of an answer on an exam, give too many prompts, or postpone uncomfortable tasks.

It's easy to understand why a caring, sensitive person would want to relieve what they perceive as the pain and suffering of children in their care. Some classroom teachers do this too. However, this results in the creation of an informal curriculum that does not push these kids to their limits—a prerequisite for academic growth. In a sense, students with LD and ADHD who get too much help are always underperforming. When these students work so much of the time with a personal assistant, they may face few meaningful challenges because the standards have essentially been lowered. They have too few opportunities to deal with stress head-on and learn from the experience. As a consequence, when they approach tasks that threaten their psychological safety, like Dr. Kandel's mice, they freeze.

I know that some of my readers would mortgage their homes to get a one-to-one aide for their child with LD or ADHD. Some probably have. This is by no means a criticism of aides, and I am certainly not arguing against providing classroom teachers with the personnel they need to address the diverse special needs of students in their classrooms. But I am arguing against the often unnecessary and inappropriate use of classroom assistants to deliver instruction or to be attached to a child who does not need this level of attention.

I need to point out that the provision of one-to-one aides is not a common practice, especially with kids with ADHD or LD, but this level of service does exist in some schools, for some kids. I think that often these adults are an underutilized resource. When teaching assistants are tied up with one or two kids, they can't help the teacher make the classroom a better place for all kids. These good people need to be educated and expected to work as part of a teaching team, serving the classroom, with a special eye on the individual kids on IEPs. They should be supporting and encouraging students in an appropriate way, but not in a manner that deprives these kids of exposure to a stress-inoculation program that will allow them to perform at levels commensurate with their intellectual ability.

I hope my implications are clear: Help only when kids need help. Intervene only when they have first struggled a bit with the challenge, but before they become immobile. Teach them to look ahead, to guess the height of the hurdle and compare it with past hurdles they have successfully surmounted. Teach them to modify their speed or the length of their stride so they engage the hurdle with the right rhythm, velocity, and lift. This is the way to break the cycle. This is the answer. If an exceptionally qualified classroom aide can do this (and I've seen many who can), I say, "How wonderful!" But to parents I say this: a one-to-one aide may seem like best service you can get for your child. Additional support may be just the thing your child needs to be successful. However, if this level of support deprives your child of the chance to learn how to recognize and master the stress that's caused by LD or ADHD, be worried about what happens when that aide leaves. Neither of us wants to see your child fall into a heap of hopeless despair because "it's all just impossible without Ms. . . ."

Thanks for letting me stand on my soapbox about this. It's a very sensitive issue, and one that's not often confronted, but I think it's relevant to this discussion. In Chapter Eight, which is written for teachers and administrators, I encourage them to deal with this problem sensitively and creatively.

The next point to consider is how to make the classroom as psychologically safe place for kids—without having to water down the curriculum.

Reduce the Threat

Many students live in a state of feeling psychologically unsafe in school. Kids who are bullied are perfect examples. Other students, especially those who have a shaky foundation kept unstable by chronic mistakes, feel threatened by a perceived or real loss of status or control. The key to success here is removing, reducing, or neutralizing the threat. To do that, we have to know what's threatening to a student. Here are some things to consider:

You Don't Have to Shout! Some sensitive, emotionally fragile students may misread a teacher's exuberance as yelling. For them, anything that goes above a quiet drone is a threat. What if the teacher is yelling at another student? Sensitive students with special needs and a long history of making errors have been fear-conditioned. They have been corrected many times in the past. Adults have raised their voices at them. This has seldom been a positive experience. Now, when they hear the teacher get louder, their brains go into protective mode—perhaps even amplifying the teacher's voice. Each of these students anxiously wonders if they're going to be the teacher's next target. There is no easy escape from this threat. Head goes down, eyes are averted. Heart rate goes up. Palms start to sweat. Breathing grows fast and shallow. Cortisol starts pouring into the blood and making its way to the brain. Learning and memory suffer.

For this reason, teachers need to find out how they are perceived by students. Teachers can ask parents what their children say about their comfort level in class, or hold private conferences with each sensitive student, introducing the topic in a creative way: "Some kids have said that when I get excited when I teach, they aren't sure if I'm happy or mad. What do you think?" Playing a videotaped recording of a recent lesson and having the students privately rate the teacher's emotional tone (happy? sad? mad?) might yield some very interesting results.

Teachers can reduce the threat by knowing which students are particularly vulnerable to stress and making the environment safe for them. When they know the triggers for certain kids, teachers can control their language and behavior so that it's perceived as being less threatening. They can demonstrate to their students the language they typically use in certain situations. Some teachers are adept at using a certain voice or tone to create a mood (of calm or excitement) or to signal transition. The key to success with anxious students is to monitor their responses to "normal" levels of communication.

Practicing or rehearsing the use of different voice levels may be necessary to train students about relative volume and the purpose of different kinds of communication. Kids can be taught that the teacher's soft voice is only used to help them get ready for transitions. *"OK, kids, we have five minutes until we have to get ready for art class."* Soft-spoken teachers tend to have quieter classes. Quieter classes tend to decrease the stress quotient of the classroom and the kids in it. It's one more easy way to help kids with ADHD and LD deal with stress. A louder "stage voice" is only used for instructional purposes: *"I've got some very exciting information I want to share with you today, class!"* Kids tend to listen carefully when they know that the loudest or warning voice will only be used when things are getting out of control or when students are in danger. *"Children, I need you to quietly and quickly get in line; we are having a fire drill."*

Silence is golden. Virtuoso teachers understand the power of silence and how to use the absence of sound creatively. Requesting that students take a moment for silent reflection before responding may give one who is a slow processor the time needed to formulate and answer to share without fear. Requests or directions given quietly (rather than called out across a room) are more effectively received and processed by a child who gets anxious as the focus of attention.

Lunch . . . Fun? Who Are You Kidding? Here's a scenario that highlights stress created or made worse by transitions. This time, we're in a fourth-grade classroom, just before lunch. Most of the kids are finishing the work at their desks and looking forward to the upcoming break, both the food and the fun. But one of the kids is sitting very still and not working. A mind-reader would pick up thoughts like these: *"I hate lunch. Nobody likes me. Where will I sit? Who will accept me? How can I avoid lunch? A trip to the bathroom or the nurse? My stomach hurts. I want to call my Mom. I am supposed to be doing math now. How can I do math? I'm scared about who's going to shove food down my shirt."*

Just as the impact of language or an upcoming lesson on a student's stress level can be assessed, a teacher can also have students rate their readiness to make transitions to lunch, other classes, or special activities. Many teachers have found a "mood thermometer" or "mood meter" to be a useful tool. This is a teacher-made or (better!) student-made oak tag sheet on which a child can move an arrow into a green, yellow, or red zone, either at the teacher's suggestion or whenever their mood shifts. The colors correspond to the child's readiness and willingness to make the transition. The teacher can say: "I'll look at your mood meter from time to time, just to check in and see how you're doing. You can also raise your hand to get my attention and just point to the meter to tell me your mood has changed, and we can talk about what to do." The "what to do" part is important, and implies that it's not enough just to rate your discomfort, but that the teacher will help teach the child strategies to use to get into the "green zone" and stay there.

Decrease Reliance on Reward-and-Punishment Systems Behavioral programs that promise pay-offs (rewards) when a student finishes some expected behavior or attains some goal can actually add a level of stress to a task. Most of us love to get positive reinforcements (a pay raise, a dinner out, applause from our colleagues), but the very promise of this reward has its flip side: "What if I *don't* get it??" You can see how the fear of not reaching the intended or implied goal increases pressure that impedes performance. You can see the merry-go-round rider who, when promised by a parent that catching the ring means a chance to go again, anxiously lashes out and misses the gold ring, crying out in frustrated anguish: "Oh, *no!* I missed it *again!*"

The Body Electric You know what it's like when a person stands very close to you. Depending on who it is, what you think they have in mind, or how they smell, your comfort level can range from *"Howdy Stranger"* to *"Whoa, Nelly!"* Teachers who are sensitive to the impact of their physical presence on kids can use it to assuage stress or induce a feeling of dread. Kneeling down at eye and ear level to talk to a student can be less threatening than towering over the desk. Teachers need to examine a child's reaction to them in order to know whether physical proximity is comforting or threatening to a sensitive student. Sometimes it's the other way around. Some students, especially the little ones, may come much closer to you than you expect for students at that age level. Be aware that their need to be close to you may be related to the state of anxiety they have when you move *away* from them. Especially for kids who don't have a lot of functional verbal language, body language can tell you a lot about a child's emotional state.

Attention, Attention! Yeah, I'm Talkin' to You! A teacher who tells a class to "behave or you'll lose your recess" is using a mild threat to manage behavior. Imagine that you are a child with LD or ADHD, and you have learned by experience to doubt yourself and to assume that you're the one who messed up (again). You hear this message that the teacher is broadcasting to the whole class as a statement directed just at you. You thought you were behaving OK, but now you begin to question your self-appraisal. As a result, you're back in the clutches of stress. You're thinking: *"What do I need to do to make sure I get to go to recess? What more is expected of me? How can I make this unpleasant feeling that I now have go away? I can't, and I'm getting more and more anxious."* See how easy it is for a student who is already wired for stress to get worked up and anxious about a fairly innocuous event?

Now assume that you are fortunate enough to have a perceptive, sensitive teacher who understands that you get anxious at transitions, and that your antenna picks up messages meant for the group and your brain translates them into personal directives. The fix for this problem is simple, and teachers do it all the time. Instead of uttering a blanket warning, a teacher can call attention to the positive behavior of individual kids. "Sally's sitting quietly waiting for the recess bell. I see other students putting away their work to get ready . . ." This kind of response consciously catches Sally doing the expected thing—the right thing—and rewards her with simple, sincere praise.

Ka-ching! Putting Money in the Self-Concept Account I like to use a bank account metaphor to explain the plight of many kids with LD and ADHD. Their misjudgments, their impulsivity, their processing delays and poor memory often cause actions that result in criticism. This negative appraisal may be in the form of critical or corrective comments from adults, taunts or judgmental looks from other kids, or silent self-deprecating messages like "I am such a dunce." All these negative reactions function as withdrawals from a child's self-concept account. Unless deposits (in the form of success and the positive feelings and comments that follow) outweigh withdrawals, kids are always in a time of deficit spending, heading toward psychological bankruptcy. Those of us who work with kids whose success hit rate is low need to create environments and activities that maximize the chance of success and mastery. These are the experiences that put money in their self-concept accounts. If it can stay in there for a while, it even starts to earn interest—compound interest. The feeling of being psychologically flush allows the child to take a few hits without wiping out the whole account.

Teachers can reduce the threat by learning when kids feel most confident and least anxious, and trying to replicate those conditions in the classroom. For example, a student may be relaxed and talkative with family, but communicate very little in school, especially when called on to read or answer a question in class. To give the reticent student more of a chance to interact, the teacher can have a quiet one-to-one informal conversation with the child, and can create small-group activities that prime the pump with ideas and provide opportunities for rehearsal before moving on to whole-class discussions. She can ask the student to write an answer instead of saying it out loud, or to tell a study partner an answer and then the other student can share the answer with the group. All these simple strategies can make the classroom a less stressful environment—not only for the anxious students but for all of them.

Under the "D" in DE-STRESS, I talked about the importance of identifying a child's personal assets. These are things a child does well and other people acknowledge, appreciate, and praise. It's important that a child's teacher be made aware of these strengths, since successes outside of school can serve as the foundation upon which a shaky academic self-concept can be rebuilt. Dr. Robert Brooks, noted child psychologist, speaker, and author of many books about self-esteem in children, reminds us of the importance of identifying and creating "islands of competence"—small bits of figurative land a child can visit to nourish positive self-regard before stepping off in the direction of new challenges.

Reframing Resistance Some students say or do things that seem to indicate that they see little value in the lessons or activities that teachers work so hard to prepare and present. This devaluation of a planned activity sometimes has its roots in self-protection. The student with learning or attention difficulties may have had negative experiences with a similar topic, or may be putting up a generalized defensive shield against stress that has been created by *many* unrewarding learning experiences. The underlying logic: "If I don't like this, or if I can convince the teacher it has little meaning to my own life, I might not have to do it." The real reason for this negativity is the subconscious thought, "I will not put myself in a situation in which the work is too hard or in which I will feel dumb, yet again." There are kids who, having no productive option, may claim laziness as an indelible personal trait, a character flaw "I got from my father" or "I just can't help"—which some hope will serve as a free pass to do nothing. We have to turn that belief around by creating experiences that lead to success.

Creating a Need to Know Teachers can help students reduce stress by having them focus on the importance and the relevance of a task. A three-part question can be at the heart of all learning: *Why is what we're learning important to me? To you? And to the world in which we live?* The lesson should start with activities that require students to explore and answer these questions. Doing that may either allow the student to prove the point that it's not interesting, which will give a sense of control, or it might just build interest and lead to meaningful (and therefore, less stressful) learning.

For example, students could be asked to go home and ask their parents or aunt and uncle why *they* think it's important to learn about the American Civil War. As a way to weave humor into the task and to put this war into a historic context, kids may be instructed to ask their parents how old they were during this war. Reporting the answers, and the parents' reactions, can make for a lively opening activity at the next class. This approach results in a greater likelihood that kids will get engaged than one in which a teacher announces, "I'm sure that when we finish this, you'll see the value in it," or comes out with the deadly, "I'm required to teach this, but I'll try to make it fun for you." The approach may not be enough to get the student whose fear of public failure is so entrenched that it precludes digging in to even the most exciting lesson. I addressed this problem earlier in the chapter, in my discussion of the Aye-Aye approach (in the paragraph that begins "Step into my office, please," just before the second question).

I have offered you many suggestions that are helpful for all kids, and not just those who have LD or ADHD. They are aimed at helping students develop a sense of control over their environment, which in turn reduces the stress that comes from fear based on an "I can't do this" attitude.

Exercise

Athletes train for success; why not students with LD and ADHD? Athletic coaches don't leave winning to chance. Children and adults involved in competitive sports make sure they eat right, sleep enough, and drink plenty of water.

What happens if we take this concept inside the classroom? It helps to think of the "three R's" as an educational triathlon. It should come as no surprise that the same things that give kids the competitive edge in the pool or on the track or playing field are exactly the things that help decrease anxiety and stress in all kids (not only those with LD and ADHD) and help them become more successful at school. A brisk ten-minute walk around a college quadrangle has been shown to elevate exam scores for college students. Exercise stimulates and energizes the brain to process information more efficiently, and actually makes more brain cells. A rapidly growing body of research supports the exercise-achievement connection. In *Spark: The Revolutionary*

New Science of Exercise and the Brain, Dr. John Ratey, a Harvard clinical associate professor of psychiatry, presents a compelling argument that exercise not only helps reduce obesity but also improves academic performance.

It's clearly important for teachers to build in physical activity more often during the school day. However, it's a myth that vigorous physical activity "burns off the extra energy" exhibited by kids with ADHD. It may tire them out, to be sure, but the real benefit from running around the playground or gym is that it creates endorphins, hormones that lighten mood and fight against stress-inducing hormones like cortisol. Think "runner's high." Unless you're running from a fire or a bully, it's hard to be stressed when you're running. It really works; while writing much of this book, I had the opportunity to use a device called a TreadDesk—essentially a simple electric treadmill placed under a chest-high desk (see www.treaddesk.com) designed for use while standing. TreadDesks are being used in offices around the country, and are finding their way into schools. I would like to set up a research project to measure the impact of this device on academic performance, stress, and self-esteem. I logged many, many miles while writing and editing this book, and I must say that it improved my balance and put me in a better frame of mind. I think this device holds promise for kids with LD and ADHD.

A program that has enjoyed a very positive reputation for more than twenty years and has been implemented in schools in eighty-seven countries is known as Brain Gym. The program's website (www.braingym.org) explains that "these activities recall the movements naturally done during the first years of life when learning to coordinate the eyes, ears, hands, and whole body." The twenty-six activities (along with a program for "learning through movement") were developed by Paul and Gail Dennison, respectively an educator and a reading specialist. "Even though it is not clear yet 'why' these movements work so well," the site explains, "they often bring about dramatic improvements in areas such as: concentration and focus, memory, academics: reading, writing, math, test taking, physical coordination, relationships, self-responsibility, organization skills, [and] attitude." The Brain Gym website also presents research on this approach and describes the program in greater detail.

A Note on Nutrition Successful athletes eat right. It turns out that there's a way for students to eat right too. A study reported in the *New England Journal of Medicine* in 1989 showed that students who had seventeen (!) snacks over the course of a school day did better on several measures than a comparison group who ate the same quantity of food in three meals. The students who spread out their food intake had lower cortisol levels and better glucose tolerance, and they exhibited fewer discipline problems and had an enhanced sense of well-being.

Hmm . . . Cows graze, don't they? Maybe that's why they appear to be so contented.

Go Go Go, with H_2O No one would think of sending kids onto the playing field without sufficient water. However, many kids don't get enough water during the day to keep their cells functional. Cells need water to work well, and remember, we're talking about a group of kids whose neurons (nerve cells) are already at risk as a result of stress. Why make things worse for them? When kids (and adults) feel thirsty, they are already dehydrated. Having water available for active learners is extremely important. I'm happy to report that I've seen water bottles or access to good drinking water in more and more classrooms I visit.

Reminder: *You can lead both horses and children to water, but you might have to remind little humans to drink.*

Success

> You will never find happiness if you do not
> conquer your own doubt.
>
> *—found on a Yogi Tea ginger tea bag tag,*
> October 2010

Teachers can turn distress into de-stress by using what I've termed the "language of success." By using language that promotes self-appraisal, they help students focus on the *process* they use more than the *products* they create. This is an important distinction, because product-centered self-appraisal is both fleeting and dependent on the judgment of others. By its very nature, this puts a student in an inferior position. Learning how to appraise one's efforts is a skill that serves a student well, no matter what the desired outcome.

And it can be taught. Here's how it works. When a child turns in an assignment, a teacher should say: *This looks good* (it's still OK to praise—kids expect it), but also ask: *How did you do this? What did you do to make [or write, or build] this?* If the student can't say, give some suggestions. For example: *"I see that you used a word processor. Did that help you get your words down on paper without having to worry about handwriting?"* Or: *"You folded your paper into fourths; it looks like the sections helped you organize your work—and helped you keep this math problem from running into this one."*

You should get a confirmation; this needs to be a cognitive active process. Ask the student: *"Would you agree?"*

The goal here is to get the student to self-appraise and be able to identify the behaviors or strategies that have led to success. This generates a feeling of competence and confidence that helps keep stress in check. The key is to deemphasize praise and emphasize self-appraisal. Teachers can encourage self-appraisal by asking questions like these:

- How do you think you did?
- Are you satisfied with this?
- What goal were you working on?
- Did you achieve your goal?

Consider the use of simple rating scales for students who lack language for self-appraisal—and then provide the language to go with their number rating, as in:

1 = not the best work you can do

2 = work that's OK, but not great

3 = about the best you can do

For younger kids, one, two, or three smiley faces—☺—might replace the numerical rating system.

When a student turns in work and says: *"I think this is great,"* a teacher who regards it as substandard can say: *"I have seen great work from you, and I have to disagree with you—this is not great work."* (The focus here is on comparisons with *self*; the standard here is the student's *personal best*.)

What if a student turns in work that is acceptable but devalues it (*"This sucks!"*)? After you suggest saying *stinks* instead of *sucks* (yes, we still have to be a moral compass and monitor of language), you can say: *"I'm sorry that you feel this way; I've been teaching for a long time, and what you did here definitely does not . . . stink. I can show you some examples of lousy work if you want, but this is not it . . ."* This communication establishes the teacher as an impartial judge, a giver of honest feedback.

Teachers should encourage students to keep an electronic or paper portfolio of work samples. Having this evidence allows the teacher to say: *"Here's what you did in October. Now compare that with what you just did."* (And here, resist the temptation to evaluate.) Instead, ask: *"How would you say these are different?"* You will find that over time, if you practice this method faithfully, students might ask you what you think of their work, but then will catch themselves, saying, "I know, I know—what do *I* think?" That's the goal of this approach, and it's a really great feeling (for both teacher and student) when it gets to this point.

What Do Successful Kids Do? To fully understand how accomplishments form the foundation for future success, it's important to ask how successful kids with LD or ADHD cope with stressful events. Over the years, I've interviewed hundreds of kids with learning or attention difficulties about how they handle challenges. It's a part of my neuropsychological evaluation, reflecting my strength-based philosophy of assessment. I've grouped together some of the ways kids have told me they find success, and as a consequence, experience less stress.

- *They ignore or minimize the problem:* Kids who are success-oriented say things like "What's the worst thing that could happen?" or "It's really no big deal" (and you know what? it *isn't*). This implies that they've put the problem (the outcome or the consequences) in perspective. They are not saying, "whatever!" Instead, they are saying, "There will be other challenges. It won't kill me if I don't master this one."

- *They change the subject:* Kids who feel backed into a corner might say, "I don't really know how I feel about that. I do, however, have a strong opinion about . . ." Or they might say, "You know what? Right now I'd rather talk about . . ."

- *They do something else:* Kids under pressure often manage the stress by switching gears. They do something that they do well. For example, if they are sweating math homework, they may pull out an English assignment and start writing, a task they do well. Doing something you do well creates a flow of the kind of neurochemicals that function as a biological stress-buster.

- *They prepare for all contingencies:* Successful, unstressful kids plan ahead and get the supplies, information, and resources they need to face the challenge.

- *They use "competence anchors":* Kids who couch the present challenge in the context of what similar thing they've done before are more successful and less full of stress. A student might think something like, "This is just like the biology unit we did last year. I did well on that."

Smart kids, eh? Successful kids! Un-stress-full kids!!

A Suggestion

Teachers can develop a self-rating sheet for students that contain these items followed by a 5-point scale. The results might help you develop interventions, and the scale can be used as a way for the student to measure change over time. It's all a part of helping the student gain a better sense of control—the great eradicator of stress.

Strategize

As successful students get older, there is a need to look long range, to anticipate the changes and challenges that may shake even a well-established foundation of stress-inhibiting security and confidence. So this last part of the model encourages you to *strategize*—to anticipate what lies ahead and think about how the students you care about or care for can use their repertoire of stress-management skills to better cope with the challenges they will surely face. Looks like we've come back to the Boy Scout motto here: *Always Be Prepared!*

Activities that might trigger stress could be major developmental milestones like the transition from elementary school to middle school, or from middle school to high school. We might also focus on developing "higher states of preparedness" for students who are taking the big step of graduating from high school and moving on to college or a career track. Transitions are a particularly stressful time for young adults with learning disabilities or attention deficits. In her extremely useful book on this topic, *Guiding Teens with Learning Disabilities: Navigating the Transition from High School to Adulthood,* Dr. Arlyn Roffman offers practical advice and information to help parents and guidance personnel understand the challenges faced by students with learning disabilities as they approach the transition from high school to adulthood.

No matter what the child's stage of development, certain common categories might be considered as potential impediments—activities or events that could threaten to derail the sense of competence and confidence. The following list presents a few of these demands, and the areas that might be affected by both the disability and the stress.

- *Homework demands:* Increased workload, increased complexity and variety, compatibility with a student's learning style and needs
- *Social interactions:* Expanding group of friends, more complex social demands, navigating social media, social events
- *Social pressures:* Decisions about use of free time, drug use, fashion, romantic involvement, self-image
- *Time pressures:* Deadlines, time lines, competitions
- *Environmental changes:* Lockers, complex schedules, sports, neighborhoods, schools, residences
- *Financial matters:* Spending, saving, inheritance, salary, choices or limitations, economic changes

- *Physical changes:* Size, shape, puberty, sexuality, physical prowess

Neuronal development over time changes the chemistry and architecture of the brain in ways that affect how students of different ages handle these changes. The good news is that this natural and inevitable move toward more efficient higher-level processing generally bolsters students' skills as they face new challenges. If a positive trajectory has been established through effective intervention at a younger age, we can be more optimistic about how a student will face the increased demands that come with development. Building upon a foundation of previous successes, a student is better equipped to face new challenges with greater confidence and less stress.

LATER IS BETTER THAN NEVER

If interventions aren't put into place until later in a student's life, the impact of cumulative negative experiences may prove more difficult to eradicate. However, if suggestions such as those made throughout this book are implemented, the results should be positive, even though the effects may not be as dramatic and may take longer to develop. The same thing could be said of piano lessons, couldn't it? I say this especially to parents of older children, who are reading this book and wondering whether there can still be hope for their kids. While we may not expect a late-in-life piano player to move into a career as a concert pianist, the ability to play even a few songs at social events or family gatherings can make life more enjoyable for player and audience alike. Yes, there *is* hope for your adolescents and young adults. And the more they practice, the better they play.

I hope that you have enjoyed reading about the DE-STRESS model and the examples showing how it can be put into action. Over the years, I've seen the positive effects of implementing this model in classrooms and in entire schools. Kids get happier, and they are more successful and less stressed when these principles and practices are implemented. Watching this happen over and over again strengthens my belief that this approach holds the key to reducing or eliminating stress in students with LD and ADHD. I hope that you agree.

PART FOUR

Special Messages for Teachers and Parents

8

Making Schools Stress-Less and Success-Full for Students with LD and ADHD

In this chapter I share some insights I've gained from my work in schools and offer some very practical advice for teachers and other professionals who are committed to making schools a more satisfying, less stressful experience for students with LD and ADHD. Many of the ideas and suggestions you'll find in this chapter are extensions or different expressions of the DE-STRESS model, introduced in Chapter Seven. While Chapter Eight is directed to teachers and administrators, it contains helpful information for parents as well. Research tells us that when communication between home and school improves, it almost always results in a better education for students. This is especially true when the topic is the impact of stress on kids with LD and ADHD. The more parents know about effective practices that can be implemented during the school day, the more they can do to reinforce these strategies and the language that is associated with them at home. By the same token, schools that understand and appreciate how the way stress sometimes plays out at home can be different from the way it looks in school are in a better position to help children in both environments.

Are we talking about the same child?

This is what teachers sometimes think (but may not say) when they hear parents describe their children, who are agitated, argumentative, resistant, or rude from the time they fall through the front door after school until they drop into bed at night. The teachers wonder how the well-behaved, hard-working, socially connected, star pupils that they know during the day could be the same students that parents describe as sad, teary, or with-drawn, and who retreat ritualistically behind a shut bedroom door and the apparent comfort of Facebook or computer games. How often have I heard what I've come to call a Jekyll-and-Hyde presentation. How can this be?

Remember that we're talking about students with LD and ADHD, who face a ceaseless onslaught of challenges to their perceptual, organizational, social, or emotional systems during the school day (sometimes starting with a long bus ride and ending after an arduous athletic practice). These students may have the stamina to hold up under this pressure while they are in public view. They seem to be able to "keep it together" in front of teachers they respect and admire and want to impress or please, and in the presence of friends (or those they want as friends), who seem to find school much easier than they do. It's no wonder, then, that these kids come apart the instant they throw their backpack onto the floor inside the front door. Slamming the door behind them signals that school is over, at least for now. Now they're home, where they can drop the mask of competence and confidence they've been wearing throughout a long, tough day. On some level, even if they have a kicking and screaming tantrum or hide in their room, they know that they'll still be loved. This volatility can take its toll on parents and other family members, but for these kids, like Dorothy and Toto, there's no place like home. They just need the downtime—and they need parents who can understand why.

This transition from one mood state to another is a very common phenomenon for students with LD and ADHD, who regularly use up most of the energy they have in the service of doing the business of school and protecting their image. It underscores the importance of creating an environment in school that acknowledges the impact of stress on students with these conditions, even when teachers and others may not see the overt symptoms of the reaction to pressure.

We do need to be concerned about kids who might be model students during the day and oppositional or depressed at home. But we also have to worry about the students who seem to *choose* to underperform at school when they clearly have the ability to do the required work. We need to be tuned in to the girl who unexpectedly drops out of the Spanish Club, or the previously successful boy who sabotages his performance in Honors Chemistry by failing three quizzes in a row. These behaviors may signal the presence of stress that causes kids to doubt their abilities, question the value of schoolwork, and drop out cognitively even though they physically remain in school. The "aggressive passivity" we often see in some of these students may be misread as a lack of motivation rather than a way of coping with stress. Like a nuclear reactor that's ready to blow, they shut down as a fail-safe mechanism. We want to get to these kids before they reach this point. If they have already crossed over this threshold, we have to find ways to get them operational again.

Teachers, guidance counselors, psychologists, and other professionals within the school sit at vantage points from which they can observe the tell-tale signs of stress in students who have a history of learning disabilities or attention deficits. They can then work, hopefully in a collaborative effort with parents, to create an environment that allows these students to find success without having to sacrifice their mental health or happiness.

The following story provides a dramatic example of how this was done for one high school student. It describes a somewhat fictionalized intervention program based on a composite of several I've worked with over the past three decades. For storytelling purposes, I call this program NewStart. Programs like it (with similarly optimistic names) have been successfully implemented in large urban and suburban school districts. This composite portrayal might serve as a model for other schools.

MICHAEL AND THE HUT

Based on Michael's diagnosis of ADHD, he had been on a "504 plan" in middle school (referring to Section 504 of the Rehabilitation Act of 1973), which essentially meant that his progress was closely monitored by his teaching team. While his performance and his behavior were variable, Michael was able to stay pretty much on track because of the close supervision of many adults who were working in a coordinated, collaborative way in small instructional units called "pods." His reading skills were very weak, but he had not been diagnosed with a learning disability, and he was showing some improvement. He occasionally acted up, but because he was in what amounted to protective custody in the middle school, he kept flying under the radar. But his teachers were very worried about his future.

Their fears were well-founded. Michael's transition to a 1300-student high school was a disaster. Within two weeks of his inclusion in a mainstream environment, he began to exhibit what was regarded as oppositional behavior. He actively resisted teacher direction and mumbled derogatory comments under his breath during class. At first, the other kids thought his antics were funny, but they quickly tired of his disruptions and his language. One girl confided to her guidance counselor that Michael's behavior upset her and made it hard for her to learn. Other students started acting out against him, punching him as he walked by or throwing paper wads at him. Michael's behavior had quickly made him a pariah in the classroom, and the negative attention followed him into the hallways and into the lunchroom. Nothing seemed to help; in fact, the more teachers tried to do, the worse

Michael got. He was spending more time in the assistant principal's office than he was in classes.

A teacher assistance team (TAT) meeting was called for the purpose of generating creative ideas about how to help Michael be more successful in the classroom and how to turn the tide of negativity that was being fueled by his behavior. Teachers clamped down on him, presenting him with a clear set of expectations and consequences, and for a week or so, he settled in and started to do his work. Then, as the demands for productivity increased, Michael started being late for the school bus. He often woke up claiming to feel ill, and his mother called with increasing frequency, telling the staff that Michael would not be coming in. She was a single parent who was deeply committed to helping her son find success, and she was working two jobs, which took her out of the house from early morning to early evening. On Michael's "days off" he stayed home and played video games, hung out with other truant kids who were known to be involved in drugs, and fell under the watchful surveillance of the local police. Efforts to get him to return to school failed. His academic future looked dim.

After much thoughtful deliberation among teachers, school psychologists, and his mother, the decision was made to transfer Michael to NewStart. The NewStart classrooms were housed in a hangar-type structure attached to the high school, which students referred to as "the hut." Its purpose was to identify the impediments to a student's progress and to determine what supports, programs, or interventions would lead to greater success.

Some of the students who came through NewStart returned to the mainstream educational environment with additional supports or entered classrooms that provided more highly differentiated instruction. Others returned to one of the specialized programs in the district that was a better match for their own needs. A few, whose needs were more significant, were ultimately sent to out-of-district placements so that they could receive services that were more specialized or intensive than the public school system could offer.

Michael resisted the idea of enrolling in the NewStart program, saying its students were all losers. Because his mother told him that his only other option was to be sent off to a "school for bad kids," he got on the "short bus"—complaining and cursing—and ended up at the hut.

Many of the other eleven boys and girls in the class were working on assignments that would gain them reentry to the school or program that had initially referred them to NewStart. Before Michael's arrival, there was a rhythm and flow to the daily activities in the hut. The kids in the program were, in the best sense of the word, stabilizing—getting back on track. The traumas and dramas that had been their tickets of admission to this specialized program had abated under the watchful care of a quartet of professionals that included a lead teacher who was well-connected to the staff, programs, and culture of the high school, a gifted young social worker, a caring and gentle instructional aide, and a savvy psychology intern assigned to NewStart.

Putting Michael in this program was like dropping an aggressive fish into a friendly community fish tank. His shout-outs, need for constant attention, and avoidance techniques, coupled with his incessant pleading to "go out for a smoke" (which was against the rules), sucked up a great deal of attention from the staff, and created a (for them) problematic alliance with another smoker in the group. Michael's oppositional behavior persisted in the new setting, and his clowning around increased. Despite his destabilizing impact on the community, the team members, who were well-trained and accustomed to kids like this, remained optimistic that they could crack the case and figure out how to help Michael get back on the road to success.

The team had noticed that over time, as Michael was pulled into one of the small offices that surrounded the central large work area (which was the stage upon which he put on his disruptive show), he visibly settled down, engaged respectfully with staff, and was able to get some work done, albeit in five-minute bursts. Noting that he struggled with reading, the staff looked more carefully into his educational history and found that when last tested two years ago, he had about a fourth-grade reading level. They quickly realized that when Michael went behind closed doors in a one-to-one setting with any one of them, he was protected from the shame of the embarrassment that they now felt played a very big role in the difficulties that had resulted in his referral to the hut. To test their hypothesis, all they had to do was place Michael back in the main room. Triggered by some comment from his smoking buddy, who was also relatively new to the program, Michael went back into character. Not surprisingly, asking him to read something in public would also be his cue to go on stage.

Based on their hunch that much of Michael's behavior was fueled by his desire to avoid public shame, the team developed an action plan designed to meet his needs. They referred him for a reevaluation, and this testing confirmed a diagnosis of learning disability. The school psychologist felt sitting down with Michael at this point in his life and going over his testing and diagnosis might actually push him further into a protective corner. Instead, he met with Michael in the capacity of a "brain coach," going over Michael's assignments, interpreting both his errors and his successes in light of the test findings. Michael, who had successfully played baseball in middle school, understood and respected the role (and the value) of a coach, so this form of assistance was more palatable to him than a more formal interpretation of his learning style would have been.

Michael's problems did not have a quick fix, but over time, he began to be a little more introspective and reflective, and was able to see how the strategies suggested by the school psychologist paid off. His performance was still erratic and he was easily set off by the other smoker in the classroom, but when he was able to use the techniques he had been taught, his performance improved. He began to see the connection between the test results and his efforts. The last time I heard from this team, Michael was being recommended for a return to a small program in the high school for students with language-based learning disabilities. To ensure his continued success, they were going to offer him their "warranty plan," which involved several live visits by the NewStart Staff, followed by regular check-ins by e-mail for as long as Michael felt these would be helpful.

This is a story of transition and transformation. I hope that it helps you see what can happen when a school-based team views a student with LD through the lens of stress, and how that can create a path that just might lead to a better future.

A LESSON LEARNED

I would like to share another story with you. This one helps to explain why I feel so passionate about the need for schools to help students with LD and ADHD understand these conditions and how they affect their view of themselves and their performance. Some years ago, when I was serving on the Board of the Learning Disabilities Association of Massachusetts (LDAM), I offered to make a videotape that would educate parents and kids about the impact of learning disabilities. We put an announcement in our newsletter, the *Gazette*, informing parents and teachers that we were seeking a few students with LD to appear on the tape with me to be interviewed about their personal experiences. Just by chance, we got responses from three kids who attended various public schools in the greater Boston area and three who attended a well-known and well-respected private school for students with learning disabilities.

Light(ning), Camera, Action!

This video was called *Einstein and Me* to honor the connection between kids with LD and the brilliant scientist who, according to popular lore, had that condition. It was a no-budget project, shot on a borrowed video camera one stormy October evening. Since we had no sound editing equipment, if you listen carefully you can hear the thunder booming outside the building. But the important sounds—the voices of these students—came through loud and clear. On camera, I asked the kids four questions:

- Do you have a learning disability, and can you describe how it affects you or your learning?
- Over the years, who or what helped you attain success?
- Who or what has gotten in the way of success or made life and learning more difficult?
- What advice do you have for parents, kids, and teachers who might be watching this video?

I'm pleased to say that since this tape was made (as a fund-raiser for LDAM), it has sold hundreds of copies and has been translated into several different languages for non-English-speaking viewers in the United States and for distribution abroad. It is gratifying that this video has provided information about LD for so many viewers, and that it has provided positive role models for students across the globe. I am most grateful, however, for an unexpected lesson that I learned from those kids that blustery afternoon.

Let me explain. When I asked the first question about the nature of their learning disability, the volunteer interviewees from the public school gave answers that went something like this (I'm paraphrasing here to give you the flavor of the responses): *"I guess I have a learning disability because I'm pretty bad at reading,"* or *"I've never been very good at math."* When I asked the same question of the kids from the private LD school, they sat up straight, faced the camera, and responded with something like this: "*Yes, I have a learning disability. It's characterized by a deficit in language processing and it has a significant impact on my reading comprehension. I have learned many effective strategies to help me overcome this relative weakness in my learning profile, and I . . .*"

Wow! Needless to say, I was shocked by the obvious contrast between the answers given by the two groups of students, and by the way the private school kids communicated their personal story with such confidence and poise. When asked "what or who helped you?" these articulate young scholars attributed their success to the teachers at their school, who had, among other things, "*helped me to understand the nature of my learning disability, and what I could do about it.*" When asked who had impeded their progress, they recalled "*teachers who did not believe that I had a learning disability, or those who thought that I was just lazy or stupid.*" The public school kids thanked their parents or a particular tutor or teacher for "helping them when they needed it," but none was able to explain the nature of their LD.

What I learned from this interchange was that when students are consciously taught about their LD, and, more important, given the tools to overcome their learning weakness, they develop and exude a sense of confidence and competence. They are not children under chronic stress. They know what it feels like to be right more often than they are wrong, and this cumulative success leads to a greater sense of control over how things work out in school. These are kids who have been taught to use frustration and failure as a way to gain insights about how they approach a problem and how to modify strategies based on self-evaluation. These are kids who thoroughly enjoy success because they have achieved it by working smart—not just working hard.

Rumor has it that for a while this video came to be known as the "PR film" for that excellent private school, because of the uniformly impressive and confident responses of this sample of their students. I need to point out emphatically that this is not a private versus public school issue. I have since replicated this interview format at many conferences in which I have brought in a "panel of experts," made up of students with LD or ADHD or both, coming from both private and public schools, and interviewed them in front of live audiences of parents, teachers, and kids. Through this heartwarming exercise, I have met many successful kids with LD and ADHD, and they have certainly not all attended private schools. I have learned that students' sense of confidence and feeling of competence can be attributed, among other things, to the actions and reaction of their teachers and their parents.

In the Conclusion of this book is a section called "Successful Kids with LD and ADHD: Ten Ways They Can Get There," in which I share with you the conditions that have led to success for many students with these conditions. May they serve as guidelines for you. But for now, let me offer . . .

A MINI HOW-TO MANUAL FOR TEACHERS

On the pages that follow, I share some suggestions that will help you develop students who have positive self-images, who believe in themselves and their abilities, and who know how to read the signs of stress and convert it into a positive force that will fuel their accomplishments.

Hitting the Reset Button on Stress Might Help . . . But Be Careful!

Pushing *pause* on a DVD player lets you get a snack or go to the bathroom without missing important parts of the movie. Great invention! (It explains why a lot of senior citizens use NetFlix instead of going to the theater.) Turning off a flame can stop a pot from boiling over. That's a good thing, too! But even though pulling a plug or turning off the heat can save lives, turning down the demands of a curriculum may not be particularly helpful for kids under stress.

Some students find the relative tranquility that comes from a *temporary* lowering of expectations (but not standards!) helpful. For example, a brief, *explained* hiatus can often help students get back on the track to performance commensurate with their intelligence. This is especially true if the mounds of built-up neglected homework or a spate of sub-average or failing grades can be wiped out in the name of a fresh start. But there's a problem with this practice of hitting the reset button. If this kind of "free pass" happens often, a student can learn to use it as an escape hatch from stress. It may also make other students mad, or cause some teachers to doubt a sincere student's intentions. If the classroom teacher who grudgingly caves in to team pressure to back off still regards the student as a slacker, the student will know it. Then this approach *will* backfire and may cause the student to take a giant step backward.

Intentions are not actions. Here's another warning: If the student hasn't made a sincere commitment to a new beginning, *hitting the restart button will not work.* Some students under stress will promise *anything* to get out of the hot seat they're in when teachers and adults are sitting in a conference room with them, creatively designing a plan to "help them out of a hole." While some kids want to share the adults' optimistic belief about the outcome of such a plan, the fact remains that down deep, they just can't believe it will happen. They may say yes to please the adults or to show the adults that they know the right thing to do. They may have a spurt of energy when they reengage with schoolwork, but then be unable to sustain the effort. This is why this approach is not a fail-safe method, and why performance has to be closely monitored and supported, especially when the student seems to be doing better. In situations like this, I advise teachers to start slowly, giving the student one or two discrete tasks to complete well before starting to take on the whole package. This helps to break the task of reentry into doable segments, increases the opportunities for close monitoring, and increases the chance for a full return to active duty.

Using Learning Success Partners to Build Success and Lower Stress

One technique that has met with great success in many class-rooms is called Learning Success Partners, or LSPs for short. Most teachers are familiar with the technique known as "Think, Pair, Share," developed by Frank Lyman and his colleagues at the University of Maryland. Variations of this low-risk cooperative learning strategy have been used in many classrooms to help engage students in their own learning. My approach builds on this foundation but takes it further, expanding the richness of the technique and making it better-suited for use with students who have come to doubt their abilities.

The discussion that follows assumes that a teacher has created a classroom culture in which learning from others is a shared value. The teacher has also helped students understand that *not* knowing something is a prerequisite to learning something, and not a trigger for stress. When students are asked to "find your LSP," they know that the goal of learning is to locate answers wherever you can, and that sometimes that answer is sitting right next to you. Businesses spend millions of dollars a year training employees how to work on teams that use synergistic approaches to solve problems and create new products or services. In a similar vein, teachers who use collaborative learning effectively today are helping to create the problem solvers of tomorrow. My conscious use of the term Learning Success Partners (LSPs) reflects a spirit of mutual interdependence. It also focuses on success as an outcome, which this strategy virtually guarantees.

Remember that students with LD and ADHD are all too familiar with frustration and failure. A technique that provides children multiple opportunities to *feel good about being right* will draw them into learning challenges, not make them want to run away in order to Save FASE. Here's how it works:

Consider this interaction: The teacher says to the class: *"I'm going to ask you a very important question. You may or you may not know the answer, but in about three minutes I guarantee that everyone in this room will."* Let's examine that language. The carefully chosen words first *elevate* stress ("I'm going to ask you very important question"), and then attempt to temper or reduce it ("You may or you may not know the answer"). This teacher then *assures* the student—all students—that they will experience success, and soon. And that's a promise the teacher will be able to keep.

Notice the difference between the statements in the preceding paragraph and *this* commonly heard utterance, which is also made with the intent of making kids feel more comfortable, but doesn't quite do it: *"I'm going to ask you a very important question; some of you will find it hard and others will find it easy."* See the difference? Kids' brains, especially those that are wired to be wary of challenges they cannot conquer, are tuned into the subtle nuances of language. When they hear that some students will find it hard, they automatically think, *"Yeah, that means me!"*

The savvy teacher continues, *"After I read this question, I don't want anyone to answer. I know that you might want to respond, but this time—no hands up in the air. First, I want you to turn to your LSP and tell them what you heard me ask."* (This helps both students to focus on the question and assures that the inattentive student now hears the question.) *"Then I want you to find out what your LSP thinks the answer is."* This encourages active listening, positive social communication, and interdependence. Setting the activity up this way gives each student a chance to hear or verify an answer, and it gives the teacher the opportunity to observe a student's interpersonal skills (and intervene if necessary). Think about it—at this moment, half of the students are functioning as teaching assistants. In a sense, the teacher only has to observe half as many students, since the class is now made up of groups of two!

The use of LSPs has the following benefits:

- It provides the opportunity for brief, goal-directed social interactions that the teacher can monitor and guide. This is especially important for students with social perception deficits (as in NVLD or Asperger syndrome), or those who tend to respond impulsively, derailing social relationships.

- It increases information trading, which promotes interdependence. If one student in the pair does not know an answer, it is likely that the other does. If there's doubt about this, the teacher can tell kids, *If neither of you knows the answer, or if you're not sure, just ask another team what they came up with.* (Sharing information is not only OK, it's admirable and desirable.)

- It allows an anxious child a chance to rehearse a response before going public.

The teacher can then say, *"Now raise your hand if you want to say what your partner just told you or the answer that you can both agree on."* Telling about someone else's idea reduces the possibility of public shame and decreases stress. Having the *choice* to do it reduces the stress even more.

I hope that you see how this approach can increase the likelihood that a student will be right, will feel good about it, and will therefore gain a sense of control—the great eradicator of stress. Now I'm going to introduce another technique that will also achieve this goal.

Setting a Competence Anchor

Teachers who want to reduce stress and increase learning know that getting kids into a positive mind-set will do both. They say things and do things that connect kids to the security of past positive experiences. A boat in a storm is not likely to be tossed onto a rocky shore if it has been tethered to an anchor set firmly in the ocean floor. Similarly, kids whose minds are anchored in previous successes are less likely to flounder in an anxious or distracted state. Setting a Competence Anchor is not only a brief intervention, it also involves no materials, costs no money, and benefits all students, anxious or not. What's not to like?

Here's a scene that shows how this works. We're in a class-room in which the teacher understands the connection between state of mind and learning, and knows how to get students into a positive mind-set.

"*OK, kids, I would like you to close your eyes* [thereby reducing stimuli and putting children out of public view] *and think of a time when you learned something very well; something you felt proud about. This could be something academic, like fractions, or it might be something you learned to do, like a hobby or a sport. When you get that thought in your head, simply raise your index finger a bit* [to show who's with the program and who's not] *and I'll know you're connected to that time and the feeling you had when you learned to do that particular thing.*

"*Now, open your eyes and tell us* [solo or via LSPs] *what it was that you learned and how it made you feel.*" The teacher asks the kids what was going on (place, people, timing) that made this such a positive experience. Students can also be asked to write this, or, depending on their skill level or learning strength, draw a picture of the event as the first step in the new assignment. The teacher continues: "*Today we're going to learn something new*" [anxiety rises]. "*We're going to learn about _____. I want you to tell me, based on that positive experience you just recalled* [or talked about], *what would make learning this* new *material successful for you?*" To accommodate learning style and personality differences, the students get the choice of saying the answer, telling a classmate, writing a paragraph about it, or making a representational drawing. This can also be done as a private exercise for students who are not yet comfortable in the public arena of the classroom. Here we see the power in a strategy that involves taking a student back a few steps to relive a positive memory of a past learning experience, and using this recollection to build a bridge to a new challenge. I hope that you'll be able to implement this strategy in your classroom. I've seen it help many students overcome the stress that often inhibits learning.

Happily, I'm in schools two or three times a week. In trying to better understand how kids learn and what might get in the way, I get to sit in on lots of classes and observe lots of interactions between teachers and students. Being a fly on the wall in so many classrooms over the years has allowed me to see things that a teacher whose attention is pulled in one direction after another may not observe.

Many times, after teachers spend the first few minutes of class introducing a topic as a prelude to an activity, I see students who seem to be spaced out, appearing to have no idea what the teacher is saying. Only when the teacher passes out an activity sheet or asks the students to move to their learning centers do such students become alert and recognize that something's happening. Because students in this state have been cognitively disconnected from the topic of the day, they are at these moments in a state of cognitive limbo. The explanation has to be given yet again. The teacher may have to sit with them to get them started. There is a disruption in the flow of learning for these children and for their classmates. And every time this happens, even the most committed and caring teacher gets frustrated.

For students with language-based learning disabilities or attention deficits who get lost in a sea of language, the technique of taking one step backward into competence can offer very effective engagement when introducing a new unit or learning activity. Here's what it looks like. The teacher asks the class: *"Do you remember this?"* holding up a test tube filled with red fluid; a visual prop, a reminder of yesterday's lesson. *"Turn to your LSP and tell each other everything that you remember or learned about this liquid yesterday."* Priming the pump, the teacher says: *"Things like its name, its properties, how it's used . . . If you come up with a lot of answers, you may want to write them down, so you won't forget. In two minutes, I'm going to ask both of you to decide which one thing you'll share with the class."* After the kids have had a few minutes to talk to each other, the teacher invites the students to share the answer they have agreed upon, telling the rest of the class, *"Quietly raise your hand if you or your LSP had the same answer."* This helps to make sure that the others in the class are listening. The hands going up serve as silent affirmation—positive reinforcement for the group that has shared their answer. Success abounds!

As an alternative, a teacher can invite one student in the dyad to tell *"the answer that your LSP gave, if you think it's right."* This technique gives the shy, reticent student—the one who might otherwise sit silent—the opportunity to offer an answer. If the answer turns out to be wrong, the partner shares the blame; if the answer is right, the anxious student shares the success!

RESPONSIBLE VERSUS RESPONSE-ABLE

The interventions I suggest in this chapter don't have to be used in every interaction with a child whose stress creates a disconnect from learning. In fact, the goal of using these strategies is to train students to take charge of their own learning and attention, and make them more, as I like to say: response-*able*. Just as you would not expect the person who gave you tennis lessons to accompany you onto the court each time you went out to play, a teacher or instructional aide should not be omnipresent.

I introduced this topic in my discussion of the DE-STRESS model in Chapter Seven. Let me expand upon it here. Training is training, but practice makes—well, if not perfect, at least a little better. So the goal is to give kids the training they need, and then move aside to let them practice new skills. This will decrease dependence on adults. As practice allows new skills to become more automatic, these students will begin to trust themselves. They will come to know that it doesn't take a paid professional to allow them to taste the joy of mastery—to be successful. Students with LD and ADHD will be more responsible when they are response-able, and when they know it. When that happens, teachers (and instructional aides) can stand back and watch success happen, and know they had a role in it. After all, this is the goal of intervention, isn't it?

Universal Design for Learning Turns Students into Writers

The good news is that technology is allowing thousands of kids with learning challenges or disabilities to be productive despite some impediment to learning—to be more response-*able*. According to the National Center for Universal Design for Learning (www.udlcenter.org), Universal Design for Learning (also known as UDL) is a set of principles for curriculum development that give all individuals equal opportunities to learn. UDL promotes flexible approaches that can be customized and adjusted for individual needs.

For example, a speech recognition program such as Dragon NaturallySpeaking (DNS) allows the student with physical disabilities or dysgraphia to create volumes of language just by talking. I used DNS to dictate significant portions of this book and can attest to its ease of use and its practicality. While early users were sometimes frustrated by the inefficiency of previous versions of DNS, version 11 is far easier to use than any of the three earlier versions I have tried, and it is specifically designed to be responsive to the tonal quality of adolescent speech, and according to its parent website (www.nuance.com), "Dragon lets students dictate papers and assignments three times faster than typing—with up to 99% accuracy. It also lets them control their computer desktop and applications by voice to get more done faster—whether they're sending email, taking notes, doing research on the Web, or creating a presentation." I have recommended this program for many children who balk at writing or who have difficulty with the physical aspects of written communication.

Some kids are great at telling stories that flow flawlessly from their creative lips, but dread having to write things down. Turning thoughts into handwriting is actually a very complex process, and the use of speech recognition software effectively takes out the middle man. Talking about gaining control over your environment! Think how empowering it is to see your words appear, as if by magic, on a computer screen. Editing and rewriting are made much easier by this process. I recently met an eighteen-year-old with severe learning disabilities who had had, by anyone's standards, a very traumatic past. He told me that he wanted to "write his memoirs" so other kids could learn from his experiences, but added with embarrassment "but my writing sucks." His teachers recently loaded an iPod Touch with a mobile version of DNS, and the young author is delighted. I'm eager to see how his life story unfolds in this new medium.

Ha-Ha = Aha!

Humor enhances learning and memory. Talented teachers know that students hang on to words in a joke because they want to hear the punch line. They also know that humor, in the form of funny stories, puns, limericks, or cartoons, can increase a student's enjoyment of the activity. The brains of students who enjoy learning are less anxious, less *threatened*, and more likely to retain and apply what they learn. Teachers who spend time putting the lid on a funny student's comments or antics may be missing the opportunity to use that jester as a collaborator. Comedian Jim Carrey, whose antics are enhanced by his probable ADHD, tells this story on his website (www.jimcarey.org): "My teacher in the seventh grade told me that if I didn't fool around during class, I could have 15 minutes at the end of the day to do a comedy routine. Instead of bugging everybody, I'd figure out my routine. And at the end of the day, I'd get to perform in front of my entire class. I thought it was really smart of her. It's amazing how important that was."

There's a lesson to be learned here. Students who are not natural-born comedians can be given books filled with jokes they can learn and retell to classmates. Kids can be taught limericks that they can memorize and perform at class talent shows, or at home at the dinner table. Poems that tell funny stories, like those of Shel Silverstein, for example, might be just the thing to get a student up in front of a class to present, and in so doing earn the admiration of the rest of the class. (The box presents another story of a girl who found her stage presence in a very positive way.)

Nadia on Stage

Previous experiences with success or failure are a student's script-writer. Nadia has been burned by failure over and over again. Because she has ADHD, she can be impulsive and loud, often leaping to conclusions and blurting out wrong answers in class. When she was younger, she exhibited what one teacher described as *"excited little explosions of thought"* that back then seemed funny and cute. Now in high school, these outbursts are perceived by many teachers as attention-getting disruptions. To avoid being laughed *at*, Nadia now tosses out one-liners

(continued)

---

that Leno's writers would die for. The problem is that her jokes are seldom related to the topic of the class. They create ripples of laughter among her classmates that disrupt the flow of teaching and learning, and have gotten her labeled as a student with problems rather than a girl with promise. Fortunately, Nadia's guidance counselor has found a community theater group for her that's modeled after Chicago's famed Second City. If Nadia survives high school, we may yet see her on *Saturday Night Live*.

Watch Your Language: Be Nice!

Teachers need to remember that sarcasm and ridicule have no place in the safe classroom—or in any classroom. It may seem to a teacher that a particular student can take the barbs tossed out in class, but that's usually an erroneous assumption. In parrying the teacher's remarks, the student is using up psychological energy to cope with the tension that's created in such power-unbalanced interchanges. Teachers also need to think about the collateral damage they do to the kids (especially the anxious ones) who are looking on, hoping that they're not the next target of this teacher's verbal potshots. Those students may be tempted to skip class, and they certainly won't want to come to see that teacher for extra help after school, where there's no chance of escape if the teacher starts to tease.

If you're not sure if I'm talking about you here, turn on a tape recorder and let it run for a while. Play the tape back when you're alone. Or if you're still not sure, have a trusted friend or colleague listen. Just be prepared to hear what they have to say. If you have a colleague who's guilty of this charge, maybe you can offer to team-teach a lesson. This collaboration can open the door to collegial conversations about effective teaching, something that for some teachers has not occurred since they completed their student teaching.

Desperate Students Call for Desperate Measures

Ryan's story helps me make an important point about the critical role that teachers play in this child's life. Ryan has a challenging combination of language-based learning disabilities and ADHD. The impulsivity that often characterizes ADHD is not always a liability, but in Ryan's case, it is. Think of a frog, throwing out its tongue to catch a fly. This is rapid, goal-directed behavior that has a purpose and a payoff. Some people with ADHD use that trait to their advantage. Like the frog, Ryan's intentions may be good, but unlike the frog, his ability to plan and deliver is way off. In the classroom, the language he uses when his tongue goes into action lacks order and does not send a clear message. If Ryan *were* a frog, his tongue would fly out of his mouth, only to miss its mark and get stuck with a sizzle on the side of a sun-baked rock or a hot BBQ grill. Day after day, Ryan tries to join in simple conversations, or attempts to say something funny in the classroom. While it comes out quickly, it often doesn't make sense. Other kids don't want to sit with him in the cafeteria because they think he's irritating. They see him as an annoying, stupid kid who won't shut up. It's not easy bein' green . . . or bein' Ryan. He's sad and lonely, and he doesn't understand why the kids are so mean to him. You can be sure that Ryan spends a lot of time Saving FASE.

Sometimes he seeks out the company of adults, who try to help him articulate his ideas by asking leading questions, or by giving him multiple-choice questions or ones that can be easily answered yes or no. This is helpful to him, but it has resulted in his moving further away from social interactions with his classmates. He tends to seek the company of younger kids who don't seem to mind or understand his sometimes confused and confusing language, but who love the way he lets them play basketball with him. Since their language is less well-developed, he has an easier time understanding them, too. When Ryan is in his regular classes, he's chronically confused by the complex language that's being used around him, both by his peers and by his teachers. For Ryan, being in there is like being on holiday in China and not speaking Mandarin. He's always looking for a flight home, but can't ask for directions to the airport.

Can you imagine how hard it is for a boy like this to keep up with the flow of communication that's ubiquitous in the classroom, in the hallways, in the cafeteria? This persistent onslaught of input he can't make easy sense of, coupled with his difficulty expressing himself clearly and his impulsive style, keeps this boy in a state of chronic stress. His only safe haven is the ride home on the bus, but only because he is wired to his iPod or playing (but alas, not so well) his portable PlayStation.

What will help Ryan? It's obvious (again). Someone needs to explain his learning disability and his ADHD to him in a clear, concrete fashion. He has to be taught that no matter how difficult it might be for him (and it will be!), there are things his teachers can do—and things that he can do—to help him better navigate this confusing word-filled terrain. The school might want to have a behavior specialist or school psychologist observe Ryan in the classroom to look for patterns of linguistic confusion or counterproductive impulsivity and come up with an intervention plan that would help him be more successful at those times. For example, if they determine he's most confused at the beginning of classes, when instructions are given, they might recommend a check-in with his LSP at those moments. Or they might suggest that the teacher use pictures or other visual graphics to supplement his poor receptive language.

It would be great to offer Ryan a social pragmatics group (to learn the rules that govern social language or the practical aspects of communication) made up of kids with typical profiles and ideally typical peer role models who don't have these vulnerabilities. Inclusion in such a group setting would provide Ryan with the instruction he needs to improve his interpersonal communication as well as a chance to practice these new skills under the watchful eye of a guidance counselor, speech and language therapist, or social worker. Ryan's parents might want to talk to his pediatrician about a trial dose of stimulant medication to see if it helps him control his impulsive behavior. He might experience more success in a classroom or program specifically designed for students with language-based learning disabilities.

Wherever Ryan is placed, his teachers should have specific training about his condition and how to treat it, and also how the ADHD thrown into the mix makes matters worse—and what to do about that. I hope that Ryan's story reminds you of other kids with similar profiles. Perhaps you will read this section and say "I know how to do that." Or, you might say, "Hmmm, that reminds me of [so and so]. Never thought of him in that way." Either way, I've achieved my goal in telling you Ryan's story.

WHEN THE GEAR SHIFT GETS STUCK: STRESS AND COGNITIVE INFLEXIBILITY

Many students who are under stress experience difficulty with both behavioral and cognitive flexibility, which can compromise the efficiency of problem solving. Individuals who have difficulty moving fluidly from one idea to another are often described as rigid or inflexible thinkers. To lessen the anxiety caused by new tasks, these kids often prefer consistent routines. It may be difficult for students like this to stop thinking about certain topics or let go of sadness about disappointments or failures. They perseverate or obsess about certain themes or ideas. This trait is often seen in the profiles of students with NVLD or Asperger syndrome. These kids' limbic systems keep sending them messages tainted by negative emotion. As a result, the chronic stress they experience has rewired their brains to be more watchful, more cautious, and more easily upset. They may find it difficult to move beyond a specific disappointment or unmet need.

Another Look at Cognitive Rigidity

Anxious students are often unable to drop topics of interest because they are at that moment operating from a place of certainty or comfort. To change thoughts would produce anxiety. This helps to explain students who have difficulty putting on the brakes when asked to write about a topic of their own choosing. Some students with poor attention or language-based learning disabilities may need additional explanations or demonstrations in order to grasp the demands of a task when it's first presented. If they are unclear about what is expected, they get anxious. Anxiety clouds cognition. Hard-working (or perfectionistic) students with LD or ADHD may plug away at a task, trying to make it right, but because of weak executive functions (their ability to think, organize, and execute), they don't find success. They are on a slippery slope.

Some kids may approach tasks in a haphazard fashion, awash in anxiety, getting caught up in the details and therefore missing the big picture. This cognitive style may explain why some students have great ideas but can't express them efficiently on tests and written assignments. Interviewing a child like this can provide abundant evidence of knowledge about a subject, whereas the same child's written work may only provide evidence to support the diagnosis. Difficulty in seeing new ways to think about something can lead to perseverating on content or having difficulty shifting from one idea to another. This rigidity can also make it hard for a student to go from micro to macro, or move from a focus on details to the big picture and back again.

Stress to Go

Students under stress may also carry over a problem-solving approach, a response style, or information from an earlier task that does not relate to the new challenge. Their cognitive rigidity makes it difficult for them to clear out old ideas or old strategies. Even if they are not applicable, they are familiar; they are comforting. This helps to explain why it might be difficult for students with LD or ADHD to internalize and apply suggestions given by their teachers and their therapists. I have often heard teachers say something like: "She seemed to get it when I explained it to her, but the next day, or even later in the same day, the memory seems to have gone up in smoke." This is often interpreted as poor memory or weak executive functioning, but stress is the most likely culprit.

In the Event of an Emergency . . . In fulfilling its protective mission, a brain under stress is looking for an escape route. If it can't find one, it closes down or it retreats to what is known, what is comfortable. Stress shuts off the mind to new ideas. It impairs memory. Sometimes an inflexible or rigid style is a defense against anxiety-producing ambiguities. When we begin to look to stress as the culprit here, it becomes clear why learning new information is so hard for these kids. Unless the brain is convinced that the new information will make it safe, or make it feel better, it holds tenaciously to its old ways.

You're Not the Boss of Me! How often in the lives of kids with significant LD and ADHD do they have the chance to be in charge of anything? How much control do they really have over their lives? They are surrounded by paid professionals telling them what to do, when to do it, and how to do it. When they get it wrong, there is always someone there to witness it. When they get it right, the reward is more hard stuff to do. This underscores the importance of helping students attain a sense of mastery—defined as the consistent ability to get something—anything—right, all the time. It also speaks to the importance of giving students the opportunity to excel in nonacademic areas, like art, music, sports—or, say, ham radios. Remember: the more unusual the skill is, the less likely that someone else can do it well—or do it at all! This virtually guarantees a sense of mastery. I mean, how many people can make "Sailor's Valentines"? (If you're not from a seacoast town in New England, get Google to tell you about it.)

STRESS SOMETIMES FUELS SUCCESS

Fortunately, some kids under stress look for a positive outlet and become the best that they can be in this environment.

Meet Blake

Take Blake, for example. He's chronically anxious at school. He's a very poor reader trying to keep from being embarrassed in a reading-rich environment. He does not like to hang out with the smart kids for fear of being found out, and he's sensible enough to avoid the many temptations of the potheads and skateboarders. He's good at math computation, but word problems trigger high anxiety and frequent trips to the bathroom or the nurse's office. He misses a lot of school, particularly on exam days. He loves science but never does his homework. He has a language-based learning disability that makes it hard for him to speak in a fluid fashion, but he's the person you want to have with you on a nature field trip or on a fishing trip in Alaska. He is a Daniel Boone in a Daniel Webster world.

It comes as no surprise then that Blake is very confident and competent when it comes to working with horses and in his 4-H Club activities. This culture allows for kids to be alone with animals, who, despite their intelligence, do not read, and who are low-demand in terms of social interaction. (And their math skills are limited to the number of scrapes they can make on the ground with a hoof.) As a member of the 4-H Club, Blake regularly engages in group activities that are marked by regularity, ritual, and a common language that might even qualify as a form of social scripting. While there are certainly surprises and unexpected events in the world of animals, their activities are generally delineated by the domesticated rituals of the barn, trail, and paddock.

Many students with LD and ADHD have difficulties planning and organizing their work. This cognitive style may explain why Blake can have good ideas that he fails to express efficiently on tests and written assignments. He often feels overwhelmed by large amounts of information and may have difficulty retrieving material spontaneously or in response to open-ended questions. His compulsive, overworking style comes into active duty in the service of quelling anxiety created by the task. This helps to explain why he does better on "limited guess" activities, such as True/False or recognition (multiple-choice) questions.

Ahh, the liberation that comes from success! The key to the success of kids with ADHD and LD who are shutting down, acting up, or acting out because of academically induced stress is to give them opportunities to be successful and to enjoy the feelings that come with success. Kyesha's journey explains how this can happen, and what teachers can do to help.

Meet Kyesha

Kyesha had been receiving services under the provisions of an IEP since first grade, when she was diagnosed with a learning disability. Enrolled in a self-contained classroom for LD students, she had received specialized instruction with supplemental speech and language therapy and occupational therapy. As a result of these intensive services, Kyesha did fairly well in elementary school. She clearly benefitted from the specialized instruction and the additional support services, and acquired skills that the team felt would serve as the foundation for continued success in middle school.

For that reason, Kyesha was assigned to an "inclusion class" in the sixth grade. This was a class of twenty-seven students, co-taught by Ms. Grisham, a general education teacher, and Mrs. Brewer, a veteran special education teacher. Mrs. Brewer had fourteen years of experience working with students with learning disabilities. Kyesha was a little nervous about the transition to middle school, but her older sister was in eighth grade there and this helped pave the way. She started off doing well in the new class, but by mid-October, things started to go downhill.

In elementary school, Kyesha's curriculum had been modified, which in her case meant that some of the assignments were abbreviated so that they would take less time, and the introduction of new vocabulary was purposefully controlled by the teachers. The focus in elementary school had been on having students develop a sense of mastery over their work so that they would feel good about school and proud of their accomplishments. This approach worked well for Kyesha, who by the time she reached fifth grade felt both competent and confident as a student. Things started off well for Kyesha at the beginning of her sixth-grade year, probably because her teachers deliberately got things off to a slow start. However, the demands of a statewide curriculum and the lurking promise (threat?) of statewide standardized testing ramped things up rather quickly. Kyesha still possessed the skills that she had learned all through elementary school, and she knew what she had to do to master the individual assignments, but she began to feel overwhelmed by the volume and complexity of the sixth-grade curriculum.

She was also using a lot of energy trying to negotiate the sometimes perplexing social environment of middle school. What was in fashion one week was out the next. A popular girl could miraculously become a social outcast, seemingly overnight, because of something someone wrote or didn't write on Facebook, or because of a look given in the lunchroom. Kyesha watched her older sister breeze through school, always surrounded by a group of the coolest kids, and although she never told anyone, she was sure that she would never achieve such a status in this place in which rules, styles, and language changed so unpredictably. Kyesha, who had played soccer for several years, did not try out for the school team when the opportunity presented itself because she was sure she would mess up. Normally a talkative, bubbly, outgoing girl, she began to seem tense and troubled.

After hearing Kyesha sobbing uncontrollably in her bed one night, her mother asked her what was wrong. Through her tears, Kyesha proclaimed, *"Mom, I hate middle school! I feel like I've landed on another planet. I can't breathe there."* Alarmed, Kyesha's mother immediately contacted the school and set up a meeting with Kyesha's teachers and the school psychologist. The team was troubled to hear that Kyesha was so upset at home. They shared her mother's concern, but believed that Kyesha was just going through a difficult transition to middle school, and that she would soon become acclimated. They promised to monitor her performance and her emotional state very carefully and provide whatever supports she needed. The psychologist agreed to see Kyesha for a weekly check-in. Kyesha's mother shared the results of the meeting with her daughter, and was able to persuade her to go back to school and "give things another try."

After two months of reluctant attendance, even though she was well-supported by a team of qualified and caring professionals at school, Kyesha shut down. She ultimately refused to go to school, complaining one morning of a severe headache. After a visit to her pediatrician, who could find no physical reason for her pain, Kyesha's mother sought out a consultation with me.

I interviewed Kyesha about why she thought school was so much harder for her this year. It was clear to me that she felt overwhelmed, and had no sense of being able to turn this around. "What worked before isn't working now," she told me. I contacted Kyesha's teacher, Mrs. Brewer, whom I had met some years before during a consultation about a child in her class. After we talked, both of us agreed that as much as everyone hoped that Kyesha would be able to get back on track, this would not happen without some significant changes. I found it hard to imagine how Kyesha's needs could be addressed in a twenty-seven-student class with a fast-paced curriculum—even one taught by two talented teachers. If the right kind of support could be provided now, it could help to put her back on a positive trajectory. Perhaps with more intensive supports, she would be able to return to a more integrated program in short order. But for the moment, I felt that she was at significant risk. Troubled by Kyesha's precipitous downturn, I wrote the following letter advocating for an immediate change in her program:

> I have met several times with Kyesha S. and her parents. This little girl appears to be under a great deal of stress and I am deeply concerned about her mental health. It is my opinion that without a more intensive and specialized program of support, Kyesha's chances of performing at a level commensurate with her intellectual capabilities will be limited. It is difficult to imagine her being successful in a mainstreamed educational environment, especially as the curricular demands increase. I believe that Kyesha's mental health will deteriorate further, and that she is at risk for depression, if changes are not made immediately. I understand that the school has considered hiring a full-time instructional aide to support Kyesha in the integrated classroom, but it is my recommendation that she have the opportunity to experience a specialized learning environment designed for intellectually capable students with significant learning disabilities. Such a small

> group setting will be well-suited to her
> educational and emotional needs, and will allow
> her to access a curriculum that might be so
> complex and rapid-paced that it would otherwise
> leave her far behind her classmates.

I knew that this school strongly supported inclusion, or the education of students with special needs in as typical environment as possible. I have spent much of my career supporting responsible inclusion, but I did not think that Kyesha should go back to the integrated program; at least not yet. So I also wrote:

> While I am a staunch supporter of inclusive
> educational environments for children with
> special needs, I don't feel that even the most
> qualified instructional aide would be able to
> make the necessary modifications in curriculum
> delivery that would be an integral part of a
> self-contained LD classroom. Such a placement
> need not and should not preclude Kyesha's access
> to kids without significant learning difficulties.
> Indeed, she will continue to benefit from an
> inclusive educational environment, both socially
> and academically (through collaborative
> learning projects and shared educational and
> extra-curricular experiences), but she needs to
> have her education delivered in a small,
> substantially separate program.

Fortunately options were available, and a place was found for Kyesha in a classroom for students with language-based learning disabilities that was housed in the same middle school. The teacher was a charismatic young man who was like the Pied Piper of Special Education. He was so entertaining and he made the classroom such a fun place to be that typical students came by to ask if they could take science or social studies in his room.

This could have turned out differently, but sometimes the stars align, don't they? The brightness of this star teacher proved to be attractive enough to Kyesha that she agreed to return to school. She told her parents that she hoped this class would help her feel like she had during the past few years in elementary school—successful!

By the end of her sixth-grade year, Kyesha was generally staying one step ahead of the curriculum, had signed up for the girls' softball team (where *guess who* was the coach?) and was taking one of her courses in Mrs. Brewer's classroom.

The only way that the problem that I talk about in this book will be improved or eradicated is if administrators of special education are able to change the paradigm for delivery of service to students who have learning disabilities and ADHD. If school districts continue to provide services to kids with learning disabilities and ADHD without understanding the real problem underlying their difficulties, we will do more than perpetuate the problem. We will make it worse. If we, in the name of inclusion, pretend that we are going to meet the needs of students who have significant, neurologically based deficits of processing and attention in large classes with insufficient support for teachers and students, we will fail. By offering these students dribs and drabs of specialized instruction delivered in the guise of inclusive education, we are depriving thousands of kids of the "appropriate education" called for in federal legislation for students with special needs.

SYNERGY RULES!

I recently met man who told me that his specialization was "User Friendly." Hal is a psychologist specializing in human factors engineering. He spends his time making devices, software, and support services easier to use. I told Hal that a problem I was having with my computer had been described by a technician in an Indian call center—in a moment of candor—as "lying somewhere between the CPU and the chair." The implication was that it was I—and neither the computer nor the software—that was to blame for the problem. I of course interpreted this to mean that I was stupid. While I must admit that that is exactly what I was feeling at the time, Hal explained to me that human factors engineers who are committed to making things user friendly *never* see the problem residing within the user. Rather, the problem is always seen to lie in the software, the program, or the device that a user was, well . . . using.

In an epiphany, I asked if this concept could be or had ever been applied to the classroom. Without skipping a beat, Hal proclaimed, "As a matter of fact it *has*." He explained that back in 1987, Steve Mariotti was a math teacher working with disenfranchised urban youth. Trying to gain both the interest and the motivation of students in this class, Steve quickly discovered, much to his chagrin, that the students had no interest whatsoever in math. They were, however, interested in the economics of buying and selling things, both legal and illegal. *Oh, oh.*

Game on! While one might debate the relative merits of using an illegal substance as the basis for curriculum development, these students were absolutely "turned on" by a discussion about how they could maximize their profits on the street. Seizing this opportunity, Mariotti tapped into these kids' interests and got them hooked—not on crack but on business. Motivated by this experience, he created a program known as the Network For Teaching Entrepreneurship (NFTE), which according to its website has resulted in the education of more than 350,000 young urban adolescents in the basics of marketing economics. You can read more about this phenomenal project and the incredible stories of students involved in it at www.nfte.com.

What struck me as particularly relevant about the genesis of the NFTE was the clear message that unless the educational environment understood and responded to the needs of its clients, it was doomed to fail. In Hal's parlance, education, to be successful, had to be user friendly. Once a curriculum is matched to the learning style and interests of the students, success appears inevitable—perhaps *unstoppable*.

How might this line of reasoning be applied to the thesis of my book? Doesn't it make sense, I thought, that the classroom teacher—understanding the learning style of a particular student—should be able to design a curriculum that is well-suited to both the interests and the cognitive style of that student? Doesn't interest override anxiety? If this were true, as I believe it is—wouldn't success be virtually guaranteed? Then I was hit by the sobering reality that despite the best intentions of teachers and administrators in many schools, this explosion of potential seldom happens!

No doubt millions of IEPs have been developed with the intent of building a bridge between the characteristics of the learner and the characteristics of the curriculum. How many times, one must ask, does this actually happen? Far too infrequently. So what's the big disconnect? How hard can it be to teach kids in the way they learn?

How many classes are based on the theory of multiple intelligences advanced by that brilliant researcher Howard Gardner? How many classes are based on this intuitive, revolutionary, knock-your-socks-off concept, which attempts to capitalize on the natural strengths of learners? A thousand? Ten thousand? Clearly, not enough. If classrooms or schools were built on the premise that "we will teach children how they learn" and "we will ensure all students in our school will have the opportunity to experience mastery, at whatever level they can," I submit that we would have many more successful students and much less stress among our student population.

It's as I said earlier: students with learning disabilities and ADHD are actually easy to teach. We have decades of research that tells us how to do this with a reasonable degree of success. If we were to simply assume that all kids sitting in front of us have learning disabilities or attention-deficit/hyperactivity disorder, and we did what we are supposed to do—what research tells us to do—this stress issue would fly out the window. If we did that, you wouldn't be reading this book, and I would be off somewhere making jewelry or large, bizarre welded metal sculptures (which is what I do to relieve my own stress).

THOSE WHO CAN, DO!

I'm thinking back to the *Einstein and Me* video I described earlier in this chapter. Why is it that schools that are *created* to meet the needs of students with learning disabilities and ADHD seem to be able to do this job so well? Is it because they have more talented faculty? No! There are gifted teachers in every school in the world. I have observed that both schools that have more money and those that are struggling financially are able to create the kind of environments that reduce stress in kids, so it's not related to school budget. It may be because many of these schools do not live under the shadow of the standardized tests that control (yes) the curricula of many public schools and the teachers who work in them. There is a nearly universal belief on the part of public school teachers that "I have to get them ready for this test." As long as the performance of a teacher or a school is based on raising test scores and not on their ability to create successful, self-confident lifelong learners, a huge group of students, including those with LD and ADHD, will continue to fall behind. The dropout rate for these kids is notoriously high, and the percentage of students with LD or ADHD who fill our prisons give us the data to know that what we're doing for or to millions of students is just not working.

Performance that is self-motivated and not controlled by others is more creative and produces higher-quality work. Higher-quality work creates a better self-concept. A better self-concept creates more confidence. Increased confidence instills a sense of competence. *And the beat goes on* . . . (Sonny and Cher, 1967).

Teachers and administrators have the power to make changes that will enable kids with LD and ADHD to feel more competent, be more confident, be less stressed and more productive. It doesn't take more money to do this. It doesn't take miracles. It requires a paradigm shift. And that requires enlightened leadership. So I ask: are *you* an enlightened teacher or leader?

INTRODUCING THE HYBRID TEACHER

One of the major contributions of inclusion, when well conceived and well supported, has been the transformation that takes place when talented and motivated regular and special educators work together on a team. In my roles as a consultant and as a teacher educator in a university that embraced an inclusive philosophy and the practices that support it, I have witnessed the emergence of what I call the "hybrid teacher"—a new kind of professional who creatively builds bridges between curriculum and all kids, especially those with LD and ADHD. Let me use this opportunity to list some of the characteristics of this teacher, so that you will recognize one when you see one.

This is the kind of teacher who knows how to build kids up from the inside out, and in so doing enhances confidence and reduces the stress that affects the lives and learning of so many kids. In my view, a professional with many of the traits listed here is the closest thing I can find to a great teacher for kids with learning disabilities and ADHD. This list of traits is not intended as a report card for teachers, nor is it an effort to describe the ideal teacher. It is offered as a way to acknowledge both the challenges and the opportunities that exist for teachers working in tough times.

The Hybrid Teacher . . .

Understands the relationship between emotion and cognition. Except when working with a child who is known to have primary emotional disturbance, the first assumption is not that learning difficulties are the consequence of being upset. Instead, emotional reactions and in many cases negative behaviors are recognized as coping mechanisms triggered by the stress generated by frustration and fear of what a child sees as inevitable failure. This understanding is neither an excuse nor a reason to allow the student to excuse this behavior; it is a way to help explain it and work through it or around it. The hybrid teacher also understands that many of these negative emotions and troubling behaviors go away when students feel competent and successful.

Knows that students learn in different ways, but does not trivialize this by offering a simplistic explanation like: "Lee's a visual learner." The hybrid teacher says things like: "Because testing and my observations have confirmed that Jamilla can't hold on to the auditory images of [sounds, syllables, words, sentences, paragraphs, my voice, the voices of many kids and teachers in the cafeteria, the sequence of directions, and so on and on], I need her to understand that (1) this task is going to be difficult and (2) that she has the skills, or that I am going to teach her the skills to handle this task, and (3) that some of the other kids may not have to use these tools, but that she does, and (4) that she will be successful if she does."

Focuses on the learner first and the curriculum second, taking the student to a place of cognitive and psychological safety before venturing into deeper waters of new material. Reviews focus not on what was taught yesterday but on the student's feeling of success with that material. This teacher understands the importance of creating a positive connection to prior learning, of tapping into a student's positive emotions about a task or a topic, and helping students recognize and reduce negative influences on learning (for example, automatically saying or thinking: I can't *do* math!") by practicing thought-stopping techniques and generating positive self-statements that are tied to actual successful experiences.

(continued)

Demonstrates the ability to expose students to a variety of stimuli, knows when students are connected emotionally and cognitively to the experience, and also gives students the opportunity to demonstrate what they have learned in a variety of ways, publicly valuing these alternative ways to display knowledge and skills.

Is guided and energized by finding out what facilitates effective learning and what gets in the way. The focus of teaching is to minimize the impediments by educating learners about their own cognitive styles, modifying the curriculum without lowering standards, and creating a learning space in which students can feel safe and competent.

Praises the process that students use as often as the product, or more, since the product may be substandard (in the child's perception or in reality) even if the process is right. Teachers who ask kids "how did you get that answer" generally get a scowl or a "huh?" response, which isn't very reinforcing. When hybrid teachers get a blank stare in response to this question, they give the student a couple of possible choices ("because you took all the distracting things off your desk," or "I noticed that you put on the headphones to block out the noise from the classroom"). This can generate an "Oh, yeah" response; the next time the question is asked, that student is more likely to come up with an answer that addresses the process of figuring something out. That's the behavior of a successful learner.

Understands that it's not about having kids work harder, but rather that they work smarter. Hybrid teachers ask kids what strategies they have used in the past to be successful in any kind of learning (in school or outside it) and help to translate that skill and recreate that positive learning experience in the classroom. We all know the student who can take apart and rebuild a computer but can't read. The hybrid teacher focuses on how the student learned to do the former and uses that knowledge as a basis for specialized instruction in reading. If a child says "I remember everything I see," this teacher ought to be able to capitalize on that strength by developing a sight word vocabulary that will jump-start more difficult reading.

Knows that it's important to separate skill instruction from content acquisition. A blind student may not be able to read small print, but can certainly learn content. Making modifications in that case is a no-brainer. Hybrid teachers keep that image in mind when they work with students with visual perceptual difficulties that get in the way of fluent reading. Remember that when poor readers rely on reading to gain knowledge, they miss a lot of information. Students who have problems holding words or sounds in working memory simply cannot benefit from a lecture that's not supported by visual cues. Remember what it's like to know just a little Spanish when you try to understand those rapidly delivered directions to the airport in Mexico City.

Is willing to take a risk when it comes to advocating for a student with LD or ADHD in the classroom. It takes courage to tell an administrator, "This kid will just not be successful without some significant supports— more than I'm able to give in this classroom even though I'm awesome."

Examines classroom practices to identify what works and what doesn't. These teachers are more likely than other teachers to want to work with another adult, ask for feedback about performance, go to professional conferences and in-service training with the needs of individual students in their heads, and be willing and able to teach others what they know.

Knows how to work in a team with the student as the key member. Building and maintaining relationships with the family takes time and a sincere desire to hear the family's story. Giving the family the time to tell a teacher what worked and what didn't in the past, or what the struggles are around homework, yields data that may be more important than any test score. Reaching out to physicians to get and give information if medication or health issues are involved is another important skill. Working with ancillary personnel in the school (speech therapists, occupational therapists, and the like) and helping them help the teacher incorporate therapeutic interventions in the classroom is critically important.

Understands that cultural and language factors play an important role in learning. Just because a student speaks good English, that doesn't rule out the possibility of confusion between the first and second language or that delays in language processing or reading are related to the simultaneous translation that's going on in the student's head. Hybrid teachers are able to read subtle but important behaviors such as eye contact or physical proximity, and accurately interpret them in the social and cultural context of the child. They know how to differentiate a language difference from a learning disability—or who to ask.

(continued)

Is able to cover the curriculum by understanding the child. To consider each child as a unique individual is for these teachers not just a euphemism; this belief is acted upon minute by minute, even in large and diverse classrooms. Each child is connected to the teacher by a line. For some students, it's a gossamer spider's thread that registers every movement of the learner; for others it's a ship's cable that takes a powerful action to get it to move. The hybrid teacher is connected to kids and kids are connected to this teacher most of the time. This allows the teacher to be responsive to not only the student with LD and ADHD but to all learners in the classroom.

Author's note: I know that there are other traits that distinguish the hybrid teacher. The reader can add to this list, as I will as time goes on. *By the way, I forgot to mention: The hybrid teacher is always a twin, or has been cloned, so that one of them can sleep, eat, do research on best teaching practices, and go to the toilet while the other teaches.*

In all seriousness, it is a delight to watch these teachers in action. They are everywhere if you look. They may be young or old or professionally trained or natural teachers. Parents need to seek them out, reward them, advocate for more time, money, and resources to support them, praise them for their work, and bring them flowers. If your child gets one of these teachers every two or three years, school is probably going to be OK. Administrators need to pay these people more money, praise them more, show them off more. They are the hope for children with learning disabilities in these challenging times, and my experience suggests that we have reason to be hopeful.

If you are a teacher, I hope that you embody the traits I have outlined here. If not, I hope that you aspire to become a hybrid teacher—that multitalented professional who holds the key to success for the children about whom this book was written—and that this book helps you attain your goal. If you are an adminis-trator, I hope that you oversee or plan to create an environment in which both teachers and their students with LD and ADHD can attain their highest potential. I wish you well.

In the next chapter, I speak directly to parents, offering them some words of advice and messages of hope.

9

Parents and Families

Home Is Where the Heart (and the Heartache) Is

> I got a lot of support from my parents. That's the one thing I always appreciated. They didn't tell me I was being stupid; they told me I was being funny.
>
> —Jim Carrey

> I attribute my success to my parents. No matter how bad things got for me, no matter how frustrated or defeated I felt, I was always sure they believed in me. They knew that I was smart and capable. While I was growing up, they were my anchor. Now that I'm an adult, and they're not around anymore, they still are.
>
> —John H., age forty-six

Some kids have enough personal glue to keep things together during a long school day, but absolutely combust when they walk through the front door of the family home—*your home*. No matter how well your kids handle their day at school, it's often at home where the proverbial stuff hits the fan. Your child may have managed well enough to get by in school, but finds it impossible to keep up this front all day long.

Kids need some down time to process what has happened to them during the past seven or eight hours. They need to recharge their personal batteries so they can get up the next morning *and do this all over again*. It's seldom pleasant when your son or daughter crashes when they walk through your front door, but as you've come to appreciate how much energy it takes to make it through a long and challenging day, you might be able to understand this reaction. Since LD and ADHD tend to run in families, it's quite likely that you might have had a similar experience. In this chapter I introduce some families whose stories bring to life the challenges typical around a child with LD or ADHD (or both) who's under stress. More important, I'll give you some practical advice about what you can do to help children recharge their batteries at home, so they're ready to face the both the challenges and the joy of success that tomorrow holds in store for them at school.

WHAT FAMILIES CAN DO AND UNDO

ADHD and LD-related stress affects not only the child but the whole family—parents, brothers and sisters, even the extended family. By focusing on LD and ADHD at home, I hope to offer parents and other caregivers some very practical advice about how they can help children with LD and ADHD take control over their anxiety and experience a greater sense of mastery. As a result, children can be happier and more productive not only at home but at school and on the playground or playing field.

I also take a look at the role other children play in the home. Younger and older siblings and the way they interact with a brother or sister can literally make or break a child with special needs. The same can be said of parents who are impulsive or grandparents who muck things up when they just want to help. Even aunts, uncles, and cousins can have a positive or negative influence. This chapter will help you understand the relationship between home and school, how different individuals in the family circle view learning or attention difficulties and their treatment, and what people say and do that can make things worse . . . and especially, how they can make things *better*. First a little background.

LD and ADHD-Related Stress: A Family Affair

It's quite likely that children with ADHD and LD live in families with others who have these same conditions. While estimates vary depending on which research you read (and when it was done), it is generally acknowledged that genetics plays a role in about 50 percent of children diagnosed with ADHD. This means that for about half of the kids who have this diagnosis, one or more family members likely have it too. The family connection holds true for LD as well; about a third of the children born to a parent with dyslexia are likely to have this type of learning disability. There's another confounding factor: depending on the source you read, recent research suggests that there is about a 30 percent to 50 percent overlap between these two conditions. That means that one-third to one-half of the children who have LD are also likely to have ADHD as a comorbid condition.

This means that in many families, one or both parents or one or more siblings may have LD, ADHD, or a combination of the two. Climbing out farther on the branches of the family tree, you are likely to find a grandparent or even a great-grandparent who displayed the symptoms of either condition, or both. Since the terms are relatively new, any diagnosis will have to be inferred by looking back at accomplishments or difficulties that these older folks may have had. Old report cards (or their absence) and family lore often paint a picture of a relative who most certainly had either or both conditions. The point here is that LD and its close cousin ADHD both tend to run in families, and fairly often they live together under one roof, sometimes within one or more people who live under that roof. Let me now tell you a story that underscores the impact that ADHD can have on families, especially when more than a couple of people have it.

Rick's Story

Many years ago, I had the opportunity to work with a family that stayed together by living apart. The dad, Rick, was an electrician. The nicest guy you'd ever want to meet. A stalwart, hard-working provider; a quiet, even-tempered rock for his family. Mom was an upbeat, funny, and energetic woman who flitted from one clever and witty idea to another like a butterfly on speed. This was a great couple. In family therapy sessions, their love and respect for each other was palpable, and their concern for their kids was profound.

I got to know these folks after I had done an evaluation of their youngest daughter that confirmed a diagnosis of ADHD. She had been having increasing difficulty in school and the parents were pretty sure that ADHD was a factor. The parents were very familiar with this condition, since the mom and one of their two sons had been given this diagnosis two years prior, before they had moved from another state. After I had carried out the evaluation, the parents asked if I would see them for family therapy to help them quell some of the chaos that reigned in their home. Much of the time, three-fifths of the family members were forgetting things, losing stuff, being late for school, getting into scraps over frustrating homework, and negotiating or arguing endlessly about things that even they said, in retrospect, that were of little real significance. The kids' friends seldom came to this house to play—way too much confusion, yelling, and mess. Yet in all of this chaos, people seemed to have fun!

Well, *most* people . . . Remember Rick? Thank goodness for his constellation of character. Rick was the force that often stabilized his family, which could have served as the "poster family" for the genetic basis of ADHD. Even though medication had been helpful for the mom and one son (and they would be exploring its use with the little girl), guess when the effect generally wore off? Right. Just about the time Rick came home.

Now imagine this scene: Dad, who specializes in rehabbing old houses for resale, has been working since dawn, stringing miles of wire through ancient dusty walls, testing circuits, climbing on ladders, putting up fixtures, working with and around his contracting crew, dealing with inspectors, and connecting high-voltage lines from the street to house, confident that everything he had touched would work well once he threw the main switch. He was a man in his element; a master of his craft. It was only when this confident, competent electrician walked through his front door that sparks began to fly!

One evening, when the mom and kids were scheduled to be three places at once (!), she called to cancel a scheduled family therapy session. Apparently, Rick had not gotten this message, because he showed up at my office right on time, having come straight from work. He was dusty, disgruntled, and disappointed to find out that the family would not be coming. "This clinches it," he muttered, shaking his head sadly. Leaning forward, fingers drumming nervously on his knees, he said, "I guess I better tell you about this." *How many secrets have I heard behind my office door? How many confidences shared? This one was big.*

Rick told me that he had been retrofitting a three-family house down the street from theirs, and that instead of selling it, he was going to rent out two floors, and . . . keep the other one for himself. He and his son Robby (the only child without ADHD, and a *lot* like dad) were going to live there! This was not about a separation, Rick said, "It's about sanity." He explained, with much sadness, "I love my wife. I love my kids. But I feel so stressed all the time when I'm there. I can't stand the constant ruckus. Each morning I go to work and when I'm on the site, I am in total control of everything I see. I can figure out what's wrong and I have the knowledge and the skills to fix it. I feel good at work. But when I get home, it's like I walk into a hurricane—and not the eye. There is no peace, no quiet. And you know what, Doc? . . . I can't fix it."

Rick said that he had been struggling with this for a long time. He was worried because Robby was falling behind in school because of the chaos at home and because the other kids needed (and got) so much attention. He had talked to his parents (who always stayed in a hotel when they came to visit his family!) and to his minister, who knew the kids (well!) from Sunday school. Rick told me, "If I were a drinker, I'd be going to a bar every night before I came home to get courage from a bottle—but I'm not." It was obvious to me that this was tearing him up inside. One night as he lay in bed sleepless, Rick said the answer came to him, accompanied by sense of relief mixed with grief. He and his son Robby would use the house down the street as their apartment. Rick, pragmatist that he was, said he figured this was just like putting an addition on his house, but making it far enough away that he wouldn't hear the screaming, running, crashing, and arguing that seemed to go on nonstop.

He had the plan well thought out. The other kids could come and visit, but at first, only one at a time. Their friends could come over too, attracted to the calm and quiet of the new space. They could do sleepovers; have normal kid fun. He'd have frequent meals with the family in the main residence, and sometimes they'd all come to what he was going to call the "annex" to eat with him. He also looked forward to the times when they'd get a sitter for all the kids at the main house, so that he and his wife could re-connect with each other at the annex and enjoy quiet conversations (and sex), neither of which they had had much time or energy for in the big house.

A Drastic Measure? Yes, perhaps—but this story points out how ADHD can impact a family's life. It's not surprising that the rate of separation and divorce is so high in families that have a child with a disability. When I hear from frustrated teachers, "Things would be so much better for this child if the parents would only . . ." I tell them Rick's story. They always get the point. Whether parents are trying to help a son or daughter cope with the stresses of school and playground, or it's about finding peace and quiet, or trying to avoid the blame and shame that often factor into the family life of a child with disabilities, this is hard, hard work.

How Did Rick's Story Turn Out? Sadly, I don't know. Shortly after his poignant disclosure, I learned that Rick's dad had been diagnosed with cancer. The family was moving back home, and Rick was going to take over the family business with his brother. Maybe Grammy's house became the new annex.

Language Matters

Our unique human capacity to use language can make stress worse or make it better. While a fish reacts reflexively to imminent danger (and probably does not think about it too much), we humans (and other primates who use sign language, like chimpanzees, gorillas, and orangutans) can use language to calm ourselves down—or to work ourselves into a real frenzy. The language-trained chimp can hold up a hand and wildly gesticulate the sign for "trouble." The anxious student may be heard saying things like, "This is way too hard!" or "This is boring [or stupid]," or "This is stressing me out!" Even if they are not saying these things out loud, their behavior tells us that they may be thinking, "Where's the exit? This is way too hard for me!" Or "I remember how awful I felt that last time I had to do something in public like this."

When we can talk to ourselves about solutions ("I know what I can do about this") or when we can use language to offset our perceptual weaknesses, success is more likely. That's why it's important for parents to try to get their kids to talk about their learning problems, *and* the ways to make them better. A child who speaks about solutions is a child headed down a road to success. By reacting to a child's difficulties with positive suggestions and messages of hope, family members can keep a boy or girl on a positive path toward improvement. The moral of this tale is this: Parents, watch your language. What you say can make all the difference in the world. Remember to invoke "I can and I will" when you talk to your children about their difficulties.

In the next story, you'll read about how the superior verbal skills of a young man not only offset his visual-perceptual weakness, it gave him the tools to talk it out with his parents, his teacher, and his tutor.

Like Son, Like Father

The apple indeed does not fall far from the tree . . . Seventeen-year-old Daniel tended to tense up whenever he had to do math or anything that involved numbers or calculation, especially in his math class (with twenty-six students), but also in a one-to-one situation with a tutor in a quiet room. A neuropsychological evaluation had revealed that Daniel had a learning disability, characterized by slow processing speed and significant weakness in visual-perceptual skills. His working memory (the ability to hold images or words or thoughts) was in the average range, and his verbal skills (his use and understanding of language) were in the superior range. This uneven neurocognitive profile had resulted in challenges in math over the years, and his frustration and failures had caused him to be wary when any task involving numbers came into his path.

His language-based skills helped him a bit in algebra, which presented mathematical concepts in a linear manner. The equations could be thought of almost as number sentences with a beginning, middle, and ending (with some information left out just to make it interesting). Geometry was another story. On the testing, when Daniel was asked to copy a complex figure (in the Rey-Osterrieth Complex Figure Drawing assessment), he drew the figure piece by piece. The pieces didn't fit together in a cohesive way. As a result, his rendition was filled with so many distortions that his drawing barely resembled the model he was copying. When asked to draw the design again from memory, the distortions and misplacements became worse and the essence of the drawing went up in smoke. There was no similarity between it and the model he had seen just minutes before.

This evaluation confirmed a diagnosis of dyscalculia, a specific disability in math. His parents told me that although Daniel had written stories from an early age, he would "never get anywhere near puzzles or Legos." It's easy to understand the impact of this lifelong weakness on geometry, which involves the perception and manipulation of shapes and designs, and explains why this boy might not love math.

After the testing, I explained to Daniel and his parents how his difficulty with short-term visual memory for complex shapes was a big factor in his struggles in geometry. I also explained to them how after years of challenges in math, his brain had learned to regard anything related to math or visual perception as a threat. Any task that might have required the perception and manipulation of shapes now served as an automatic trigger, signaling his brain to put up its defensive shield. I also pointed out how his early frustrations with math had created a negative mind-set about numbers in general, and how he was caught up in a vicious cycle of fear, avoidance, confrontation, frustration, and failure, a pattern that had repeated itself thousands of times over the years.

Hmmm!?! It was at this point in the process that Dan's dad learned forward and said, "Forgive me for interrupting, Doc, but this is amazing! You could be describing *me!* I always knew math was hard for me, and I had to hire personal tutors to help me get through graduate school—but as I listen to you talking about Danny—you could be talking about *me!*"

Since learning disabilities often run in families, this revelation did not come as great shock to me, but Dan's father's recognition that he might have suffered from the same kind of math disability as his son hit him like a tsunami. He leaned forward and implored, "Go on . . . Go *on!* I think I'm getting a two-fer here," referring to the evaluation I had completed. Daniel smiled in wonderment as he began to realize that he and his dad might be members of the same club.

As I continued to explain my findings, I noticed that Daniel's father sat wide-eyed in apparent recognition of the symptoms I was describing. He nodded in acknowledgment when I talked about how, when Daniel faces tasks he believes might be difficult, his brain puts up its defenses to prepare him to deal with the stress-producing situation. I pointed out how this may give rise to negative self-talk. Daniel told me that he often said to himself things like, "This is going to be difficult" or "I can't do problems like this" or other comments that are associated with the flight reactions of someone under stress. His father just sat back and listened as the boy told the story that was in many ways his own.

I pointed out that during the testing, when I asked Daniel to do anything that involved numbers, there was a notable increase in his anxiety (heavy sighing, erasing and redoing several problems, uttering disparaging comments under his breath about his dislike of math). This transformation was rapid and dramatic—

and reversed itself when we moved back into the domain of language. Dan's father, an attorney, smiled and said, "Thank God for the Law." He told his son that math had been the bane of his existence, but that his language and problem-solving skills served him well in school and now in his chosen career. He said that this difference between his verbal skills and his math skills probably had a lot to do with his ultimate career choice. When we discussed the pattern of math and geometry becoming automatic triggers for defensive shields, creating a vicious cycle of fear, avoidance, confrontation, frustration, and failure—a pattern that had repeated itself thousands of times over the years—Daniel's father instantly replied, "I know exactly what you're talking about. That's why my wife does the taxes for our family!" At this point, Daniel's mother, who had been listening to this conversation with a knowing smile, simply nodded.

Daniel was intrigued by my interpretation of his learning disability, and was clearly a little surprised but encouraged by his very successful father's disclosure. As a result of this evaluation and the discussion that ensued, Daniel was highly motivated to learn new strategies to overcome his weaknesses. Both father and son were intrigued when they heard the approach that the testing supported, which involved the purposeful pairing of visual symbols with more abstract numbers.

The parents subsequently hired a tutor who served as Daniel's learning coach. She helped him mentally prepare for math in order to gain a positive mind-set before he faced the challenge of new material. She built bridges of competence by helping Daniel achieve success on progressively more difficult problems, and by helping him use his strong language skills to counteract the anxiety-filled messages that his brain had been sending to him.

I learned later that Daniel had started to take a morning yoga class with his dad, partly because it gave him some time to bond even more with his father (whose physician had suggested the yoga), but also because his soccer coach had told the players that it could improve their mental attitude and their game. His mom began to present "mental math challenges" to Daniel on the ride home from school. Because this activity was done in the privacy of the car and was fun, Daniel's negative reactions to math began to decline in frequency and duration.

Daniel took his newly acquired self-understanding and turned it into self-advocacy. Because of his exceptional verbal skills, he was able to articulately explain his learning disability (dyscalculia) to his teachers and tell them about the strategies he had learned from his tutor that helped him to be more successful. In this way, he felt a sense of mastery over the condition, even if his brain-based learning disability continued to present him with challenges. His father was proud of his son's ability to "state his case," and acknowledged that he was just a little jealous that Daniel had been able to find out relatively early in his life why some aspects of math were so challenging.

Daniel's parents supported him throughout this process, suggesting that he drop computer-assisted design, an extracurricular activity that was not well-suited to his learning style and that was frustrating him. Instead, they encouraged him to try out for the school's debate team, through which he achieved some degree of fame throughout the district and in national competitions for his incredible ability take any side in an argument and convincingly drive this point of view home to others. In a follow-up visit, he was a self-assured and confident young man. He told me that he was thinking about law as a career (surprise, surprise!), and he expressed his own understanding about his vulnerabilities (and how to overcome them): "I hope that if I have children someday they won't expect me to help them put together model planes." He added with a smile, "And I guess I'd better find a wife with great eye-hand coordination!" His father smiled, looked sweetly at his wife (an accomplished knitter), and said: "That's what *I* did!"

Stories about LD don't always have such happy endings. Unless they are properly addressed, these neurologically based differences in processing style, especially when paired with variable attention, create stress not only in students but also in their families. A child who is operating under stress during the day often brings emotional baggage home on the school bus. While it's the child who has the problem, this is very much a family matter.

WHEN A CHILD NEEDS MORE HELP THAN PARENTS CAN PROVIDE

If a child is really down in the dumps about the situation in school, a supportive family atmosphere, while very important, might not be enough to stop a nosedive into sadness and depression. Parents may seek out a therapist who specializes in stress reduction techniques such as thought-stopping and thought-shifting, methods that allow a child to put the brakes on negative self-statements and turn these into self-directed cheerleading. Under the care of a qualified therapist, your child can be taught how to tune in to and change those negative inner messages that, protective as they may be on one level, still impede learning and have a deleterious impact on memory.

Therapists who practice cognitive-behavioral psychology use this method extensively. Thought-stopping involves realizing that what we're saying to ourselves is preventing us from finding success. The next step is thought-shifting, the conscious substitution of a positive message to self. This can be something like "I can and will do this," or "My brain is reading this as a bigger challenge than it is," or "I've done things like this before," or "What's the worst thing that could happen if I mess this up?" Thought-stopping is kind of like when you realize that you're driving way too fast, and you take your foot off the gas. That action immediately slows down the speeding car, and if it's not quite enough, a gentle foot on the brake pedal will take care of the rest. If kids like Daniel are helped to realize when they are using negative self-talk and how to stop the thought in its tracks and change it into something else, they can shut off some of the language that not only reflects but also fuels the fires of stress.

Meditation is also a helpful technique to reduce the stress associated with performance anxiety. Relaxation-inducing, success-oriented mantras can be brought into service when needed. Kids who are into sports but plagued by anxiety might enjoy learning about managing stress by thinking positively from *The Mental ABC's of Pitching*, a short book by H. A. Dorfman. The ideas and strategies found in this excellent little book, which have improved the game of many major league pitchers, can be easily transported to academic work.

"I CAN'T HELP IT. EVERYONE IN MY FAMILY IS TIGHTLY WOUND"

Like LD and ADHD, anxiety can run in families—another example of a comorbid condition. It's quite possible then that a child who has a learning disability or ADHD might also have the genes that predispose him or her to generalized or situational anxiety. So now we're talking about the combination of performance-induced anxiety and stress with biologically endowed anxiety layered on for good measure. Anti-anxiety medication, therapy, meditation, yoga, and vigorous exercise can all be helpful ways to reduce anxiety in a person who is biologically predisposed to it.

What if someone (or OMG, *everyone!*) in the family *is* tightly wound? And a child with LD or ADHD lives in that same house? What is the impact of environmental stress on LD and ADHD? You know that one of the first things a parent hears at "back to school night" is to "make sure your son or daughter has a quiet, organized space in which to do homework." What if your house is always in state of anxiety-ridden chaos? What then? Difficult as it is, you need not only to address the stress created by toxic learning situations but also to work on the environment at home to minimize the effects of anxiety pollution and contagious anxiety.

Shhh! She's Listening!

The observation that family stress makes anxiety worse is especially important when that anxiety is generated by serious concerns about the difficulties a child with LD or ADHD is having at school. Things really get bad when parents (or grandparents) can't contain their worry and it spills over into the environment of the child. I can't tell you how many times I've been talking with a parent on the phone about a child's problems, only to hear a side comment addressed to the child, indicating that the subject of our conversation is right there in the room. This means that child has been in earshot of the parent's agitated and often tearful communication with me. In such situations, I actively intervene, asking the parent if we can talk privately, or if we can reschedule a telephone appointment at a time when a child is at school, or asleep. Most parents respond positively to this suggestion, saying something like, "You are so right, what were we thinking?" Their anxiety, fueled by their legitimate worries about their child, has taken a front seat and has clouded their judgment.

In the early years of my practice, I used to be surprised when parents brought a child to my office for an interview prior to a neuropsychological evaluation and talked freely about their anxieties in front of their child. Driven by their desire to find someone who could help, a parent often launched into an upsetting stream of worries about their son or daughter. Sometimes they spoke about the disappointment they felt about the child's lack of progress, or relayed a story about a very negative relationship with a teacher or administrator—all while the child was sitting, often teary-eyed, in the chair next to them. This happened so regularly early in my practice that I changed my approach to interviewing families. In addition to speaking to the parent and child together (which gave me a wonderful opportunity to see how they communicated, and how they both dealt with the stress produced by being in a strange new setting), I also make time to speak to the parent individually, and let both the adult and the child know that prior to the first visit. I tell the child that we'll have lots of time to talk alone during the testing, which generally takes place in two three-hour sessions, spaced a week apart.

Contagious Anxiety

A parent who is an anxious person may have a particularly difficult time keeping anxiety-generating information private. Here's a story that helps paint a picture of how this plays out. A teacher recently sought my advice about how to help the parents of one of her five-year-old students. The little girl, Jamie, was exhibiting a delay in speech and language, having difficulty keeping up in school, and had begun to call herself "stupid." Jamie's mom, who was by the teacher's account "a very nervous woman," worried aloud and often about her child. The teacher was concerned about the impact of the mom's anxiety on her little girl, and wanted my advice about how to talk to the parent about this.

I told her that as the little girl's teacher, she might be able to help just by giving the mom the time to talk about her worries. Once the teacher has established a level of trust, she might be able to explain that she understands that any parent could get upset about these things, but that it's important to try hard not to let this worry show when Jamie is around. I told the teacher, "Someone needs to let this woman know how important it is not to let Jamie overhear her talking about her worries with her husband, friends, grandparents, or with professionals on the phone." I also told her that the parents may need to talk with a psychologist or social worker who can help support and guide them through this very difficult time. I suggested that the teacher tell the mom that she should not discuss her concerns about this problem with Jamie, other than to assure her that "we'll do everything we can to make this better." In the meantime the mom should be encouraged to reinforce what Jamie is doing well, and praise her publicly (and sincerely—don't blow it out of proportion) for her accomplishments. If Jamie's dad is a calming presence, her mom might want to let him take some of the action steps that will help their daughter get the help she needs, like talking to the therapist or communicating with the teacher or others working with Jamie. Whereas mom's anxiety might act as a filter that keeps her from finding comfort in their comments, perhaps dad will be able to hear the reassuring words of these folks and reinterpret them to his wife. Of course this situation could be reversed. An anxious and reactive dad, ready to do battle with any enemy of his daughter's happiness, might be encouraged to keep his sword in its scabbard by his calm and even-tempered spouse.

Work Behind the Scenes

Parents need to work quietly in the background, doing whatever they are going to do with as little fanfare as possible. Promising a child that you are going to "fix the problem" may seem comforting, but it may in fact create an expectation, and the child may then focus obsessively on the promise. "When are you going to talk to Mrs. Johnson, Mommy?" "Did you call my teacher today? I've been thinking about this all weekend. What do you think she'll say, Mommy?" Parents need to act calm and relaxed around their child, and stay focused on the child's positive features and actions. Kids like Jamie deserve and need to have a happy childhood, and shielding them from parental stress and anxiety is a part of creating an environment that will allow them to meet their fullest potential. This is also the foundation for a positive self-concept, which could be eroded very quickly if they sense their parents' worry.

WELL-MEANING? RELATIVELY SPEAKING . . .

I will tell you that being a grandparent carries with it joys that my wife and I could not have imagined years ago. Seeing these little wonders spring forth from our gene pool is confirmation that miracles do in fact happen. Grandparents often tell you why this position is so great: "You can spend a few hours or days with the grandkids, spoil them rotten, and then give them back."

There's a bit of a conflict of interest at work here, though. The parents of your grandchildren are your children. Even as a grandparent, you can never stop being a *parent*. And although the kids are in their thirties, forties, and fifties, some grandparents can't turn off the parenting switch, which they believe gives them the right to weigh in on just about everything from naptime to nuptials. For better or worse—and it varies from culture to culture—elders have an incredible amount of *potential* influence on the lives of the next two (or three, if they stay healthy) generations. Whether they exercise this influence, or more specifically *how* they exercise it, is the source of much consternation in the lives of young parents.

There are probably a few folks who have worked out this delicate balance of roles very well. Most, I think, are still working on it. My wife and I were reminded of our status by our younger daughter's gentle but frank reminder: "You had your turn, Mom and Dad. This one's *ours!*" She's right, and we did. And somehow, together my wife and I created an environment that turned out a pair of open, honest, self-assured daughter-mothers who, with their wonderful husbands, are creating the next generation of our family, and doing it exceptionally well. That helps us be content standing back and watching how they do it, and "kvelling" from a respectful distance (if you don't know what *kvelling* means, you can *kugel* it). I know. Bad joke. I got that from *my* father.

But enough about my family. What about yours? If you are a parent of a child with LD or ADHD, are *your* parents—the grandparents of your kids—helpful? Does their behavior or the language they use make things better or worse? Are you in the market for an intergenerational family therapist? Evan's mom is . . .

This question came in via my website. I've changed it a little and am reprinting it with her permission. When I got it, I felt like the Dear Abby of Dyslexia.

> Dear Dr. Schultz,
>
> My son Evan has a learning disability. He is 15 and has had multiple evaluations by school psychologists, clinical neuropsychologists, neurologists, etc., etc. There is no doubt in my mind about this disability. I myself am dyslexic. I understand Evan's struggles, and his teachers "get" him. Evan understands his problems very well and in fact, he's a great self-advocate—but Doc, my husband's parents just don't get it. They, in particular my ex-marine father-in-law, think that the diagnosis is a "crock" and insist to me (and on the times when we let them see him, to Evan) that all he has to do is buckle down and work his "a _ _" off. I am so upset by this constant barrage of denial and promises/threats ("We'll take you to Europe with us if you pull yourself out of this 'slump'"). Doc, this boy works harder than any kid I know, and he works "smarter" too. He's pulling B's in honors courses and is the captain of the varsity basketball team.

I want my in-laws to back off, but my husband,
at 46, is still under the influence of "The Great
Santini." How do I break this cycle and get these
demons off my son's back? They come
(uninvited, mind you) to our place every
Thanksgiving and Christmas and launch into this
theme as soon as they walk past the mistletoe.
My husband tells me to "just keep quiet." What
do I do???

Signed, Desparate [sic] Dyslexic

A factor that leads to frustration in the life of a child is the attitude held by some adults (including, unfortunately, some teachers, parents, or grandparents) that the symptoms associated with ADHD and LD are caused by laziness, lack of motivation, limited intelligence, a propensity for disobedience, poor upbringing, or selfishness.

I wrote this response to the letter:

It would be ideal if your husband could tell his
superior officer to "stand down." However,
considering that the relationship between your
husband and his father goes back a long way, he
would probably be court-martialed for
insubordination and sent to the brig. It may very
well be that your talented and accomplished son
may be the hidden hero in this family battle. If
he hasn't already written an essay describing his
efforts to master the challenge presented by his
learning disability, you might want to consider
suggesting that to him. He may be able to earn
course credit for it, or it might form the
foundation of his application to a college—a
destination which seems very likely for this

young man. Then your son, brave soldier that he is, might want to send a copy of this letter, complete with his teacher's inevitable words of praise, to both his dad and his granddad simultaneously. If he likens overcoming his learning disability to defeating an enemy in battle, and describing how he did this by "*deploying appropriate resources*," and using "*an appropriate tactical plan*," he might be talking in a language these guys can understand.

Mrs. Dyslexic sent me a grateful note a few months later. She told me that after her husband read the essay, he tearily told his son how proud he is of him, and seemed to have a deeper appreciation of what the boy has overcome, and how toxic the grandfather's behavior has been. While they haven't sent the letter to "the old man," they have formed an alliance that may lead to a victory on that front for both of them.

MORE STRESS-BUSTING STRATEGIES

Give the right kind of compliments and feedback to kids under stress. Think about what you say when you compliment your child. Avoid "damning with faint praise"—backhanded compliments that highlight the problem yet again.

- *Do Not Say:* "I like how you're not pushing me away with your words."
- *Do Say:* "I like how you're letting me help you be successful. What you just said really makes me want to work with you."

Don't link the present with the unsuccessful past. Stay in the *now!*

- *Do Not Say:* "You always do that!"
- *Do Say:* "Is what you're doing right now helping you solve this problem?" or "What you're doing right now seems to me to be getting in the way of your progress."

Be proactive so you don't have to be reactive. Remember that kids who have difficulty organizing their lives may also have difficulty playing with friends. Short, project-centered or goal-directed activities are far better than open-ended play. Expecting impulsive, perceptually confused kids to structure their own environment is risky. To enable you to structure free-time activities it might be better to have kids play at your house rather than letting your child play at theirs. While this can't always happen, you might be able to share with another parent what you've been doing to structure play and why it helps your child. This advice might actually help the other parent's kids, too.

Pull the plug on mind-numbing technology. While it's tempting to let kids who can't organize their own lives sit for hours in what appears to be tranquility in front of a TV or computer game, these activities actually disengage a mind—or train it to do things wrong. If your child is poor at game playing, spending hours making mistakes is not a good way to learn ways to get better at it. If the child will let you, play together. That way you can be a video game coach. Select technology-based activities that are designed to train brains, not drain them. (Suggestions: www.cogmed.com; www.lumosity.com; Captain's Log at www.braintrain.com; Brainjogging at www.campacademia.com.)

Be a frequent flyer at reputable websites. Parents of children with ADHD and LD can be overwhelmed by an avalanche of information about these conditions. Some of the information is great and based on best practices and scientific evidence. Other sites are commercially driven purveyors of products dressed up as informational resources for parents or teachers. Let the buyer beware! There's a larger list of valuable sites in Appendix A, but here are a few very reputable sites that are always at the top of my list for parents: www.chadd.org; www.ldaamerica.org; www.ldonline.org; www.insideadhd.org; www.nldline.org; www.interdys.org. Be a regular visitor, so that you're up to date about research—and about political action on behalf of students and families affected by LD or ADHD. In general, information that's published by major hospitals with ADHD or LD programs, or by universities where research is being carried out, can be thought of as reputable. I would try to find the same or similar information on two or more sites, and always try to find the original source if an article refers to research. *A caution about Internet-based supports:* Online parent support groups or blogs can also be helpful to a worried parent as long as the discussions are positive and supportive. Unfortunately, the anxiety-filled chatter you may find at an unmonitored website can actually increase your worries. Don't get caught up in these!

Be a joiner. Most school districts have something like a Parent-Teacher Association. It might be called Parent Council or PTO, or go by some other name, but most of these groups have been established for the purpose of building better relationships between home and school.

Enjoy the PIRCs: Parent Information Resource Centers. According to the PIRC website, "The U.S. Department of Education created the first PIRCs in 1995 to provide parents, schools and organizations working with families with training, information, and technical assistance to understand how children develop and what they need to succeed in school. Today, more than 70 PIRCs operate in almost all of the states across the nation. They work closely with parents, educators and community organizations to strengthen partnerships so that children can reach high academic standards." Visit www.nationalpirc.org to find the PIRCs in your state.

Establish family meetings. Reserve one night a week when all the members of your family sit down around a table to share a quiet meal together. Consider making the meal together as an enjoyable bonding experience. If cooperative cooking is a far-reaching goal, consider having one child work with a parent each week, or have individual family members make or buy something to contribute. Compliments are welcome; critical comments have to be left at the door. To make these meetings less stressful, you should ask the same questions each week and always allow kids the right to pass (that is, to not answer them). You can also have children write down the answers before the meal and one parent can read the answers. A child who can't write can tell a parent who will then share the child's contribution. Topics for discussion should be specific to the culture of the family and the developmental level of its members. One useful topic: What's the best and worst thing that happened to me during the day? Follow-up questions for the worst thing might include: What's one thing that could have made this better? Is there anyone who could have helped you? What will you do if you face this situation again? Another good practice: "Find something nice to say to everyone at the table, look at them, and tell them. (The recipient should say "Thank you.")

Stress success. I encourage you to find different opportunities to engage your child in activities that maximize the chance for success. Often, the most effective activities are those that allow a child to compete against a personal record or only one other person (who can be strategically selected), like bowling, tennis, ice-skating, lap-swimming, diving, long-distance running, or learning to play an unusual musical instrument. (*Tip:* It's easier to be a star when you're engaged in an uncommon activity. With fewer players, you have fewer critics—no one knows if you've done something wrong.) If your kids do go out for team sports, make sure the sport fits the child. No soccer or field hockey for an uncoordinated kid who's still learning left from right—not yet, at least. And no football for a tiny boy, unless the whole team is tiny or he's vying for the quarterback's position—and can throw a football. Find opportunities for your child to be a big duck in a small pond. Even kids with dyslexia can get a lot of recognition and satisfaction from reading books or making narrated tape recordings of children's stories for preschoolers. This one's hard to do, but if you have more than one child, make sure that each has one or two areas to shine without reference to a sibling. Each child should own at least one sport or activity.

What's on your *refrigerator?* Whether it's on the fridge or in a family album or on a photo montage playing on a table-top electronic picture frame, find opportunities to showcase your child's successes in an appropriate way. This is not bragging, it's building self-esteem. Some parents say things like, "Tell Aunt Sally what you did at school." While the intent is to have kids speak strongly and positively about their own abilities, prematurely pushing them to be public about their accomplishments might make them regress. Better for you to say, "Is it OK if I tell Aunt Sally what you did today?" If they say no, you can persist a bit and ask, "Would you mind if I told her later, in private? I am so proud of you, I want to share the good news with someone who loves you." Other ways to share the success include writing letters or e-mail to relatives or texting a photo of a project well done.

Be honest. Make sure the task is praiseworthy. Telling a grandparent that a twelve-year-old child with dyslexia (whose reading is at the third- or fourth-grade level) reads really well is simply not true, and the child knows it. It's better to say, "Janelle has improved three levels in her reading since she started that new program. She's making great progress because she works really hard at it." (And don't let Grampa ask Janelle to read out loud at the next family event—unless you set this up in advance, with Janelle's approval. Even then, you might want to record the reading and have Gramps listen to the playback in private.) Teach your close relatives how to give honest praise by modeling this yourself, and by giving them the opportunity to join your child's cheering section.

Praise the process more than product. The need for honesty underscores the importance of focusing more on the process your child used to achieve success than you do on the product itself. Asking your child to say what was done to achieve a goal encourages a focus on the process. In life, it's the ability to carry out the process that leads to the product. The outcome cannot occur unless a process is followed. A good product or outcome generally implies (or demands) a good process. Your child might be shy or still learning how to analyze successes, and may not be able to identify the actions that helped achieve a goal, in which case it's certainly OK to say, "You achieved this goal because you . . ." This is a way to teach about what constitutes an effective approach to solving a problem or creating something noteworthy.

Arrange for homework that works. As a parent or caregiver, you can set the stage for nightly success by collaborating with your child's teachers. If you and the teachers have the same expectations and language, your child is less likely to be confused or resistant. If the homework is too hard for either you or your child to understand, or the directions are unclear, arrange with the teacher ahead of time that *either of you* can use a "Homework Stress Pass," and occasionally (you and the teacher decide how many you can use) skip a homework assignment. If your child has worked the expected amount of time, but has not yet completed the whole assignment, write a note on the paper, telling the teacher that despite a lot of hard work, it could not get done, and (if this is true) "that it looks like Lee understands the work." In some cases a student can find the time the next day to finish the assignment in school. At other times, a decent sample of work well done can be sufficient proof of competence.

Testing, testing! Perhaps this last recommendation is obvious by this time, and maybe I should have put it first. All the other suggestions I've offered in this book can be helpful. None of them can do any harm. But none of them will be as effective as they need to be unless and until you get a thorough assessment of your child's learning profile. Since I'm a neuropsychologist, I have a lot of confidence that this form of assessment, in the hands of an experienced clinician, can help get to the root of a child's difficulties and provide the evidence-based foundation upon which an effective intervention program can be built.

By now, you know how strongly I feel about the need to have the results of assessments spelled out to children in language they can understand by a person they can trust. A variety of professionals can play a role in helping children understand themselves better. I've included the following information to clarify any confusion that may exist about the roles of the people who might be involved in your child's life or yours.

A WHO'S WHO OF SERVICE PROVIDERS

Since many people are unfamiliar with the role of a neuropsychologist, and because there is often much confusion about the roles of the many professionals who might be involved in the lives of students with ADHD and LD, here is a bit of clarification.

School psychology is a field that applies principles of clinical psychology and educational psychology to the diagnosis and treatment of behavioral and learning problems in children and adolescents. *Educational psychology* is the branch of psychology that deals with the psychological aspects of teaching and formal learning processes. *Clinical neuropsychologists* have specialized training that prepares them to work with students whose difficulties are more serious than those often encountered in a school setting. Neuropsychology deals with the relationship between the nervous system, especially the brain, and cerebral or mental functions such as language, memory, and perception. Pediatric neuropsychologists specialize in work with children and adolescents. Neuropsychologists have an advanced degree called a doctorate (Ph.D., Ed.D., or Psy.D.), and while they study neurology as part of their training, they are not medical doctors (who have an M.D.).

There is some understandable confusion about the difference between a neuropsychologist and a neurologist. A *neurologist* is a physician (an M.D.) who specializes in neurology and is trained to study, diagnose, and treat neurological disorders. Pediatric neurologists treat neurological diseases in children. *Psychiatry*, another discipline often involved in the lives of children with LD or ADHD, is the branch of medicine concerned with the bio-psycho-social study of the etiology, diagnosis, treatment, and prevention of cognitive, perceptual, emotional, and behavioral disorders.

There is a significant amount of overlap among these professions; sometimes more than one kind of doctor works with a child. Other specialists such as guidance counselors, social workers, speech and language pathologists, or occupational or physical therapists may also work with selected students. The level of expertise all of these professionals have in working with students with LD or ADHD depends on the nature and length of their training and experience. As in other things that are good for you, in this regard too, more is better.

In this chapter, I have shared the stories of several families to show some of the different ways parents, siblings, and even extended family can feel the impact of the stress a lot of kids with LD and ADHD experience and bring home from school. I've emphasized the importance of frequent and respectful home-school communication, and why a mutual understanding of each child's needs is so critical to establishing and maintaining an appropriate learning environment. I hope that the information I've provided in this chapter will help you provide a different kind of support for your child—a network of caring individuals who are bound together by a common understanding of why children each respond the way they do, and what can be done to help them develop the skills they need to successfully navigate the multiple and ever-increasing demands of school.

This brings us to the last chapter of this book. In the Conclusion, I leave you with some parting words of hope. We are nearing the end, but I hope looking forward a new beginning for your kids.

CONCLUSION

All's Well That Ends . . . *Well* . . .

I have a confession to make. Saying good-bye has always been hard for me. As a matter of fact, my wife has given a name to the phenomenon, which has resulted in me spending much more time than is probably necessary bidding adieu to my brothers and sisters, or to our parents when they were still alive. (A few more hugs. Something "I forgot to tell you . . .") She lovingly refers to this as a "Schultz good-bye." I was going to try to avoid that as I bring this book, which in the process of writing, has come close to achieving the status of family member—my "baby," as it were—to a close. I was going to wrap it up in a few paragraphs and let you close the cover. But you know what? I just can't! So, even if you have your coat on or your car keys in your hand . . . indulge me, and let me give you a proper Schultz good-bye. I forgot to tell you something . . .

THE IMPORTANCE OF TELLING THE TRUTH

Simply stated, kids need to know what's wrong with them in order to get better. Because the research has been in flux and the terms *ADHD* and *LD* have been so popularized (or distorted), very few students really understand the nature of these conditions and how they impact their lives. Even fewer students can explain their condition to someone else. There has been much controversy about the use of the term *learning disability* because people fear its negative connotations. The euphemistic use of the term *learning differences* or the oft-invoked platitude "all kids are special" were ostensibly generated to lessen the negative impact that some people feel is associated with the term *learning disabled*. This mincing of words simply adds to the confusion. I would submit that everyone has learning differences, but not everyone has a neurologically based condition that causes an impairment in processing and retaining material that other people acquire much more easily. This neurobiological reality underscores the need not only for adults to better understand LD and ADHD but for the students who have these conditions to become more aware and educated about themselves.

Veritas vos liberabit (the truth shall make you free). I believe that every student has the right to know more about the name that's been given to the problem they have in school. Self-understanding and self-identification can lead a student to helpful resources, such as books for and about kids with LD and reputable websites that present the stories of others who have learned to deal with frustration or who have been able to attain great success despite having a learning disability or ADHD. "Ask the expert" features found on some sites can put a student in direct contact with the stories of professionals, parents, and other kids who are grappling with issues related to learning disabilities. These and other positive connections can support and sustain a student with LD or ADHD.

THE IMPORTANCE OF POSITIVE ROLE MODELS

Kids who can't see a successful future ahead need to know that others like them have transcended their difficulties and led happy and productive lives. They need to know that the struggling they have to do pays off. That's why most websites that provide information about learning disabilities contain sections with titles like "Famous People with Learning Disabilities or ADHD." While it's impossible to know for sure whether some of these people really had learning disabilities (especially the ones who aren't around to prove it, like Henry Ford, Walt Disney, Mozart, John F. Kennedy, or Albert Einstein), the lists generally include the names of contemporary artists, musicians, athletes, actors, and politicians who have at some point claimed or verified that they have a learning disability. These include people like comedians Jay Leno and Whoopi Goldberg, athletes like Magic Johnson, Olympic diving gold-medalist Greg Louganis, and Olympic swimmer Michael Phelps, and actors such as Tom Cruise and Keira Knightley. Some of these people speak openly about how learning disabilities shaped their lives. Other very successful individuals who have publicly acknowledged their LD-associated struggles and triumphs are Richard Branson, CEO of Virgin Enterprises, and Charles Schwab (yes, that Charles Schwab). The list is long and the role models many. A review of the lives of these folks can form the basis for an interesting and therapeutic term paper for the student with LD who is trying to better understand the impact of this condition. It helps kids to know that these people have overcome the negative impacts of their disabilities, or that they used the lessons they learned growing up with ADHD or LD to help them carve out successful careers.

SUCCESSFUL KIDS WITH LD AND ADHD: TEN WAYS THEY CAN GET THERE

In this book, I attempt to show how unexplained or poorly understood difficulties with learning and attention can create debilitating stress that impairs learning. By presenting the DE-STRESS model, I offer strategies that can help prevent or reverse this cycle, reducing a student's need to Save FASE. It's important to acknowledge that not all kids with LD and ADHD fall victim to the cycle of Fear, Avoidance, Stress, and Escape that plagues so many. How have some kids been protected from the negative impact of stress? From my experience, it boils down to this:

1. *They get respect:* Someone has paid these students the respect of explaining their learning disability or attention deficit disorder in easy-to-understand, developmentally appropriate language. This important task can be carried out by a variety of people, including a parent, school psychologist, neuropsychologist, therapist, or teacher.

2. *They're self-aware:* The interpretation of the conditions may need to be repeated over a lifetime, to make sure children have an age-appropriate understanding of their own unique learning or attentional style. As children get older, as their bodies and brains grow and develop, the impact of these conditions on life and learning may vary. Things that were hard in the past may become easier. Similarly, new content or new environments may pose new challenges. Children, adolescents, and young adults may need guidance at these critical points to help them understand the changes and learn new, more effective ways to cope with them.

3. *They make no excuses:* Someone has helped them understand that the LD or ADHD is not an excuse for poor performance but rather an explanation of why things are difficult. They have helped the student learn how to articulate this difference to other people, to help them understand why they may need to take a different approach to complete tasks or assignments.

4. *They work smarter:* These kids have been helped to understand that hard work is necessary for success, but that hard work alone is not enough. Because they have neurologically based difficulties, their brains process information in atypical

ways. As a result, they may have to use specialized approaches and strategies to attain mastery. They must be taught these strategies and encouraged to use them when the situation dictates. In this regard, the best teacher is success. What leads to mastery, they will use again. Teacher's prompts become less necessary over time.

5. *They learn from mistakes*: Confident, self-assured students have been taught to embrace the lessons learned not only from their success but also from frustration and from failure. They use this information to inform and guide their subsequent efforts.

6. *They have teachers and administrators in the know*: Kids who get it come from schools in which teachers and administrators also get it. Staff development efforts should be aimed at helping teachers and other professionals understand the scientific validity of these diagnoses, and the negative impact of stress on learning and performance. They should also be given the tools, techniques, and supervision that are necessary to help them become the kind of professionals that these kids must have in their lives.

7. *They are models of success for others*: To be successful, these kids not only need positive role models themselves, they should be put into situations in which their competence allows them to be role models and guides to others. Many of the confident, competent kids I have met over the years have been given the opportunity to mentor other younger students with LD and ADHD, reinforcing their status as students who have mastered this challenge and have become successful as a result.

8. *They have someone who believes in them*: All of these kids had somebody who believed in them. This might have been a parent, a teacher, a clergy person, a grandparent, or a caring neighbor—but there was someone who was this child's steadfast advocate. This was someone who was there in good times and in bad, either cheering on silently from the sidelines, writing

letters or e-mail messages of support, laboring through a tough homework assignment, or handing them a long-stemmed rose at graduation. Ask any student with a history of LD or ADHD to name the person who made a big difference in their life—and they'll have a nominee. (If they don't—find one or be one.)

9. *They have unique assets:* They have skills or talents that offset their liabilities. They compete in triathlons; they are ham radio operators; they are concert pianists; they act on stage or design the sets; they sing, they dance, they ski, they paint . . . the list is endless. Any activity where a kid with LD or ADHD can excel will help give them confidence to offset the challenges they experience.

10. *They are defined by their actions, not their label:* Successful students with LD and ADHD view themselves as capable individuals for whom a learning disability or attention deficit is simply part of who they are. They are happy with themselves and proud of their efforts. They say, "I am me, not LD. I am me, not ADHD!" They put the person first, and the disability last: "I am not a learning disabled student, I am a learner who happens to have LD or ADHD."

Note: You may wish to use the questionnaires found in Appendix B as you think about a child's environment. The results can help you generate an intervention plan designed to get the numbers up and the stress down.

A PICTURE *IS* WORTH A THOUSAND WORDS!

Most people have a story about someone or something that inspired them in their lives. I have had many such inspirations, but in closing, I want to pay tribute to a piece of art and the artist who created it. I have a lithograph hanging in my office done by the Pennsylvania-based artist Dane Tilghman. When I met this talented man many years ago, he told me that he is the descendent of slaves and that his family name was inherited from former slave owners. His family history of oppression and freedom from it is translated into the visual message of hope and the pride of accomplishment which is poignantly reflected in this work. The print depicts two little boys, one African American and the other Caucasian, sitting together, reading an open book entitled "I Can and I Will." The attributes reflected in the title represent the artist's dual messages of belief in self and self-determination, which through his art are imparted to these young boys.

I didn't realize it at the time, but many years ago when I hung this print on the wall in preparation for the opening of my clinical practice, I was accepting those positive and optimistic statements as challenges that would guide my career. It became my personal mission to instill these words in the hearts and heads of children with LD and ADHD. "I *can* and I *will*." In writing this book, I have added the subscript: *"If you will teach me how."*

In parting, that is the challenge that I present to you, my readers: to create learning environments that will help children with LD and ADHD better understand themselves as learners. Give them the tools they need to rise above their doubt and fear and to know the joy of success. Many teachers have created classrooms so infused with this spirit that they might well serve as models for others. For you, I hope this book is a validation of your efforts, and that it offers you additional ideas and strategies that will allow you to move beyond where you are. For those of you who are motivated to make a lasting difference in the lives of students with LD or ADHD, I hope that this book will serve as a road map that will change not only the way you think about kids with LD and ADHD and what they need, but also change the climate of your school. By providing students with a safe environment in which they are better able to take calculated risks and conquer new challenges, they will experience less stress and be happier at school and at home. Not only will this benefit students with LD and ADHD; all students will be raised to new levels of confidence and competence. Fear and failure erode the foundations of self-confidence. Success builds upon success.

To parents who have lovingly and selflessly given much of yourselves to help your son or daughter find greater success in school and greater happiness in life, I give to you my highest praise. To those of you who have worked alone, or with other parents, or with teachers or other professionals to create learning and living spaces in which students can know the joy of accomplishment and the feeling of competence that allows them to face new challenges with confidence, I congratulate you. I hope that the information that I have shared with you in this book helps to confirm what you have perhaps intuitively understood for years, and that I have provided new ideas and new strategies that will help you guide and support your children as they face the challenges and joys that lay ahead.

Please give your kids a message from me, will you? Tell them that there is reason to be hopeful. Tell them that they are strong, intelligent, and capable individuals who, armed with self-understanding and surrounded by people who know how they learn and how to teach them, will come to know the sense of satisfaction that comes from achievement, and the joy that comes from success. Tell them that they will no longer need anywhere to hide.

Let's take this out with a song . . .

I started this book by paying homage to the great music of the sixties and seventies that inspired and energized me in my life and in my work. I'll close this book with the words of John, Paul, George, and Ringo, perhaps the greatest musicians of our time. Let these lyrics serve as the anthem of hope for all the children and adolescents with LD and ADHD who have hidden in the shadows, besieged by stress.

> *Nowhere Man, please listen,*
> *You don't know what you're missing,*
> *Nowhere Man, the world is at your command!*

And now it's time to say good-bye.
No . . . *really.*

APPENDIX A

Resources for Families and Teachers

The printed page and the Internet are filled with a sometimes overwhelming array of resources that offer information, recommendations, and promises regarding children with LD and ADHD. Some of these are reputable sources, and some are absolute bunk. I've included sites here that have integrity, that are research-based, and that are not a front for snake oil—that is, for products of questionable value. I believe that the organizations I've listed will help you increase your knowledge of ADHD and LD, and will serve as dependable home ports in which you can take on knowledge and sustenance as you navigate turbulent waters in your journey toward greater understanding of these conditions.

SPECIAL EDUCATION AND GENERAL

American Speech-Language-Hearing-Association (ASHA)
www.asha.org

Association of Educational Therapists (AET)
www.aetonline.org

Association on Higher Education and Disability (AHEAD)
www.ahead.org

CEC—Division for Communicative Disabilities and Deafness (DCDD)
www.dcdd.us/

Council for Exceptional Children (CEC)
www.cec.sped.org

National Association of School Psychologists (NASP)
www.nasponline.org

U.S. Department of Education Office of Special Education Programs
400 Maryland Avenue, SW
Washington DC 20202
202-205-5507
www.ed.gov/offices/OSERS/OSEP

LEARNING DISABILITIES

CEC—Division of Learning Disabilities (DLD)
www.teachingLD.org

Council for Learning Disabilities (CLD)
www.cldinternational.org

International Dyslexia Association (IDA)
40 York Road, 4th Floor
Baltimore MD 21204
410-296-0232
www.interdys.org

Learning Disabilities Association of America (LDA)
4156 Library Road
Pittsburgh PA 15234
412-341-1515
www.ldaamerica.org

National Center for Learning Disabilities (NCLD)
www.ld.org

Recording for the Blind & Dyslexic (RFB&D)
www.rfbd.org

ADHD

Attention Deficit Disorder Association (ADDA)
1788 Second street, Suite 200
Highland Park IL 60035
847-432-ADDA
www.add.org

Children and Adults with Attention Deficit/Hyperactivity
Disorder (CHADD)
8181 Professional Place, Suite 201
Landover MD 20785
800-233-4050
www.chadd.org

LD OnLine (WETA Public Television)
www.LDOnline.com

National Center for Gender Issues and ADHD
www.ncgiadd.org

NLD on the Web
www.NLDontheweb.org

The Attention Deficit Information Network, Inc.
www.addinfonetwork.com

NEUROLOGY, PSYCHIATRY, AND PSYCHOLOGY

American Academy of Child and Adolescent Psychiatry
(AACAP)
3615 Wisconsin Avenue NW
Washington DC 20016
202-966-7300
www.aacap.org

American Academy of Neurology (AAN)
1080 Montreal Avenue
Saint Paul MN 55116
800-879-1960
www.aan.com

American Academy of Pediatrics (AAP)
141 Northwest Point Boulevard
Elk Grove Village IL 60007
847-434-4000
www.aap.org

American Psychiatric Association
1000 Wilson Boulevard, Suite 1825
Arlington VA 22209
703-907-7300
www.psych.org

American Psychological Association
750 First Street, NE
Washington DC 20002
800-374-2721
www.apa.org

Forms and Activities

The following tools can be used to help children articulate their views of their own status as a learner, which you know by now is a very important step toward the reduction of stress. I invite you to contact me via my website (www.jeromeschultz.com) if you have questions or would like to share tools that you have learned about or developed to help children achieve self-awareness or self-advocacy.

CIRCLES OF CONTROL

I've found that this kind of graphic organizer helps kids understand the areas in their lives over which they have some degree of control.

A child can put words or pictures in the appropriate circles, using pictures cut out of magazines or actual photographs if writing is too difficult. If a child indicates, for example, that they don't have control over who their friends are, this can be a good way to start a conversation about what's needed to have a friend and be a friend. If a child feels that how much time they spend playing video games or hanging out in the mall is controlled by parents, this can be a good way to start a discussion about appropriate behavior, responsibility, or making wise choices. You might also ask a child to describe what other kids might be in control of, and then you can talk about why these kids are allowed to or able to do these things.

The main point of these exercises is to help children take an inventory of those activities over which they have some degree of control or mastery. Pay attention to the kinds of things that end up in each circle. If reading and math show up in the circle that says "things that are out of my control," there's work to be done!

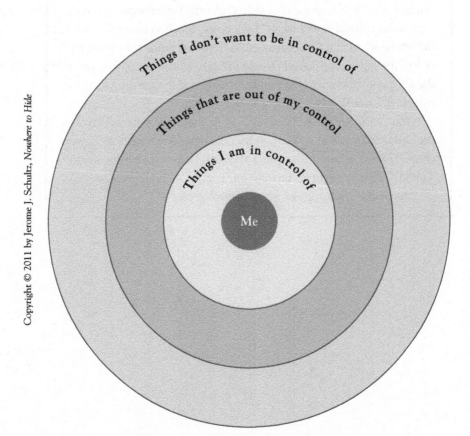

Things I don't want to be in control of

Things that are out of my control

Things I am in control of

Me

Note

You may wish to use rating scales like the ones in the "Who's in Charge of Me" form to find out what areas of life a child feels some control over. You can use this to structure an interview with the child, or you can have the child respond to it independently. For example, a 3 in the right-hand column would mean "I am a very much in control," and in the left-hand column would signify that "I am very much not in control." A 1 in the right-hand column would indicate a little in control, and in the left-hand column would signify "a little not in control." In either column a 2 would be somewhere in the middle.

You can modify this rating scale to fit the developmental level of the child, and you can add or remove items that don't apply to a given child. The information that you gather will help you identify areas of a child's life that might be brought more under a child's own control.

Remember: Stress grows when control goes.

WHO'S IN CHARGE OF ME?

I am not in control of:				I am in control of:		
3 = Very much 2 = About average 1 = Not at all			Reading	1 = Very little 2 = About average 3 = Very much		
3	2	1	Writing	1	2	3
3	2	1	Math	1	2	3
3	2	1	Spelling	1	2	3
3	2	1	Science	1	2	3
3	2	1	My dog (or any pets)	1	2	3
3	2	1	My parents	1	2	3
3	2	1	My life	1	2	3
3	2	1	My mechanical abilities	1	2	3
3	2	1	My artistic abilities	1	2	3
3	2	1	My athletic abilities or interests	1	2	3
3	2	1	My musical abilities or interests	1	2	3
3	2	1	My brother(s) or sister(s)	1	2	3
3	2	1	A medical condition that I have	1	2	3
3	2	1	My room	1	2	3
3	2	1	Taking care of my own health	1	2	3
3	2	1	Computer games	1	2	3
3	2	1	My happiness	1	2	3
3	2	1	My sadness	1	2	3
3	2	1	Other:	1	2	3
3	2	1	Other:	1	2	3
3	2	1	Other:	1	2	3

Note

A child's response to each item in "How I Feel About My Learning" provides an opportunity for parents, teachers, or therapists to

- Seek clarification of the child's perspective.
- Modify or correct misperceptions.
- Create an intervention plan specifically designed to move the response in a healthier, more positive direction.

HOW I FEEL ABOUT MY LEARNING

	Very true/usually	Sometimes/maybe	Not true at all/never
There is something different about the way I learn.			
There is something wrong with the way I learn.			
I have a learning disability.			
I understand my learning disability.			
I wish someone would help me understand why school (or this subject: _____) is so hard.			
I have ADD or ADHD.			
I have trouble paying attention but I don't have ADHD.			
I am stupid.			

	Very true/usually	Sometimes/maybe	Not true at all/never
I feel stupid.			
I act up when I'm embarrassed in school.			
Sometimes I show how I feel by acting out or acting up instead of using words.			
I am jealous of other kids who can learn more easily than I can.			
I feel a "beat behind" in school.			
I am disorganized in school.			
I am disorganized in my life.			
I am content with the way things are going in school.			
I worry about my future in school.			
My worries get the way of my schoolwork.			
I don't care about school.			
I won't do well even if I study harder.			

I wish people would: _____

_____

I'm afraid of: _____

_____

I wish I could do better in: _____

_____

Note

The "Worry and Wonder" exercise is a great way to allow kids and parents to get concerns down in writing. Parents, teachers, or therapists can use these sentence completion exercises to get a better understanding of a child's emotional state. This simple activity often yields valuable information that will help in the creation of interventions that capitalize on a child's strengths while attempting to reduce the areas of vulnerability.

FOR KIDS: I WORRY AND WONDER . . .

Please complete the following sentences:

When I think about school . . .

I Worry: _____

_____

I Wonder: _____

_____

I Think: _____

_____

I Know: _____

_____

I Hope: _____

_____

Here's an idea! Why don't you share your answers with a parent or a teacher?

Note

Parents who have completed the adult version of this have often shared their results with their child's teacher or their family therapist. It's a very helpful way to find out if both parents have the same perspective.

I have used a modification of this exercise as a development activity to help teachers assess their underlying feelings about addressing the special needs of children in their class.

FOR PARENTS: I WORRY AND WONDER . . .

Please complete the following sentences:

When I think about how my child is doing in school . . .

I Worry: _____

_____

I Wonder: _____

_____

I Think: _____

_____

I Know: _____

_____

I Hope: _____

_____

What I want my child's teacher to know about my son or daughter is:

_____

_____

_____

REFERENCES

CHAPTER 1

Amen, D. G. *Change Your Brain, Change Your Life: The Breakthrough Program for Conquering Anxiety, Depression, Obsessiveness, Anger and Impulsiveness* (New York: Three Rivers Press, 1998). See p. 117.

Goldstein, D. S. "Catecholamines and Stress." *Endocrine Regulations* 37 (2003): 69–80.

Perry, B. D. *The Neuroarcheology of Childhood Maltreatment: The Neurodevelopmental Costs of Adverse Childhood Events.* Child Trauma Academy, 2000. Available online: www.childtrauma.org/ctamaterials/Neuroarcheology.asp; access date: June 2009.

Perry, B. D. *Traumatized Children: How Childhood Trauma Influences Brain Development.* Child Trauma Academy, 2000. AVAILABLE online: www.childtrauma.org/CTAMATERIALS/trau_CAMI.asp; access date June: 2009.

Teicher, M., Samson, J., Sheu, Y., Polcari, A., and McGreenery, C. "Hurtful Words: Association of Exposure to Peer Verbal Abuse with Elevated Psychiatric Symptom Scores and Corpus Callosum Abnormalities." *American Journal of Psychiatry* 167 (December 2010): 1464–1471.

Vaillancourt, T., Duku, E., Decatanzaro, D., Macmillan, H., Muir, C., and Schmidt, L. A. "Variation in Hypothalamic–Pituitary–Adrenal Axis

Activity Among Bullied and Non-Bullied Children." *Aggressive Behavior* 34 (2010): 294–305.

Walker, D. L., Toufexis, D. J., and Davis, M. "Role of the Bed Nucleus of the Stria Terminalis Versus the Amygdala in Fear, Stress, and Anxiety." *European Journal of Pharmacology* (463): 199–216.

CHAPTER 2

Shonkoff, J., and Phillips, D., Eds. *Committee on Integrating the Science of Early Childhood Development: National Research Council and Institute of Medicine* (Washington, DC: National Academies Press, 2000).

Shore, R. "What Have We Learned?" In *Rethinking the Brain* (New York: Families and Work Institute, 1997), pp. 15–27.

CHAPTER 3

Barrett, J., Ripley, K., and Daines, B. *Dyspraxia: A Guide For Teachers and Parents (Resource Materials for Teachers)* (London: David Fulton, 2010). See p. 3.

Cortiella, C. "IDEA 2004 Close Up: Evaluation and Eligibility for Specific Learning Disabilities." SchwabLearning.org, September 19, 2005. Available online: www.sacramentoasis.com/docs/7-13-07/idea_2004_close_up.pdf; access date: April 7, 2011.

Dakin, K. E., and Erenberg, G. *Questions About Attention-Deficit/Hyperactivity Disorder and Dyslexia* (Baltimore: International Dyslexia Association, 2005).

Galaburda, A. M. (Ed.). *From Reading to Neurons* (Cambridge, MA: MIT Press, 1989). See pp. xxii and 545.

Galaburda, A. M., Sherman, G. F., Rosen, G. D., Aboltlz, F., and Geschwind, N. "Developmental Dyslexia: Four Consecutive Patients with Cortical Anomalies." *Annals of Neurology* 18 (1985): 222–223.

Hudson, R. F., High, L., and Al Otaiba, S. "Dyslexia and the Brain: What Does Current Research Tell Us?" *Reading Teacher* 60, no. 6 (March, 2007), 506–515.

"Interview with Albert Galaburda, M.D." Available online: www.nlmfoundation.org/about_autism/features/galaburda_features.htm; access date: February 16, 2011.

Kavale, K. A., and Forness, S. R. "The Politics of Learning Disabilities." LD Online, 1998. Available online: www.ldonline.org/article/The_Politics_of_Learning_Disabilities; access date: February 16, 2011.

Lyon, G. R., Fletcher, J. M., Shaywitz, S. E., Shaywitz, B. A., Torgesen, J. K., Wood, F. B., Schulte, A., and Olson, R. "Rethinking Learning Disabilities." In *Rethinking Special Education for a New Century*, edited by Chester E. Finn Jr., Andrew J. Rotherham, and Charles R. Hokanson Jr. (Washington, DC: Progressive Policy Institute and Thomas B. Fordham Foundation, May 9, 2001). Available online: www.ppionline.org/documents/SpecialEd_ch12.pdf; access date: April 7, 2011.

Shaywitz, S. E. (2003). *Overcoming Dyslexia: A New and Complete Science-Based Program for Reading Problems at Any Level*. New York: Knopf.

Snowling, M. J. "Dyslexia: A Hundred Years On." *British Medical Journal* 313, no. 7065 (November 1996): 1096–1097. Available online with registration: http://bmj.com/cgi/pmidlookup?view=long&pmid=8916687; access date: February 16, 2011.

The American Psychiatric Association DSM development website: www.dsm5.org/ProposedRevisions/Pages/proposedrevision.aspx?rid=429; access date: April 7, 2011.

Tridas, E. Q. *From ABC to ADHD: What Parents Should Know About Dyslexia and Attention Problems* (Baltimore: International Dyslexia Association, 2007).

Yoshimasu, K., M.D., Barbaresi, W. J., M.D., Colligan, R. C., Ph.D., Killian, J. M., B.S., Voigt, R. G., M.D., Weaver, A. L., M.S., and Katusic, S. K., M.D. "Gender, Attention-Deficit/Hyperactivity Disorder, and Reading Disability in a Population-Based Birth Cohort." *Pediatrics* 126, no. 4 (October 2010): e788–e795.

CHAPTER 4

American Academy of Pediatrics, Committee on Quality Improvement, Subcommittee on Attention-Deficit/Hyperactivity Disorder. "Clinical Practice Guideline: Diagnosis and Evaluation of the Child with

Attention-Deficit/Hyperactivity Disorder." *Pediatrics* 105 (2000): 1158–1170.

American Psychiatric Association, "DSM-5: The Future of Psychiatric Diagnosis." 2010. Available online: www.dsm5.org/; access date: February 24, 2011.

Atmaca, M., Ozler, S., Topuz, M., and Goldstein, S. "Attention Deficit Hyperactivity Disorder Erroneously Diagnosed and Treated as Bipolar Disorder." *Journal of Attention Disorders* 13, no. 2 (2009): 197–198.

Barkley, R. A. (1997). *ADHD and the Nature of Self-Control* (New York: Guilford Press).

Biederman, J., Faraone, S. V., Keenan, K., Knee, E., et al. "Family-Genetic and Psychosocial Risk Factors in DSM-III Attention Deficit Disorder." *Journal of the American Academy of Child and Adolescent Psychiatry* 29 (1990): 526–533.

Hallowell, E. M., and Ratey, J. J. *Answers to Distraction* (New York: Bantam Books, 1996).

Hallowell, E. M., and Ratey, J. J. *Driven to Distraction: Recognizing and Coping with Attention Deficit Disorder from Childhood Through Adulthood* (New York: Simon & Schuster, 1995).

"Increasing Prevalence of Parent-Reported Attention-Deficit/Hyperactivity Disorder Among Children—United States, 2003 and 2007." *Morbidity and Mortality Weekly Report* 59, no. 44 (November 12, 2010): 1439–1443. Available online: www.cdc.gov/mmwr/preview/mmwrhtml/mm5944a3.htm?s_cid=mm5944a3_w; access date: February 23, 2011.

JAMA and Archives Journals. "ADHD Appears to Be Associated with Depressed Dopamine Activity in the Brain." *Science Daily* (2007, August 8). Available online: www.sciencedaily.com/releases/2007/08/070806164505.htm; access date: November 19, 2010.

Levy, F., McLaughlin, M., Wood, C., Hay, D., and Waldman, I. "Twin-Sibling Differences in Parental Reports of ADHD, Speech, Reading and Behaviour Problems." *Journal of Child Psychology and Psychiatry* 37, no. 5 (July 1996): 569–578.

Sachs, G., Baldassano, C., Truman, C., and Guille, C. "Comorbidity of Attention Deficit Hyperactivity Disorder with Early- and Late-Onset Bipolar Disorder." *American Journal of Psychiatry* 157 (March 2000): 466–468.

Schultz, W. "Predictive Reward Signal of Dopamine Neurons." *Journal of Neurophysiology* 80, no. 1 (1998): 1–27.

Shea, S. E., Gordon, K., Hawkins, A., Kawchuk, J., and Smith, D. "Pathology in the Hundred Acre Wood: A Neurodevelopmental Perspective on A. A. Milne." *Canadian Medical Association Journal* 163, no. 12 (December 12, 2000). Available online: www.cmaj.ca/cgi/content/full/163/12/1557; access date: April 7, 2011.

Sonders, M. S., Zhu, S. J., Zahniser, N. R., Kavanaugh, M. P., and Amara, S. G. "Multiple Ionic Conductances of the Human Dopamine Transporter: The Actions of Dopamine and Psychostimulants." *Journal of Neuroscience* 17, no. 3 (1997): 960–974.

Teeter, P. A. (1998). *Interventions for ADHD: Treatment in Developmental Context* (New York: Guilford Press).

CHAPTER 7

Brooks, R., and Goldstein, S. *Understanding and Managing Children's Classroom Behavior: Creating Sustainable, Resilient Classrooms* (New York: Wiley, 2007).

Csikszentmihalyi, M. *Flow: The Psychology of Optimal Experience* (New York: HarperCollins, 2008).

Jenkins, D. S., Rao, A., Jenkins, A., Buckley, G., Patten, R., Singer, W., Corey, P., and Josse, R. "Nibbling Versus Gorging: Metabolic Advantages of Increased Meal Frequency." *New England Journal of Medicine* 321 (October 5, 1989): 929–934.

Ramirez, G., and Beilock, S. L. "Writing About Testing Worries Boosts Exam Performance in the Classroom." *Science* 331 (2011): 211–213.

Ratey, J. *Spark: The Revolutionary New Science of Exercise and the Brain* (New York: Little, Brown, 2008).

Roffman, A. *Guiding Teens with Learning Disabilities: Navigating the Transition from High School to Adulthood* (New York: Random House, 2007).

Sammons, W.A.H. *The Self-Calmed Baby* (Boston: Little Brown, 1989).

CHAPTER 8

Bonwell, C., and Eison, J. *Active Learning: Creating Excitement in the Classroom AEHE-ERIC Higher Education Report No. 1* (San Francisco: Jossey-Bass, 1991).

CHAPTER 9

Dakin, K. E., and Erenberg, G. *Questions About Attention-Deficit/Hyperactivity Disorder and Dyslexia* (Baltimore: International Dyslexia Association, 2005).

Dorfman, H. A. *The Mental ABC's of Pitching: A Handbook for Performance Enhancement* (Lanham, MD: Diamond Communication, 2000).

Tridas, E. Q. *From ABC to ADHD: What Parents Should Know About Dyslexia and Attention Problems* (Baltimore: International Dyslexia Association, 2007).

OTHER REFERENCES

"Asperger's Stress Hormone 'Link.'" BBC News, April 2, 2009. Available online: http://news.bbc.co.uk/2/hi/health/7976489.stm; access date: February 26, 2011.

Gartner, A., and Lipsky, D. K. *Inclusion: A Service Not a Place, a Whole School Approach* (Port Chester, NY: Dude, 2002).

Giangreco, M. *Quick-Guides to Inclusion: Ideas for Educating Students with Disabilities*, 2nd ed. (Baltimore: Brookes, 2007).

Jorgensen, C. *The Inclusion Facilitator's Guide* (Baltimore: Brookes, 2005).

Snell, M. *Collaborative Teaming: Teachers' Guide to Inclusive Practices* (Baltimore: Brookes, 2005).

ABOUT THE AUTHOR

Jerome (Jerry) Schultz, Ph.D., is a former middle school special education teacher who currently works in private practice as a clinical neuropsychologist. He is on the faculty of Harvard Medical School in the Department of Psychiatry, and serves as a neuropsychological consultant to several large school districts in the Boston area.

For more than three decades, Dr. Schultz has specialized in the neuropsychological assessment and treatment of children with learning disabilities, attention-deficit/hyperactivity disorder, and other special needs. He was on the faculty of Lesley University in Cambridge, Massachusetts, for almost thirty years, and served there as the founding director of the Learning Lab, a diagnostic clinic. He then became the co-director of the Center for Child and Adolescent Development, which was part of the Cambridge Health Alliance. Missing direct contact with children and families, he returned to private practice in 2009.

In addition to his clinical and educational work, Dr. Schultz serves as an international consultant on issues related to the neuropsychology and appropriate education of children and young adults with special needs. For several years, he was the resident expert on learning disabilities and ADHD at www.familyeducation.com, a website for parents and teachers. He was on the Board of Directors of the Learning Disabilities Network, and was vice president of the Board of the Learning Disabilities Association of Massachusetts. He currently serves on the Editorial Board of the journal *Academic Psychiatry* and is on the professional advisory boards of the Learning Disabilities Association of America and Inside ADHD.com.

Dr. Schultz has written many articles about children with learning challenges and created award-winning videotapes on the topic. He lives in the Boston area with his wife, Marlene.

INDEX